ENGLAND

AND THE

FRENCH REVOLUTION
1789—1797

ENGLAND

AND THE

FRENCH REVOLUTION
1789—1797

BY

WILLIAM THOMAS LAPRADE

AMS PRESS
New York

Reprinted from a copy in the collections of the Brooklyn Public Library
From the edition of 1909, Baltimore
First AMS EDITION published 1970
Manufactured in the United States of America

Standard Book Number: 404-03878-6

Library of Congress Card Catalog Number: 77-109922

AMS PRESS, INC.
NEW YORK, N. Y. 10003

CONTENTS.

PREFACE.

This study was originally undertaken with the purpose of showing to what extent the English social and political life of the period contemporaneous with the French Revolution was influenced by that event, or, in other words, whether the popular agitations in England, which attracted the attention of the English government at this time, owed their origin to the revolution taking place in France. In the course of investigating the subject it became apparent that these agitations were due to conditions existing in England itself rather than to outside influences, and consequently the policies and methods of William Pitt became the primary themes of the study. However, in spite of this change of view, it has seemed best to adhere to the original plan of presentation, and to regard the English social organization as a whole, discussing its economic, political, and religious aspects, but stressing the administration of the government and the measures of those at its head.

It is easy to forget, more than a century after the event, that the French Revolution presented a constantly changing aspect to those watching it from England, and one must give due weight to the fact that until the Tories and Whigs definitely took opposite sides of the questions supposed to be at issue in France, the views which Englishmen held varied according to the characters of the individuals themselves. Moreover, it is so difficult to classify such individual views, expressions of opinion, or private actions, or to draw from them any generalizations of value, that no attempt has been made to do so here, but the discussion has been confined to those influences only which took the definite form of word, deed, or movement the evidence for which clearly appears in the documents of the period. It is manifestly impossible to ascertain the effect on people in general of isolated pamphlets or speeches unless the evidence proves that in consequence of them a considerable body of men meditated taking action or unless some collective expression of opinion or collective action resulted therefrom.

This investigation covers the period from 1789 to the spring of 1797 when a change appeared in the attitude of the English ministers toward the war with France. The author regrets that he has been unable to examine all of those records preserved in the Public Record Office bearing on the subjects which are discussed in this monograph and are to be treated more fully in a larger work now in course of preparation. Though in consequence of this fact some of the conclusions regarding the diplomacy of the period are in a measure tentative, yet they seem to represent the most reasonable interpretation of the evidence at hand and are not invalidated by anything found in the work of those who have hitherto examined the materials in the Public Record Office.

The author acknowledges with appreciation the assistance of Professor John M. Vincent, at whose suggestion this inquiry was undertaken, and of Professor Charles M. Andrews, who has also given helpful advice. Finally, he acknowledges the many courtesies shown him by the library staff of the British Museum, of the Library of Congress, and of the Peabody Institute of Baltimore.

ENGLAND AND THE FRENCH REVOLUTION.

CHAPTER I.

PRELIMINARY SKIRMISHES.

When, in the summer of 1789, it became evident that a new régime was about to be inaugurated in France, the general attitude of the English public, if we may accept the expression of the writers for the press as typical, was one of approbation. The people were ready to welcome France as a free nation. Sometimes it was suggested that Louis XVI was merely receiving what his interference in the American war had merited.[1] It was said also that the prospective change of affairs in France would not result in an ultimate advantage to England, since France, possessing freedom, would become a more formidable rival than she had hitherto been.[2] Yet few doubts were expressed that the final disposition of the affair would be beneficial to France.

In all of these discussions, however, the writers maintained the attitude of disinterested spectators, and no one had yet imagined that England would be directly concerned. The events which were taking place in France were regarded as merely wonderful phenomena, and therefore proper subjects for speculation. Not until 1791 was the French Revolution to become a party question in England. Previous to that time, the newspapers which represented the views of the party in power were fully as extravagant in their praise of the progress of affairs in France as those

[1] Morning Post, July 8, 17, 1789. The Oracle, July 2, 1789.
[2] The Oracle, July 4, 1789; August 25, 1789. Morning Post, July 24, 1789. Whitehall Evening Post, August 20–22, 1789. Public Advertiser, December 27, 1789.

which were the organs of the aristocratic Whigs. Both
alike deprecated the excesses of the populace, and approved
only of the underlying purpose which was supposed to give
rise to them. The means were to be justified by the end.[8]

By the close of the year 1791 no question in English politics
received greater attention than did the French Revolution.
The first thing that requires explanation in this discussion,
therefore, is the process by which the domestic affairs of
France became in so short a time the vital question on which
the political parties in England were divided. Several
events which took place in the latter part of 1789, in 1790,
and in the early months of 1791 prepared the way for the
introduction of this troublesome question into the party
politics of Great Britain. Chief among these events was
the publication of three pamphlets. It is not likely that
any one of these productions had the effect which its author
anticipated. Probably no one of them, if left alone, would
have exerted any considerable influence on the English
people. Their importance lies in the subsequent events to
which they had been a necessary prelude, and we cannot
understand these events without some knowledge of the
nature of the pamphlets and the circumstances which attended their publication.

The first of these pamphlets to make its appearance was
that of Dr. Richard Price, a nonconformist minister, entitled "A Discourse on the Love of Country," an address
delivered by its author, November 4, 1789, before the

---

[8] For such expressions of opinion see: St. James Chronicle, July
30–August 1, 1789; August 4–6, 1789; September 12–15, 1789; Oc-
tober 27–29, 1789; November 26–28, 1789; December 18–20, 1790.
Bristol Journal, July 11, 1789. The Gazetteer; and New Daily
Advertiser, January 27, 1790. The Oracle, July 23, 25, 31, 1789;
August 8, 12, 13, 14, 15, 1789; September 22, 26, 1789. Public
Advertiser, July 25, 1789; September 7, 12, 1789; December 3, 1789;
April 9, 1790; May 24, 26, 27, 28, 1790; June 30, 1790; July 14, 1790;
August 21, 1790. Morning Post, July 22, 1789; August 31, 1789;
September 1, 4, 12, 24, 1789; October 2, 17, 27, 1789; December 23,
1789. The Diary; or, Woodfall's Register, August 7, 1789. White-
hall Evening Post, July 30–August 1, August 20–22, 1789; September
10–12, 1789; May 27–29, 1790; June 24–26, June 29–July 1, 1790. The
World, February 11, 18, 1790; June 1, 1790; July 22, 1790; September
13, 1790.

Society for the Commemoration of the Revolution in Great
Britain, and immediately published. This society was composed of a considerable body of men who had been accustomed for a number of years to meet on the anniversary of
the Revolution of 1688 to partake of a dinner and listen to
a sermon. Naturally, a majority of the members of the
society were Dissenters, but some members of the established church were included, among whom were several
peers and members of Parliament. The previous year had
been the centennial of the revolution, and naturally the enthusiasm which had attended the celebration of that event
had not entirely subsided by November, 1789. Lord Stanhope presided at the dinner, which was held at the London
tavern. These enthusiastic English patriots declared themselves pleased at the turn which affairs had taken in France,
and sent a congratulatory address to the National Assembly.
This communication did no more than express to the body
to which it was presented the felicitations of those who
drafted it on the prospect of constitutional government
in France, and up to this time there was nothing which
could justify a suspicion that the members of this English
society had any desire to imitate those who were making
trouble across the Channel.[4]

Dr. Price's sermon was chiefly a concise statement of his
political philosophy, from the point of view of the English
constitution.[5] The only specific reference to the French
Revolution was in the peroration, which was a somewhat
exaggerated exultation at what had taken place and an exhortation to friends of liberty to persevere in their efforts.
It is impossible to see in it more than the enthusiasm of an
orator who was influenced by the spirit of the occasion.[6]

[4] For accounts of this meeting and copies of the resolutions, etc.,
see: An Abstract of the History and Proceedings of the Revolution
Society in London, etc., 1789. The Diary; or, Woodfall's Register,
November 6, 1789.
[5] Price, Discourse on the Love of Country.
[6] The following is the paragraph in question:—
"What an eventful period is this! I am thankful that I have
lived to see it; and I could almost say, *Lord, now lettest thou thy
servant depart in peace, for mine eyes have seen thy salvation.* I

This is not the place to appraise the correctness of the conclusions which the preacher reached with regard to government. However, since Burke's "Reflections on the French Revolution" were intended chiefly as a reply to this pamphlet, it is necessary to describe briefly the character of these conclusions, which were not new and, for the most part, had been expressed before by the same author. The latter, after defining a country as a community of inhabitants rather than an area of territory, declared that man's highest obligation was one of benevolence toward all countries; but to his own country, because of his residence in it rather than because of any superiority it possessed over other countries, he owed a peculiar devotion, which should cause him to seek to make the three "chief blessings of human nature," truth, virtue, and liberty, universal in his community. Here lay the first duty of a citizen. Virtue and truth, the preacher argued, should increase coordinately, since "virtue without knowledge makes enthusiasts and knowledge without virtue makes devils; but both united

---

have lived to see a diffusion of knowledge, which has undermined superstition and error—I have lived to see the rights of men better understood than ever; and nations panting for liberty, which seemed to have lost the idea of it.—I have lived to see thirty millions of people, indignant and resolute, spurning at slavery, and demanding liberty with an irresistible voice; their king led in triumph, and an arbitrary monarch surrendering himself to his subjects.—After sharing in the benefits of one Revolution, I have been spared to be a witness to two other Revolutions, both glorious.—And now me-thinks I see the ardour for liberty catching and spreading; a general amendment beginning in human affairs; the dominion of kings changed for the dominion of laws, and the dominion of priests giving way to the dominion of reason and conscience.

"Be encouraged, all ye friends of freedom, and writers in its defence! The times are auspicious. Your labours have not been in vain. Behold kingdoms, admonished by you, starting from sleep, breaking their fetters, and claiming justice from their oppressors! Behold the light you have struck out, after setting America free, reflected in France, and there kindled into a blaze that lays despotism in ashes, and warms and illuminates Europe!

"Tremble all ye oppressors of the world! Take warning all ye supporters of slavish governments; and slavish hierarchies! Call no more (absurdly and wickedly) reformation innovation. You cannot now hold the world in darkness. Struggle no longer against increasing light and liberality. Restore to mankind their rights; and consent to the correction of abuses, before they and you are destroyed together."

elevates [sic] to the top of human dignity and perfection."
Last of all he would have liberty, but he contended that it
ought to follow and not precede virtue and knowledge,
since it might otherwise become mere license.

The preacher next undertook to point out, in order to
comment on them more specifically, some of the more important duties which a man owes his country. The first of
these was the obligation of a citizen to obey the laws and
magistrates of the community in which he resides. Civil
government he defined as "an institution of human prudence for guarding our persons, our property, and our good
name, against invasion; and for securing to the members
of a community that liberty to which all have an equal
right, as far as they do not by any overt act use it to injure
the liberty of others." Civil laws he described as "regulations agreed upon by the community for gaining these
ends;" civil magistrates as "officers appointed by the community for executing these laws." From these premises he
argued that obedience to the laws and magistrates was a
"necessary expression of our regard to the community,"
without which anarchy would result, and therefore it was
the office rather than the person of the magistrate that
deserved to be honored. In advancing this argument the
author took occasion to declare that the king of England
was "almost the only lawful King in the world, because
the only one who owes his crown to the choice of his people."

This remark naturally led to a discussion of the Revolution of 1688. Dr. Price announced that the three chief
principles contended for in that revolution were, "The right
to liberty of conscience in religious matters; The right to
resist power when abused; and, The right to chuse our own
governors; to cashier them for misconduct; and to frame a
government for ourselves." After discussing these principles, he went on to remind his audience that there remained other abuses which would have to be removed before
the ends striven for in the revolution could be said to have
been attained. This reference was, of course, to the Test

Act and Penal Laws and to the existing state of representation in the House of Commons.

It is not probable that this pamphlet would have received any more attention than would naturally have been bestowed on a work by a man of the eminence of Dr. Price if it had been left without any further advertisement than the replies of minor writers such as any publication was sure to call forth in this period. Such was its fate indeed until October 31, 1790, when Burke published his Reflections. Within little more than a month after that date ten new editions were sold.[7]

The reply that Burke made to Dr. Price's discourse has become a classic among political pamphlets. But as Morley has pointed out, half of the "impressive formulæ and inspiring declamation," of which the work is largely composed, were "irrelevant to the occasion which called them forth, and exercised for the hour an influence that was purely mischievous."[8] We have no desire here either to criticize or to analyze Burke's political philosophy, but in order to estimate correctly the influence of this particular work on the events that followed, it is necessary to determine as far as possible the methods by which the author reached his conclusions and his intentions in presenting them to the world. A series of curiously unrelated elements seems to have entered into the composition of the Reflections and the result was a literary hodgepodge which compelled attention because of the eminence of its author, the general interest in the subject which was supposed to be discussed, and the hyperbolical language in which it was set forth.

Perhaps it is not necessary to observe that in writing this pamphlet Burke was not primarily concerned with the French Revolution. One of his ambitions was, as he put it, to "illustrate" himself and his family.[9] A man who covets such honors is naturally ready to defend the institu-

---

[7] Public Advertiser, December 7, 1790.
[8] Morley, Burke, 153.
[9] Fitzwilliam, Correspondence of Burke III, 389.

tions which favor his ambitions and to resent any criticisms which are aimed at the objects of his desire. Probably Burke was sincere in his belief that a titled aristocracy is a beneficial and almost a necessary element in a state, and it is not to be inferred that he was consciously influenced by his ambitions in reaching this opinion. Yet these ambitions are a factor that cannot be disregarded by a student of his career.

Assuming that monarchy was a logical if not a necessary accompaniment of nobility, Burke was bound to become a strong supporter of the rightness of kingly rule. Not that he accepted the doctrine of divine right; on the contrary, he specifically disclaimed it; but his theory seems to have been that whatever is has a divine sanction, provided it be the result of an historical process and bear the marks of time. He profoundly distrusted popular government and had a horror of radical reforms. He accepted the philosophy of Hamlet, preferring to bear existing ills rather than hazard a remedy which might call for change. He never would believe, he said, that because people had lived under an absolute monarchy, with all its inconveniences and grievances, they had a right to ruin their country on the chance of regenerating it in some other way.[10] He would have had the French go backward and revive their old States General with its historical limitations, and he even suggested that they might modify it slightly to meet the exigencies of the crisis which confronted them at that time. But he could not bring himself to admit the validity of an institution which did not have the approval of centuries; he would not agree that a time could ever come when it would be proper to disregard precedents.

One element which influenced the writing of the Reflections was the temperament of the author. Two years after the pamphlet was published Fanny Burney noted in her diary that it was not permissible to discuss political questions with him in polite society on account of his terrible

---

[10] Fitzwilliam, Correspondence of Burke III, 176.

irritability. To approach a subject of that character, she
said, gave his face the "expression of a man who is going to
defend himself from murderers."[11] Apparently, he placed
such a high estimate on his own perspicacity that it was
difficult for him to consider a thing from any other point
of view than that which he had already attained.[12] He seems
to have been encouraged in this vanity by his son, for whose
sake a title was chiefly desired, and who needs to be considered in any discussion of his father's course with regard
to the French Revolution.[13]

We have already remarked that Burke in his Reflections
was not primarily concerned with the French Revolution.

---

[11] Barrett, Diary and Letters of Madame D'Arblay V, 92.

[12] Fitzwilliam, Correspondence of Burke III, 130, 139. In February,
1790, Burke submitted a proof of the Reflections to his friend Sir
Philip Francis, who criticized the work frankly and severely.
Among other things he wrote to Burke, "In my opinion, all that
you say of the queen is pure foppery." Burke's reply to this
criticism is the only illustration that there is space to give of his
infatuation with his own prepossessions: "I tell you again,—that the
recollection of the manner in which I saw the queen of France, in
the year 1774, and the contrast between that brilliancy, splendour,
and beauty, with the prostrate homage of a nation to her,—and the
abominable scene of 1789, which I was describing,—*did* draw tears
from me and wetted my paper. These tears came again into my
eyes, almost as often as I looked at the description;—they may
again. You do not believe this fact, nor that these are my real
feelings; but that the whole is affected, or, as you express it, down-
right foppery. My friend,—I tell you it is truth; and that it is
true, and will be truth when you and I are no more; and will exist
as long as men with natural feelings shall exist. I shall say no
more on this foppery of mine."
This conceit which Burke had of his own opinions makes it
easier to understand his strong resentment when Fox and his
friends ridiculed the Reflections.

[13] Fitzwilliam, Correspondence of Burke III, 133. Richard Burke
wrote to Sir Philip Francis after his father had received his friend's
letter criticising the Reflections. The son requested Francis not to
oppose any more of his father's opinions. He went on to say:
"There is one thing, however, of which I must inform you, and
which I know from an intimate experience of many years. It is,
that my father's opinions are never hastily adopted, and that even
those ideas which have often appeared to me only the effect of
momentary heat, or casual impression, I have afterwards found,
beyond a possibility of doubt, to be the result of systematic medi-
tation, perhaps of years; or else, if adopted on the spur of the
occasion, yet formed upon the conclusions of long and philosophical
experience, and supported by no trifling depth of thought. . . . Do
I not know my father at this time of day? I tell you, his folly is
wiser than the wisdom of the common herd of able men."

To understand his real purpose we must review briefly several circumstances which preceded its composition. In the debate on the Regency question, arising from the temporary insanity of the king in the winter of 1788 and 1789, many differences of opinion on the constitutional points at issue were expressed, some believing that if the Prince of Wales should be allowed to assume the government with all the rights which pertained to his father, he would immediately dismiss the existing administration and summon another composed of his Whig friends. Burke endeavored to persuade his party associates that since the crown was hereditary, the prince became regent automatically during the period of his father's incapacity, without the necessity of the intervention of Parliament. He therefore strongly urged that the prince be allowed to take the initiative and communicate with Parliament without waiting for the action of the existing administration.[14] Fox, however, who was the leader of the party, was too good a Whig and estimated too highly the rights of Parliament to advocate such a step, even though it would have advanced his own interests. He contended that although the prince had a right to the Regency, it would be better for him to await a formal notification from Parliament before assuming the reins of government. But Pitt and his party, whose offices were at stake, had no intention of adopting the views of either Burke or Fox. They contended that while it might be expedient for Parliament to select the prince and to define his powers, in reality the latter had no more right to the position than any other Briton.[15] The effect of such assertions on a man of Burke's opinions is easy to understand. They were to him nothing short of revolutionary and almost treasonable. It was at this time, he tells us himself, that he formulated the theory of the English monarchy which he presented in the Reflections.[16]

[14] Fitzwilliam, Correspondence of Burke III, 90.
[15] For the debates on the Regency see: Hansard, Parliamentary History XXVII, 653–1160.
[16] Fitzwilliam, Correspondence of Burke III, 399.

2

As early as October, 1789, Burke had conceived for the French Revolution an intense dislike founded largely on the theory that the revolution was a result of the agitations of unscrupulous leaders who were actuated by selfish motives.[17] A development of this idea led him to the conclusion, expressed in detail in the Reflections, that the confiscation of the church lands was the result of the combined efforts of a literary cabal and the French monied interests. The purpose of the men of letters was to discredit the Christian religion by weakening the church; that of the capitalists, who held government loans as a part of their newly acquired wealth and were also envious of the position of the nobility, was to reimburse themselves for their loans to the government and to strike a blow at the nobility who controlled the patronage of the churches.[18]

It is manifest from what has been said that when Burke came to London in the late autumn or early winter of 1789 he had already formulated his opinions with regard both to the French Revolution and to the English constitution. The only thing lacking was some reason for giving them publicity. According to the account which he himself gave of it, the missing element was supplied in the following manner. Acting in accordance with Burke's own advice, Fox had been endeavoring to conciliate the Dissenters, who had not been disposed hitherto to give him a very cordial support,[19] since their liberal views made them rather inclined to agree with Pitt's course on the Regency question. On the day that Burke reached town he met a prominent Dissenter at a dinner, and engaged him in a discussion of the

---

[17] Fitzwilliam, Correspondence of Burke III, 115. For a more explicit statement of the same view, see his letter to Francis, November 19, 1790, in the same work III, 176 :—

"I charge all these disorders, not on the mob, but on the Duke of Orleans, and Mirabeau, and Barnave, and Bailly, and Lameth, and La Fayette, and the rest of that faction, who, I conceive, spent immense sums of money, and used innumerable arts to instigate the populace throughout France to the enormities they committed; and that the mobs do not disgrace them, but that they throw an odium upon the populace, which, in comparison, is innocent."

[18] Burke, Reflections on the French Revolution, 161–170.

[19] Russell, Memorials and Correspondence of Fox II, 359.

reasons why his coreligionists were not favorably disposed toward the Whigs. This gentleman gave Burke the impression that the Dissenters withheld their support because of the supposed private immorality of Fox. Burke warmly defended his friend and party associate. On the same night, after he reached home, he read for the first time Dr. Price's sermon, which contained a veiled reproof of Fox for his failure to be as virtuous in his private as in his public conduct. This paragraph naturally tended to confirm the notion which Burke had got from the discussion earlier in the evening as to the attitude of the Dissenters. Price's views on the constitution differed widely from those which Burke himself held, and, as the latter thought, from those held by Fox also. The introduction of the French Revolution into the peroration of the sermon gave further food to Burke's vivid imagination, and led him to conclude that Dr. Price was one of a cabal plotting to effect a similar revolution in England.[20] He immediately began to prepare a reply. By the middle of February, 1790,[21] the manuscript of this reply was in the hands of the printer.

Burke's primary intention was that his pamphlet should contain a confutation of the views held by Dr. Price, Lord Lansdowne (Lord Shelburne), and others with regard to the principles on which the English government was based. In a letter to Sir Philip Francis he wrote: "I intend no controversy with Dr. Price, Lord Shelburne, or any other of their set. I mean to set in full view the danger from their wicked principles and their black hearts. I intend to state the true principles of our constitution in church and state, upon grounds opposite to theirs. If any one be better for the example made of them, and for this exposition, well and good. I mean to do my best to expose them to the hatred, ridicule, and contempt of the whole world; as I always shall expose such calumniators, hypocrites, sowers of sedition, and approvers of murder and all its triumphs."[22]

[20] Burke, Reflections on the French Revolution, 13.
[21] Fitzwilliam, Correspondence of Burke III, 394–398.
[22] Fitzwilliam, Correspondence of Burke III, 140.

An examination of the Reflections will show that the author has here clearly expressed his purpose in writing the pamphlet. [He desired to discredit the opinions of Price and others concerning the English constitution; to show that in expressing their admiration for the French Revolution and for the new constitution which was then in the process of incubation they had approved of conceptions of government which differed radically from the views which were accepted as orthodox in England; to prove that the proposed French constitution was not only wrong in theory but could not possibly work in practice, and that for Englishmen to engage in the pursuit of this political will-o'-the-wisp was both foolish and dangerous.]

There was no possible chance of reconciling the opinions of the two authors. Their differences were fundamental. Price contended that government derives its proper sanction from an explicit or implied compact of the governed. He believed that since the Revolution at least, the English government had had the authority of such a compact. Burke denied that the authority of the English government could be referred to such a compact. He looked to history for civil sanctions, and was not concerned about origins. His argument, perhaps not without weight, was that the continuation of an institution or custom for centuries was prima facie evidence that it was suited to the needs which it was supposed to supply. He professed to desire laws and institutions which would promote justice and the public welfare. He merely denied that the popular will was a proper criterion by which to determine what these laws and institutions were. And he denied that the English constitution looked to this criterion as a final arbiter.

Burke believed that he was a representative of the aristocratic party, and that when his pamphlet was published it would at once receive the approval of his associates, since the nobility had been one of the first objects of attack in France. He believed that if the principles of those who admired the French Revolution were permitted to spread

unopposed in England, one inevitable consequence would
be an attack on the English nobility, and that therefore he
deserved the thanks of his aristocratic friends for coming
to their defense.   Again, he argued that since French revolutionists, while adhering to the monarchy, had repudiated
any rights which the king might claim as inherent, and had
made him the mere executive head of the nation, it was
important for the interests of Fox, who could scarcely hope
for the favor of George III, that the rights which the Prince
of Wales had as the heir of his father should be defended
and kept secure.   He saw in the principles on which the
new French monarchy was to be established, and of which
Dr. Price approved, a menace to the doctrine that the king-
ship of England was necessarily inheritable, and he believed
that he was serving both Fox and the prince in attempting
to prove that even in times of revolutionary stress the principle of heredity had been adhered to in the selection of
those who should occupy the English throne.[23]   As a logical
result of this argument he was obliged to deny categorically
that Dr. Price had been correct in his statement that by the
Revolution of 1688 the English people had established their
right to frame their own government, to choose their own
governors, and to cashier them for misconduct.   Indeed,
Burke ridiculed such a notion as without the shadow of a
foundation.

The distinguished author soon found that his opinions
were not shared by all of his party associates.   In the
discussion of the army estimates, February 5, 1790, Fox
casually remarked that "the example of a neighbouring
nation had proved, that former imputations on armies were
unfounded calumnies; and it was now universally known
throughout all Europe, that a man by becoming a soldier
did not cease to be a citizen."[24]   This led Burke, a few days
later, to give the first public expression of his views on the
French Revolution and his fears of its effect on England.
Fox replied in a conciliatory speech, repaying in kind the

[23] Fitzwilliam, Correspondence of Burke III, 387–407.
[24] Hansard, Parliamentary History XXVIII, 330.

complimentary remarks which Burke had made with respect to him personally, but carefully refraining from giving explicit utterance to his opinions concerning the French Revolution. Sheridan, however, insisted on declaring his disagreement with the views that Burke had stated, and the latter rejoined that as a consequence they two must henceforth travel different political roads.[25] At the time no one dreamed that this debate marked the beginning of a permanent separation between the two political leaders. On the contrary, it was popularly supposed that Sheridan would virtually if not formally withdraw from the party.[26]

Burke seems to have thought that this debate clearly demonstrated the need for his pamphlet. A few days later he submitted the proofs to Sir Philip Francis, who, as has been intimated, advised strongly against publication.[27] So the matter rested for several months. But in the meantime another discussion was in progress which emphasized still more the difference of opinion between Burke and Fox and furnished the occasion for the first introduction of the French Revolution into English politics.

In 1787, and again in 1789, Beaufoy had moved in the House of Commons the repeal of the Corporation and Test Acts.[28] In the latter year the motion had been defeated by a majority of only twenty votes, and Fox had been persuaded to renew it in 1790, with the hope that under his championship the measure might be carried. There was the usual wealth of pamphlet discussion on both sides,[29] supplemented by local meetings and newspaper comments.[30]

---

[25] Hansard, Parliamentary History XXVIII, 323–374.
[26] The World, February 11, 12, 1790. Public Advertiser, February 12, 1790.
[27] Fitzwilliam, Correspondence of Burke III, 128. Burke gave the proofs to Francis on February 17. They were returned with the criticism the next day.
[28] Hansard, Parliamentary History XXVI, 780–832; XXVIII, 1–41.
[29] For titles of many of these pamphlets see the appended bibliography.
[30] For typical newspaper comment, see: St. James Chronicle, August 8–11, 1789; September 8–10, 1789. Public Advertiser, January 14, 1790; February 1, 5, 6, 10, 16, 18, 22, 23, 25, 1790; March 1, 1790. The Gazetteer; or, New Daily Advertiser, January 20, 1790. The Diary; or, Woodfall's Register, January 16, 1790.

Of course, the bulk of the discussion, since it came from the aggressive party, was in favor of the repeal. On February 4, 1790, less than one month before the motion was to be made, an administration newspaper announced that the government would have to take some stand on the question "unless the friends of the established church exert themselves more than they have hitherto done."[31] Thereupon meetings of the clergy were held, petitions circulated, and instructions sent, even to members of Parliament who favored the repeal, requesting them to vote against it.[32] Naturally, in the discussions which attended this agitation, attention was called to the fact that prominent Dissenters had expressed their admiration for the French Revolution; and it was equally natural that they should be accused of having the same attitude toward the established church in England that the revolutionists had manifested toward the Roman Catholic Church in France. The agitation was terminated for the time by the debate in the House of Commons on March 2, 1790. Pitt did not appear at his best in the speech in which he opposed the repeal, since, as was well known, his motives were political rather than the result of any real conviction with regard to the subject. Fox and Burke appeared on different sides of the question, the latter using Price's sermon, to which he had already prepared his reply, as the chief basis of his argument. The two Whig orators, however, took care to make it evident in their speeches that they were acting as was their custom concerning parliamentary reform and similar questions, and had agreed to disagree with regard to the particular topic which was being discussed. The combined administration and ecclesiastical interests easily defeated the motion by a vote of 105 to 294.[33] But this agitation portended more than

---

[31] Public Advertiser, February 4, 1790.

[32] St. James Chronicle, February 4–6, 1790. Public Advertiser, February 5, 1790. The World, January 16, 1790; February 23, 1790. The Diary; or, Woodfall's Register, January 21, 26, 29, 1790; February 3, 6, 9, 18, 19, 23, 24, 1790; March 1, 1790. General Evening Post, February 18–20, 1790; February 27–March 2, 1790.

[33] Hansard, Parliamentary History XXVIII, 387–451.

was realized at the time. The sinister specter of the French Revolution had appeared for the first time in English politics, and it had been openly charged that there was a party in England who wished to imitate its worst examples. To complicate matters still further, Burke and Fox had again appeared on opposite sides of the question.

Although it was now generally known that he was preparing a work on the French Revolution, Burke had as yet refrained from giving his pamphlet to the public. On July 14, 1790, the first anniversary of the fall of the Bastille was celebrated by a dinner at the Crown and Anchor tavern. Several prominent Whigs attended and took a conspicuous part in the exercises.[34] This fact and some attendant circumstances caused Burke to hesitate no longer, and the Reflections made their appearance on October 31.[35] The character of the work has been made apparent in the account which has preceded. It was a defense and a justification of the monarchy, the nobility, and the established church as they existed in England, and a condemnation of the French Revolution as involving principles which, if accepted, would result in the downfall of these institutions. The author viewed the English constitution as the product of an historical development, and in no sense designed to secure the people in the possession of any innate or natural rights. Privileges possessed by the people as well as the institutions of government were, in his opinion, inherited from antiquity. " We have," he said, " an inheritable Crown; an inheritable peerage; and a House of Commons and a people inheriting privileges, franchises, and liberties from a long line of ancestors." Even the reformations which had been made hitherto "proceeded on the principle of reference to antiquity." "From Magna Charta to the Declaration of Rights," he continued, "it has been the uniform policy of our constitution to claim and assert our liberties as an *entailed inheritance,* derived to us from our forefathers, and transmitted to our posterity; as an estate specially belonging to

[34] Public Advertiser, July 16, 1790.   The World, July 16, 1790.
[35] Fitzwilliam, Correspondence of Burke III, 398.

the people of this Kingdom, without any reference whatever to any other more general or prior right." Even the
revolution had been made " to preserve *ancient* indisputable
laws and liberties, and that ancient constitution which is our
only security for law and liberty.'

Since Burke had long been prominent in public life, since
the subject which he had discussed was one which had
excited the curiosity of the people, and since it was known
that the views which he held were radically different from
those of most people at that time, it was only natural that
the Reflections should be widely read, and should give rise
to many replies. A majority of these replies had no
other effect than to afford employment for contemporary
publishers and reviewers, and to serve as topics for conversation. But among them appeared, in the early months
of 1791, a pamphlet worthy of notice because of a certain
influence that has been attributed to it.

Thomas Paine, the author of this pamphlet, " The Rights
of Man," the first part of which appeared at this time, was
a republican whose egotistical, undisciplined mind led him
to estimate far too highly his own common sense. However, he seems to have had the merit of believing in himself,
and to have been actuated by a desire to change society
into what he considered to be a more desirable state. When
comparing his opinions with those of Burke, we must remember that the two men looked at the questions at issue
from opposite points of view. Burke accepted things as
they were, and believed that they were in the main good,
because they were results of a long period of development.
Paine, with little respect for antiquity, conceived of things
as he believed they ought to be, and considered it his duty
to effect their transformation. " It is out of the question,"
he said, "to say how long what is called the English constitution has lasted, and to argue from that how long it
is to last.'

Before many months had passed after the publication of
the Rights of Man, it had become a favorite ruse of both
Burke and Pitt to class with the supporters of Fox the

imaginary disciples of Paine. We must therefore understand at the outset the character of the doctrines propounded
by the "trans-Atlantic republican." Certainly he did not
attempt to disguise his opinions. He boldly affirmed that
"civil government" was synonymous with "republican
government." He ridiculed Burke's arguments, and developed at even greater length the ideas which he had formerly advanced in Common Sense. We need not detail
his theories here. They were based on the doctrine of the
social contract that pervaded the political writings of the
time. He was, however, explicit in his opposition both to
the monarchy and to the nobility. He could find no justification for either, and did not hesitate to conclude that
"the romantic and barbarous distinctions of men into kings
and subjects, though it may suit the conditions of courtiers,
cannot that of citizens; and it is exploded by the principle
upon which governments are now founded. Every citizen
is a member of the sovereignty, and, as such, can acknowledge no personal subjection; and his obedience can only be
to the laws."

This pamphlet was widely read, the notoriety of the
author and the subject insuring a hearing. It received further advertisement at the hands of both Burke and Pitt,
but its doctrines were far too sweeping to receive the
approval of any considerable number even of the most
radical reformers who were active in England during this
period.

These preliminary discussions and differences had not
yet occasioned the division of the English people into two
parties with the French Revolution as, ostensibly, the chief
point at issue. They were merely the first of a series of
events which, in the exigencies of politics, were to lead to
that result. It will appear in the next chapter how the
condition which had been thus brought about was utilized
by a minister who, to extricate himself from an unpleasant
situation, and apparently for the purpose of preserving his
own political fortunes, plunged incontinently into a discussion of this foreign issue.

CHAPTER II.

THE FIRST ATTACKS.

In October, 1790, Burke and Fox were apparently bound by permanent ties of amity as members of a great party whose chief excuse for existence was to oppose the political measures of William Pitt. Within less than a year from that date Burke and Pitt were working together, either tacitly or by specific agreement, to compass the disruption of the party of which Fox was still the leader. The object of Pitt was perfectly clear: he desired as nearly as possible to control personally every department of the English government. Of Burke's motives it will be necessary to say something hereafter; they are not so easy to understand.

Let us recall for the moment a few familiar facts. The party in power, the Tories, was at this time composed of two elements: one, which was representative of the commercial and financial interests, was dominated by Pitt; the other, a less numerous body of men, including the Duke of Leeds, secretary of state for foreign affairs, and the lord chancellor, Lord Thurlow, supported the king. The Whigs, as the opposition party termed themselves, were composed of the more prominent members of the nobility under the nominal leadership of the Duke of Portland, but really looking for political guidance to Fox, who with Burke and Sheridan made up their great triumvirate of orators. There was also a younger element (of which Charles, afterwards Lord, Grey was a type) which was inclined to support reforms and to hold different views from the majority of the party with which they were connected. It is essential to note these facts, since, as was said by a contemporary journal, this was a period when the majority of English people took their opinions from leaders or prominent men,

27

and did not question seriously the authority of their accepted oracles.[1]

A man of Pitt's character naturally looked askance at those of his party associates who did not submit to his leadership. Therefore he only waited for a provocation to rid his cabinet of several members who were friends of the king rather than of the minister, holding himself ready to take advantage of the occasion when it should offer itself. As far as mere numbers were concerned, he had assured himself of ample support in the House of Lords by the process of creating new peers. But, in matters that required oratorical or managerial ability, he had hitherto been obliged to depend on Thurlow, who was somewhat weakly assisted by Lord Hawkesbury. Such a state of affairs was not satisfactory to the minister, particularly as he and the lord chancellor frequently disagreed.[2] In order to remedy this difficulty, and to prepare for a withdrawal of Thurlow's support, he requested the king, in November, 1790, to elevate to the peerage his relative, William Grenville, the younger brother of the Marquis of Buckingham.[3] This step, which was taken without the advice of the rest of the cabinet, was by no means satisfactory to all of his colleagues, and when he heard of it the Duke of Richmond remonstrated in a private letter to the minister, saying that it was an act ill calculated to alleviate the troubles with the lord chancellor.[4] But Pitt was looking farther ahead than to a mere reconciliation with Thurlow. The king granted the request, though he complained that the House of Peers was certainly becoming too numerous,[5] and Pitt reaped the

---

[1] Evening Mail, February 25–28, 1791.

[2] Stanhope, Life of William Pitt II, 43. Harcourt, Diaries and Correspondence of George Rose I, 98. Browning, Political Memoranda of the Duke of Leeds, 139–141. Auckland MSS. XXXII, 308.

[3] Salomon, William Pitt I, 589. This is an appended letter from Pitt to the king.

[4] Stanhope, Life of William Pitt II, 75–80. The letter from Richmond to Pitt is quoted.

[5] Stanhope, Life of William Pitt II, Appendix XII–XIII. The letter from the king to Pitt was dated November 21, 1790.

reward of his foresight. Eighteen months later he dismissed the chancellor and thereby secured the needed bait to gain the support of a prominent Whig lord. The next step was the substitution of Grenville for Leeds in the foreign department and the appointment of Henry Dundas in Grenville's place, thereby greatly increasing the personal power of the minister. The circumstances which attended these changes in the cabinet introduced a strenuous era in English party politics. The crisis came in the early months of 1791.

Russia and Turkey were at war. England's ally, Prussia, desired that the English government join with her in a demand that peace be made on the basis of the status quo ante bellum, that is, without the necessity of Turkey's ceding to her enemy any conquered territory. The question turned on the possession of the fortress of Ochakov. After considerable preliminary discussion, it was finally decided by the British cabinet on March 21, 1791, to send a fleet to the Baltic for the purpose of overawing Russia and compelling her to accede to the terms of the allies. On March 25 notice was given in Parliament that an address from the king would be presented requesting a grant of money for this purpose. Two days later a despatch was sent to the English minister at Berlin informing him of the line of action determined upon. This course had been championed by the Duke of Leeds and supported by Pitt, but had been opposed by both Grenville and the Duke of Richmond. However, all had finally agreed to it.[6]

When, on March 29, the king's message was discussed in the House of Commons, the proposal was carried by a vote of 228 to 135.[7] But the Whigs were active in their opposition, and in the division several of Pitt's adherents voted with them.[8] Two days afterward the minister called

---

[6] Browning, Political Memoranda of the Duke of Leeds, 148–152. Auckland MSS. XXIV–XXVI. Leeds MSS. IV–VIII. These collections contain numerous despatches, letters, etc., which give a detailed account of the entire negotiation.
[7] Hansard, Parliamentary History XXIX, 31–79.
[8] Browning, Political Memoranda of the Duke of Leeds, 152–155.

on Leeds, and informed him that on further inquiry he had found that many who had voted with him were not inclined to support the measure which had been proposed.[9] Additional inquiries served only to confirm this opinion, and at the cabinet meeting of April 16 an entirely different policy was considered and adopted. The government decided to withdraw the offer which had been made to Prussia, and to send to Russia a special agent authorized, if necessary, to yield every point that the empress claimed.[10] Since Leeds refused to sign the necessary despatch to Berlin, Grenville acted in his stead. A short time afterward the cabinet changes mentioned above took place. Pitt now had a secretary of state for home affairs of whom he later said, "Every act of his is as much mine as his."[11] If he had not been writing to Grenville he might with equal propriety at that time have affirmed the same thing of the new head of the foreign department. The result, as Grenville's under-secretary saw it, was that Pitt practically gained control of the departments of home and foreign affairs in addition to his own.[12]

Thus, though Pitt's personal influence in the administration was heightened by the outcome of the Russian fiasco, the Whigs appeared on the surface to have triumphed in their opposition. A less astute politician than Pitt might have been at a loss how to proceed. To make matters worse, Thurlow regarded the new home secretary as "the most impudent fellow he ever knew."[13] In fact, the lord chancellor had told Leeds some time before that he was sure he would be dismissed as soon as a successor could be found.[14] Leeds thought that the entire administration should admit their defeat and follow his example. Moreover, the

---

[9] Browning, Political Memoranda of the Duke of Leeds, 159–160.
[10] Browning, Political Memoranda of the Duke of Leeds, 165–166. Auckland MSS. XXV, 451, 452; XXVI, 239, 258.
[11] Dropmore Papers II, 596.
[12] Hutton, Selections from the Letters and Correspondence of Sir James Bland Burges, 174.
[13] Browning, Political Memoranda of the Duke of Leeds, 149.
[14] Browning, Political Memoranda of the Duke of Leeds, 149.

king was reported to have intimated that "he was not so
wedded to Mr. Pitt as not to be willing to give his confidence to Mr. Fox if the latter should be able in a crisis like
the present to conduct the government with greater advantage to the public."[15]   In self-defense, Pitt assumed the
aggressive, and immediately began to attack his enemy.   In
looking for the weak point in his opponent's armor, he
found an ally who was a welcome addition to his forces at
this juncture.

Pitt had joined in the chorus of dissent from Burke's
theories which began to be heard soon after the publication
of the Reflections.   The World, which was extremely partizan in its support of the administration, repeatedly criticized the book, sometimes using ridicule.[16]   There was

---

[15] The Argus, April 22, 1791.

[16] The World, November 3, 1790:—

"The manner in which Burke holds forth on the 'horizontal
beauties of the queen of France' is the newest kind of praise in a
publication dedicated to the national Revolution that has ever appeared.   Added to this, the number of swords that were to 'leap
out of their scabbards' is another living image which has not yet
made its way into politics!   Don Quixote now falls into nothing
before Burke!   And it may fairly be expected that, the impeach-
ment being over, he will now employ himself in rescuing distressed
damsels about the different parts of the country."

Two months later the same paper contained a more serious
criticism:—

"Possessing, as we do, the highest opinion of the splendid talents
and private worth of Mr. Burke, we most sincerely regret that his
last production was ever given to the world; as, in our opinion,
it detracts, in point of composition, from his merits as an argu-
mentative writer, and is (a matter of much greater moment), in
its political tendency, subversive of those principles which form the
basis of our excellent constitution, and which he long supported
with so much firmness and warmth as a British Senator.   The
rhetorical flourishes with which it abounds might give promise of
future eminence to any youth who wrote it as a college exercise,
and whose unformed judgement might be allowed the privilege of
substituting flowery declamation and pathos for substantial rea-
soning.   Its principles are those of the once happily exploded
Filmer.   There is nothing in them original, no trace of superior
political genius or learning.   It can only be said that the same
excreable sentiments are obtruded upon us in a more elegant and
fashionable dress.   In this pamphlet, we lament to see the author
of Thoughts on the present Discontents;—the declaimer against the
American war—the peace, etc., contend that any form of government is preferable to innovation; and that the many were formed
for the convenience of the few.   Heu! quantum mutatus!   Who

certainly little in common in the views which had hitherto
been held by the Whig orator and the minister. The
former had not swerved a whit from his opinions; but Pitt
gave mere theories or principles little consideration when
his own power and influence were concerned. He did not
necessarily accept Burke's opinions now. He merely found
in his former antagonist a convenient instrument to serve
his own purposes, and he did not hesitate to make use of
him.

His method of doing so was as follows. We know that
Burke published his pamphlet in spite of the advice of one
friend. Another friend of his, on the day he received a copy
of the work, noted in his diary that the writer was "a man
decried, persecuted and proscribed; not being much valued,
even by his own party, and by half the nation considered as
little better than an ingenuous madman."[17] This being so,
we are surely not justified in believing that a work by such
an author could in the course of a few months change the
point of view of a nation. It is not strange, therefore, that
when Fox openly dissented from his opinions, and his supporters did the same, Burke should have become melancholy
and dejected, and could find only comfort not joy in the
large sale of his book.[18] Perhaps his feelings on the subject may be best expressed in his own words:—

could have supposed that the philosophic eye of Burke was capable
of being dazzled by the taste, the politeness and magnificence of
that cruel despot, Louis XIV? Yet, to judge from his book, that
prince's patronage of letters, the splendour and gaieties of his
palaces and his camps, not only (in Mr. Burke's opinion) palliated,
but amply compensated for the havoc and desolation which marked
his infamous passage through a world which he filled with carnage
and despair. We feel, in common with Mr. Burke, for the fallen
and distressed. But is beauty an apology for enormous profligacy?
The king of France draws forth his sympathy—but he drops not a
tear to the memory of the miserable martyrs of despotism, who
ended their days in the horrid dungeons of the Bastille." The
World, January 7, 1791.

See also the same paper, November 25, 1790; January 4, 12, 1791.
[17] Baring, Diary of Rt. Hon. William Windham, 213.
[18] Life and Letters of Sir Gilbert Elliot I, 365, 371. Burke wrote
to Sir Gilbert on November 9, 1790:—
"The public has been so favourable that the demand for this
piece has been without example; and they are now in the sale of

"According to the common principles of vulgar politics
this would be thought a service not ill intended, and aimed
at its mark with tolerable discretion and judgment. For
this, the gentlemen have thought proper to render me obnoxious to the party, odious to the Prince, (from whose future
prerogative alone my family can hope for anything)[19] and
at least suspected by the body of my country. That is, they
have endeavoured completely and fundamentally to ruin
me and mine in all the ways in which it is in the power of
man to destroy the interests and objects of man, whether
in his friendship, his fortune or his reputation."[20]

In other words, Burke had intended to serve his party
and the prince by his pamphlet. Instead of receiving
thanks for the service, the author believed that Fox and
Sheridan had so damaged his reputation with both the
prince and the aristocratic Whigs that any further advancement of his fortunes from these sources was put in jeopardy.
Having such a belief, it was only natural that his resentment should cause him to discredit those who, he imagined,

---

the twelfth thousand copies. I know very well how little elated I
ought to be with this, perhaps, momentary opinion, which time
and reflection may change, and which better information from those
who are preparing to give it may dissipate. In truth, everything
rather disposes me to melancholy than to elevation. It is comfort
and not joy that I feel. It is indeed necessary for me to have
some, and that not a little support when a man like Fox declares
his entire disapprobation of the work in the most unqualified terms,
and thinks besides that in point of composition it is the worst I
ever published. When Fox disapproves and Sheridan is to write
against me, do not I want considerable countenance? "
[19] In this parenthetical statement Burke probably referred to his
ambition to become a peer. It is well known that for the services
he rendered the Pitt administration from this time to his death it
was the purpose of the minister to gratify this ambition. It is
said that the patent was actually being made out when the death
of Burke's son caused the title to be no longer a thing which the
father desired. Therefore he contented himself with a pension
which was said to have had a present value of thirty-six thousand
pounds.
  For correspondence and other matter relating to these facts see:
Fitzwilliam, Correspondence of Burke IV, 239. Stanhope, Life of
William Pitt II, 244–250. Morning Chronicle, October 1, 1794;
November 13, 1795. It is unnecessary to mention here Burke's
pamphlet in defense of his pension and the debate in Parliament
which occasioned it.
[20] Fitzwilliam, Correspondence of Burke III, 402–403.

3

were seeking to injure him. He therefore readily played
into Pitt's hands, and in that way helped the minister out
of a perplexing political situation.

The first public notification of the fact that the two eminent Whig orators would no longer act together was given
on the floor of the House of Commons. Burke had been
accustomed to hold opinions different from those of Fox
and Sheridan on several questions, such as parliamentary
reform. On these occasions they had maintained their party
relations, though disagreeing on the question at issue. Fox
seems to have seen no reason why they should act otherwise
with reference to a matter as purely speculative as he believed the approval or disapproval of the French Revolution
to be at that time.[21] On April 8, 1791, in the first debate
on the Quebec government bill, he expressed himself as
opposed to reviving in Canada "those titles of honour, the
extinction of which some gentlemen so much deplored," and
referred to the fact that the territory had formerly been a
French colony.[22] Again, a week later, in a debate respecting the proposed Russian armament, he incidentally described
the new French constitution as, all things considered, "the
most glorious fabric ever raised by human integrity since
the creation of man."[23] Burke attempted to reply at the
time, but was prevented by cries of "Question!" Six days
later, when it was proposed to renew the debate on the
Quebec bill, Burke called on Fox, and informed him that
he intended to take part in the debate and discuss the French
Revolution. It was reported that he also informed Pitt of
his intention. At any rate, when the order of the day was
proposed, Sheridan asked that the consideration of the
measure be postponed. When Pitt refused to grant this
request, Fox made a brief speech in which he lamented that
what he had said previously had been misunderstood, and
affirmed that while he admitted his admiration for the

---

[21] Hansard, Parliamentary History XXIX, 378, 390.
[22] Hansard, Parliamentary History XXIX, 107.
[23] Hansard, Parliamentary History XXIX, 249. Fox afterwards
asserted that he had referred to the French Revolution and not to
the constitution, as was reported. See the same work, 377.

French Revolution he had never, either in or out of Parliament, defended republican principles where England was
concerned. Burke began his speech by recalling his friendship with Fox, but went on to say that his principles " were
even dearer to him than his friendship." Fox made no
reply, and the matter rested until May 6, the next date set
for consideration of the Quebec bill.[24]

It will be observed that these discussions were taking
place at precisely the time when the minister was most embarrassed by the outcome of the Russian imbroglio. The
brief and entirely incidental panegyric on the French Revolution which escaped Fox on April 15 gave Pitt his opportunity of widening the breach between the Whig orators,
and in conjunction with Burke of drawing away from Fox
a large body of his aristocratic supporters.

The next move came when on the appointed date the
speaker put the question whether the Quebec bill should be
read paragraph by paragraph. It is difficult to see how the
occurrences of that day can be interpreted as anything but
deliberate manœuvers on Burke's part. Immediately after
the announcement of the speaker, Burke rose and began a
speech which bore little relation to the question before the
house. At the outset he proceeded to deny the proposition
that " all men are by nature free, and equal in respect of
rights, and continue so in society," and persisted in this line
of discussion in spite of repeated attempts to call him to
order. Fox ironically remarked that he did not think his
right honorable friend out of order, since it seemed to be a
day of privilege when any gentleman might stand up and
select his mark and abuse any government he pleased.
After considerable discussion of the point of order, during which Burke, declaring that " he was fully convinced
as he could be that no one gentleman in that house wanted
to alter the constitution of England," continued his
former discussion, Pitt suggested that some one move

---

[24] Hansard, Parliamentary History XXIX, 359–364.   Morning
Post, April 23, 1791.

that it was " disorderly to avert to the French constitution
in the present debate." When Burke persisted in his dis-
quisition, Lord Sheffield acted on Pitt's suggestion. The
natural result of such a motion, as the minister probably
foresaw, was to afford a more suitable pretext for the discussion which it was designed to prevent. In the debate
that followed, Fox again defended himself from the insinuation that he had maintained republican principles, and
insisted that there was no more reason for discussing in the
house the constitution of France than there was for discussing the constitutions of Athens and Rome. Burke, now
clearly in order, proceeded with his speech. Toward its
conclusion he said that " it certainly was indiscretion, at any
period, but especially at his time of life, to provoke enemies,
or give his friends occasion to desert him; yet if his firm
and steady adherence to the British constitution placed him
in such a dilemma, he would risk all; and, as public duty
and public prudence taught him, with his last words exclaim, ' Fly from the French constitution.' " At this point,
Fox, who sat near the speaker, whispered that there was no
loss of friends. Burke continued: " Yes there is a loss of
friends. I know the price of my conduct. I have done my
duty at the price of my friend. Our friendship is at an
end."[25] This entirely uncalled-for outburst could have had
but one meaning. It was a declaration of war against Fox.

There was little delay on Burke's part in continuing the
struggle with his former friend and ally. Within a few
days after his public avowal on the floor of the house, he
endeavored, through Sir Gilbert Elliot, to have the Duke of
Portland demand an explanation from Fox. With that
purpose in view he sent to Elliot minute instructions concerning the proper procedure for the duke to use on the
occasion of such an interview. According to these instructions, Portland was not to be misled by any general assurances. " The point to be explained," his instructor went
on to say, " is not whether he [Fox] means to introduce the

---

[25] Hansard, Parliamentary History XXIX, 364-401.

French Revolution here, but why, if he does not, he extols and magnifies it in the language and sentiments of those who do." Not content with this, the instructions continued, " The truth is, that no explanation can give satisfaction." However, Elliot did not agree with Burke's suspicions of Fox, and declined to perform the task thus imposed upon him.[26]

Having failed in his first attempt, Burke had recourse to a pamphlet which he published late in the summer.[27] The occasion for this work was, as he explained it, a paragraph in the Morning Chronicle, which he regarded as the authentic exponent of the views of the supporters of Fox. This paragraph stated that the Whig party had decided the question between its two orators, and concluded in these words, " The consequence is, Mr. Burke retires from Parliament."[28] In this pamphlet Burke referred to his Reflections where he had attempted to prove that the existing state of things in France was " not an undigested, imperfect, and crude scheme of liberty, which may gradually be mellowed and ripened into an orderly and social freedom; but that it is so fundamentally wrong, as to be utterly incapable of correcting itself by any length of time, or of being formed into any mode of polity of which a member of the House of Commons could publicly declare his approbation."[29] He further said that he was ready to show " that those who could, after such a full and fair expression, continue to countenance the French insanity were not mistaken politicians, but bad men."[30] He next proceeded to quote at length some of the more radical statements made in Paine's Rights of Man, which, it will be remembered, was a pamphlet confessedly in favor of republican doctrines as that

---

[26] Life and Letters of Sir Gilbert Elliot I, 376–378.
[27] " Appeal from the New to the Old Whigs in consequence of some late Discussions in Parliament relative to the Reflections on the French Revolution." This pamphlet was published anonymously, but was immediately accredited to Burke. In fact, Richard Burke had had a part in its composition.
[28] Morning Chronicle, May 12, 1791.
[29] Burke, Appeal from New to Old Whigs, 11.
[30] Burke, Appeal from New to Old Whigs, 14.

author understood them.   These quotations Burke professed
to believe representative of the views of those in England
who admired the French Revolution.[31]

There are two possible explanations of Burke's course on
this question.   One impeaches his moral and the other his
mental integrity.   We might conclude, and not without
plausibility, that when the author of the Reflections discovered that, as a result of the publication of his pamphlet,
he could hope for little further advancement from his
former associates, he deliberately decided to support the
ministry, with the design of retrieving his political fortunes.
But there is another view more favorable and probably more
nearly correct.   It was patent to any well-balanced mind
that there certainly was not at this time, if there ever was
afterward, any considerable party in England that desired
to reenact the scenes of the French Revolution in their own
country.   Pitt, even when dealing with Burke, was not so
hypocritical as to profess to believe that there was.[32]   Yet
Burke was unable to rid himself of the notion, which he had
hastily adopted, that there was such a party and that the
established government in England was in imminent danger
of overthrow at its hands.   He was so possessed with this
idea that in his frantic efforts to thwart this imaginary
party he entered into a political alliance with the most
eminent exponent of the constitutional views which the
Reflections had been intended to combat.   That he acted in
conjunction with Pitt with the definite intention of furthering the interests of that minister, the evidence at hand does
not, perhaps, warrant us to conclude.   Yet, at any rate, he
must have understood that his efforts to stigmatize Fox,
both in his instructions to the Duke of Portland and in the
Appeal from the New to the Old Whigs, as far as they
were to have any effect at all, must inevitably result in
advantage to Pitt's interests and that too at a time when the
minister stood in sore need of such assistance.   Furthermore, though no official cognizance had been taken of the

[31] Burke, Appeal from New to Old Whigs, 85–100.
[32] Fitzwilliam, Correspondence of Burke III, 344.

project, Pitt and Dundas had tacitly acquiesced in the mission which the younger Burke had undertaken in favor of the exiled French princes. The son had assisted his father in the preparation of his last pamphlet, and was quite as enthusiastic in the matter as his sire. All of this necessitated frequent communications between the Burkes and the minister, and gave ample opportunity for any agreements they might have deemed it advisable to reach. Whether or not the advice of the ministers had been sought or any suggestions received from them before the publication of the Appeal from the New to the Old Whigs, it is certain that the author expected them to approve of it and thank him for it after its appearance. In view of these facts, it mattered but little whether or not there was an explicit understanding among the members of the new coalition opposed to the French Revolution.[33]

It is certain that Burke had not labored alone and without encouragement in his efforts to induce the members of the aristocratic party to separate from their leader, Fox. The supporters of Pitt were ready to welcome him with open arms into their camp. The World, which since their publication had been busy in its efforts to ridicule the Reflections, by June 4, 1791, began to give more credence to the opinions of one who had "manfully torn himself from connections dishonourable to the interests of his country."[34] After the publication of the Appeal from the New to the Old Whigs, and after the author had been received at Windsor, the same paper felt constrained to recant openly and explicitly its former views:—

---

[33] For Burke's correspondence with his son while the latter was on the Continent in 1791, and other information regarding his mission, see Fitzwilliam, Correspondence of Burke III, 201–383. In a letter to his son, dated August 16, 1791, Burke referred to the mission on which the younger man had gone to the Continent. and said, "I ought to be cautious of seeking the ministers on this business, because they have made no advances whatever to me on the subject; no, not so much as to thank me for my pamphlet." Further on in the same letter he said: "I told you that the ministers had taken no notice of my book. It was then true. But this day I had the inclosed civil note from Dundas."

[34] The World, June 4, 1791.

" However we might have censured many parts of Mr. Burke's political conduct while he disgraced himself and his ability by a uniform concurrence with the rest of the party, it is but justice at present to announce our hearty absolution. His candid avowal of lurking mischiefs in the minds of certain dangerous men, and his beautiful communication of sentiment upon the French Revolution, preponderate all his former political tendencies. . . . By a noble secession from treason intended against the constitution of his country, Mr. Burke has reinstated himself in the high opinion of those who formerly disapproved of his politics : by an open declaration of his motives, he has put the nation on its guard ; and by asserting the just privileges of monarchy he has obtained the peculiar favour of his sovereign." [35]

This was not purely a tribute to Burke's newly acquired zeal on behalf of the administration. The supporters of the minister were busy with their endeavors to supplement the efforts of their ally, and this paragraph was part of a propaganda which had been begun soon after Fox made the avowal in the debate on the Russian armament. The evident purpose of the paragraphs appearing almost daily in the administration newspapers was to create a popular belief that since Fox had confessed his admiration for the French Revolution, he must therefore desire to compass the destruction of the British constitution. These attacks were soon directed against the proposed celebration of the second anniversary of the fall of the Bastille. A similar celebration had been held the year before and had received a rather favorable notice from the administration papers.[36] These festivals were designed to afford an opportunity for conviviality to those who attended. Usually such functions began in the afternoon and continued far into the evening, during which time twenty-five or thirty toasts were drunk. The advertisement for the second banquet specifically re-

[35] The World, October 27, 1791.
[36] Public Advertiser, July 16, 1790. The World, July 16, 1790.

quested that the participants refrain from political discussions.[37] Therefore it is difficult to imagine any unfavorable results from such a celebration except, perhaps, injury to the reputation for sobriety of those who attended. Yet this proposed assembly was now held up as a political red rag to frighten the aristocratic supporters of Fox. Taking their cue from the wild rhetoric of Burke, the writers for the press endeavored to connect this celebration with the intentions of the Whig leader, and to imply that an event of this kind would lead to the most mischievous consequences. For example, as early as May 9, 1791, the World said:—

" We are told by Mr. Burke that plots and strategems are ripening—and we all know that pamphlets, speeches, public meetings and public toasts, of the most seditious kinds are setting afloat by a few artful and designing men, who would plunge their country in ruins for the purpose of ambition or enthusiasm. It behooves Englishmen to watch over such men ; they are easily known—they carry their dark lanthorns in their faces—their half speeches, hesitations and innuendoes—' Willing to wound, but yet afraid to strike.'

" The anniversary of the 14th of July too is approaching, (the memorable anniversary of Mr. Fox's glorious fabric, the French Revolution)—From these beacons, therefore, let Englishmen take warning, and guard that constitution, which has been for ages the nurse of heroes, the pride of nations, from being trampled on, or annihilated by ambitious democrats or canting republicans."

As the date for the celebration approached, these implications became more specific, and the suggestion was repeatedly made that if any disorders should result they must be laid to the charge of the admirers of the French Revolution.[38] One of the papers most active in its efforts to

---

[37] The Star, July 11, 1791.
[38] The World, April 27, 1791; June 4, 8, 18, 1791; July 14, 1791. The Oracle, June 15, 1791; July 4, 1791. Evening Mail, June 17–20, 1791; June 29–July 1, 1791. The following quotations are from these papers. Only a few of those found have been cited. The Evening Mail said:—
" A few false patriots, clothed in the masquerade dress of liberty,

convince the public that the approaching celebration would
be made the occasion for carrying into effect "some seditious projects" on the day that the feast was to be held,
took the precaution to announce that the government, instead of betraying any dread of a dinner, would labor to
avoid the slightest appearance of any such apprehension.
"The Bank Guard has even been forbid to march through
the Strand, that no irritation might be given to inflame the
popular mind; and a field day of the first regiment of foot
guards, destined for today, is, to remove the slenderest pretext, postponed."[39]   The most plausible interpretation of
this editorial is that it was a case of protesting too much,
since such popular excitement as existed had been aroused
solely by the supporters of the administration.   Those concerned in the celebration insisted that they only intended to

---

and concealing beneath it the spirit of the most daring licentiousness, shall in vain attempt to plunge their murderous daggers into
the side of a common venerable parent.   A vigilant ministry will,
no doubt, take timely precautions for the prevention of those
tumults and disorders which afflict the miserable kingdom of France;
and into the net which treacherous *soi-disant* patriots may rashly
spread for others will their feet be taken;—the danger will fall on
their own heads."
      The World:—
"The respectability of the house of the Crown and Anchor in
the Strand, and the number of men of fashion who are to meet
there on this occasion put it out of our power to believe that anything can be meant beyond what is fair and proper.   But it will
undoubtedly be well deserving the attention of the directors of that
meeting to prevent every possible tumult, lest they should share the
odium which any such circumstance would properly deserve."
      Again: "St. George's Fields will be double guarded, it is said,
on the 14th of July next, for reasons too obvious to mention."
      Again: "But the stronger reason why any man who bears the
name of Englishman should watch over such an intended celebration, is when the chief of the party declares in the face of the
world that he looks upon the French Revolution to be one of the
most glorious fabrics ever raised by the wisdom of mankind.   Such
declarations should put every man on his guard, for if he and his
adherents really think so, as good patriots, they should endeavour
to make this country (which they do not seem to admit so glorious
a fabric) something like it.   Therefore, it is to meet this intended
reformation in the bud, that remarks and observations are made
on this unnatural fete, and which we trust will be followed up by
the prudence and foresight of government as well as by the public
at large."
      [39] The Oracle, July 14, 1791.

spend a social evening together, and in fact they did nothing more.   Because of the feelings already stirred up the
principal Whig leaders did not attend,[40] and for the same
reason the diners broke up somewhat earlier than was customary on such occasions.   After they had nearly all gone,
at the time when attendants on such functions were apt to
be considerably under the influence of the beverages used
on the occasion, a mob, seemingly bent on mischief, appeared at the tavern, but finding that the party had dispersed, caused no serious disturbance.[41]

In order to understand the real significance of this dinner in English politics, we must consider it in connection
with a riot which took place in a neighboring town on the
same day.   On July 13 the World announced that seditious
handbills had been posted in the vicinage of Whitehall and
in other towns in England, "evidently with a view to excite
the populace to riot tomorrow."   As Birmingham was the
only place at which such an event actually occurred, it will
be necessary to consider at some length the disorders at
that place, but we must acknowledge at once that because
of the mystery which still envelops the origin of these riots
it will not be possible to reach positive conclusions.   The
best that can be done is to give the circumstances in detail.
Any explanation of the event demands the adoption of
one of two hypotheses.   It is possible that these seditious
handbills and the riots at Birmingham were the work of
revolutionary enthusiasts who failed entirely to appreciate
the real attitude of the English public.   The other explanation is that these seditious notices were a part of the
furtive efforts of some of the supporters of the ministry to
make the celebrations on July 14 the occasions for popular
disorder, with the design of attaching the responsibility for
such disorders to those who admired the French Revolution.
Neither of these conclusions can be completely substantiated
by the evidence at hand, therefore a statement of the case

---

[40] Morning Post, July 13, 1791.
[41] Morning Post, July 15, 1791.   The World, July 15, 1791.   The
Oracle, July 15, 1791.   General Evening Post, July 14–16, 1791.

is all that will be attempted here.   The facts, briefly, are
as follows.

Dr. Joseph Priestley, the celebrated theologian and chem-
ist, lived in Birmingham and was the minister of a dissenting congregation at that place.   On account of his polemical
abilities, he was much disliked by the orthodox clergy in
the community, who were frequently engaged in discussions with him.   The fact that while the established church
was at a standstill in Birmingham the dissenting sects were
growing rapidly and contained the people of the most considerable means in the town,[42] only served to add fuel to
the flames of discord.   Priestley not only disagreed with
the doctrines of the established church but was also frankly
opposed to any state church.   As he himself expressed it,
his teachings laid "grains of gunpowder" which would
finally "blow up the established hierarchy."[43]   He had taken
an active part in the efforts to secure the repeal of the
Corporation and Test Acts, and had thereby aroused additional opposition on the part of the clergy of the Church of
England.   The discussions went to such length that the
ministers of the establishment, in speaking to the lower
classes, charged Priestley with the design of blowing up
the churches.   The agitation was kept up in Birmingham
even after the motion for repeal was defeated in March,
1790.[44]

Under these circumstances, on July 7, 1791, at about the
same time that such notices were appearing in the papers
of the other towns in England, the friends of the French
Revolution in Birmingham advertised that they would have
a dinner on the anniversary of the fall of the Bastille.
With the proposed celebration, however, Priestley seems to
have had nothing to do, nor did he attend the function when
it was held.   It is unnecessary to observe that those in

[42] Morning Post, January 11, 1791; December 24, 1791.   The
Oracle, July 29, 1791.   The Diary; or, Woodfall's Register, July
22, 1791.   Evening Mail, July 27-29, 1791.
[43] Priestley, Letters to Rev. Edward Burn, Preface.
[44] For the titles of some of the pamphlets published, see the appended bibliography.

Birmingham who were friendly to the French Revolution
were, in a large measure, Dissenters, and that an agitation
directed against the Dissenters was also directed against the
admirers of the French Revolution, and vice versa.   It
was said at the time that reports were industriously circulated among the lower classes charging the magistrates with
being unfriendly to the Nonconformists and likely to impose
no punishment for destroying their houses of worship.   A
few days after the announcement of the proposed dinner,
the following notice was circulated:—

"On Friday next will be published, price one half penny,
an authentic list of all those who dine at the hotel, Temple
Row, Birmingham, on Thursday the 14th instant in commemoration of the French Revolution.   Vivant Rex et
Regina."[45]

On the morning of July 11 there appeared in one of the
taverns and on the streets, from some unknown source, a
handbill which was certainly of a seditious character.[46]   On

---

[45] Authentic Account of the Riots in Birmingham, etc.   This
pamphlet was published in September, 1791, and it contains a collection of documents and contemporary accounts pertaining to the
riots.   See the first two pages for the information contained in
the above paragraph.

[46] London Gazette 1791, 431.   Copies of this handbill may be
found in any of the contemporary papers and in many other places.
The following copy is taken from the official proclamation of the
king offering a reward of one hundred pounds for the arrest of
its author:—

"My Countrymen!   The second year of Gallic Liberty is nearly
expired.   At the commencement of the third on the fourteenth
of this month, it is devoutly to be wished that every enemy to civil
and religious despotism would give his sanction to the majestic
common cause by a public celebration of the anniversary.   Remember that on the fourteenth of July the Bastille, that high altar
and castle of despotism, fell.   Remember the enthusiasm, peculiar
to the cause of liberty, with which it was attacked.   Remember
the generous humanity that taught the oppressed, groaning under
the weight of insulted rights, to save the lives of the oppressors!
Extinguish the mean prejudices of nations; and let your numbers
be collected and sent as a free will offering to the National Assembly.   But is it possible to forget that your own Parliament is
venal!   Your Ministers hypocritical!   Your Clergy legal oppressors!
The reigning family extravagant!   The Crown of a certain great
personage becoming every day too weighty for the head that wears
it! too weighty for the people who gave it!   Your taxes are partial
and excessive—your representation a cruel insult upon the sacred
rights of property, religion and freedom.—But on the fourteenth

the same day another tract was distributed under the cap-
tion, " An Incendiary Refuted," which was intended as an
answer to the first paper, and was calculated to arouse the
popular mind against the admirers of the French Revolution, who were supposed to have been the authors of the
tract to which the reply was addressed. It is certainly
noteworthy, if true, that this reply was written and printed
in time to be circulated on the same day that the other
handbill made its appearance. The only alternative to this
conclusion is to assume that the papers were the work of
the same author, or, at least, that there was a previous
concert between the writers.[47]

of this month, prove to the political sycophants of the day that
you reverence the olive branch, that you will sacrifice to public
tranquility till the majority shall exclaim—The peace of slavery is
worse than the war of freedom. Of that moment let tyrants
beware."

The authorship of this document has never been determined.
There are two hypotheses, which are probable according to the
theory adopted to explain the origin of the disturbances. It may
have been the work of a misguided enthusiast for liberty, who
vastly mistook the sentiment of the people. If such was the case
and the authorities were desirous of apprehending the author, in
view of the rewards offered by both the king and the Dissenters
it offers a difficult problem to explain how a person of that character was able so successfully to conceal his identity. On the
other hand, if the publication of this handbill was merely a part
of a preconcerted plan to instigate disorder by furnishing a ground
on which to carry on the agitation in such a manner as to fix the
blame on the supposed revolutionists, it must be admitted that it
was a daring undertaking executed with phenomenal success.

[47] Authentic Account of the Riots in Birmingham, 3. The following is a copy of the second paper :—

" A paper having been distributed in the town this morning,
evidently calculated to weaken the attachment of the people to the
present excellent form of government, and to excite tumults similar
to those which have produced the most atrocious murder, anarchy,
and distress in a neighbouring kingdom, it is thought proper to
apprize the good and peaceable subjects of this place, that every
position in that seditious hand-bill is as false and fictitious as the
wretch who composed it. The present enjoyment we now experience, of every blessing, freedom and protection a mild government
can bestow, is the best refutation of the detestable calumnies of
the author of this hand-bill; and whatever the modern republicans
may imagine, or the regicidal propounders of the Rights of Man
design, let us convince them that we are not so destitute of common
sense, as not to prefer the order, liberty, happiness and wealth,
which is diffused through every portion of the British Empire, to
the anarchy, the licentiousness, the poverty and misery which now
overwhelm the degraded kingdom of France."

The gentlemen who had published the advertisement for
the dinner now, on July 13, offered a reward of one hundred
guineas for the author of the first handbill. In the same
notice they declared their entire ignorance of its origin, and
expressed their firm attachment to the government as it
existed, vested in the three estates of King, Lords, and
Commons.[48] They had written and were preparing to publish another advertisement recalling the notice of the dinner
when they were visited by the proprietor of the tavern at
which it was to be given, who argued that the excitement
was subsiding, and that he could not afford the loss which
would be entailed if the dinner should not be held after
the preparation which had been made for it.[49] It was thereupon decided to adhere to the plan for the celebration, but
to refrain from speeches, and to disperse at an early hour.
This was accordingly done. The company met at three
o'clock in the afternoon and by seven o'clock had all dispersed. A considerable number of bystanders had been
present, and had groaned and hissed as the diners went
into the tavern. However, they then left, and did not return
until more than an hour after the dinner was over and the
hall entirely empty. An effort was made to convince the
mob that the celebration had been concluded, but they de-
molished the windows and otherwise injured the hotel.
Next they proceeded in turn to both the " New " and " Old "
dissenting meeting-houses, and destroyed them. In the
midst of the attending disorder, precautions seem to have
been taken not to endanger the adjacent property. The
seats and woodwork of the Old Meeting-House were torn
out and burned in the churchyard near by, and it was said
that the engine was permitted to play on the adjoining
houses, but not on the church, which was in flames.[50] The
rioters, gaining recruits from the colliers, now proceeded to

---

[48] Morning Post, July 23, 1791. Authentic Account of the Riots
in Birmingham, 3.
[49] The Star, July 21, 1791. Gentleman's Magazine LXI, 599.
[50] Hutton, Life of William Hutton, including a particular Account
of the Riots in Birmingham, 244.

demolish the residences of Dr. Priestley and other prominent Dissenters. Among other unfortunate circumstances
was the almost total destruction of the books and laboratory
of the distinguished scientist. But, even when engaged at
these tasks, the mob furnished a remarkable example of
order amidst confusion. They carefully protected the
property of Methodists and followers of the Countess of
Huntingdon, as well as of the members of the established
church. It was only those who would not join their cry of
" Church and King " who suffered.[51]

In response to the requests for protection and offers of
assistance in quelling the disorders by those whose property
was being destroyed, the magistrates replied, " Pacific
measures are adopted."[52] These same magistrates, from
either design or neglect, had already failed to read the Riot
Act, as was their duty whenever such outbreaks occurred.
This omission was an item of not a little importance when
the time came for the trial of the rioters.[53] At length, on
the third day of the riots, the magistrates and some of the
more prominent churchmen printed and circulated among
those who were taking part in the disorders the following
extraordinary broadside, which they styled, " Important Information of the Friends of the Church and King : "—

" Friends and fellow churchmen, being convinced you are
unacquainted with the fact that the great losses which are
sustained by your burning and destroying the houses of so
many individuals will eventually fall on the county at large,
and not upon the persons to whom they belonged ; we feel it
our duty to inform you that the damage already done, upon
the best computation that can be made, will amount to
upwards of one hundred thousand pounds, the whole of
which enormous sum will be charged upon the respective
parishes and paid out of the rates : We therefore, as your
friends, conjure you immediately to desist from the destruction of any more houses ; otherwise the very proceedings

---

[51] Evening Mail, July 15–18, 1791.
[52] Hutton, Life of William Hutton, 248.
[53] The Star, August 24, 1791.

which your zeal for shewing your attachment to the Church
and King inspired, will inevitably be the means of most
seriously injuring innumerable families who are hearty supporters of the government, and bring on an addition to taxes,
which yourselves and the rest of the friends of the church
will for years feel a grievous burden.   And we must observe to you that any further violent proceedings will more
offend your King and country, than serve the cause of him
and the church.   Fellow churchmen, as you love your King
regard his laws and restore peace."[54]

The "friends and fellow churchmen" either differed
from the opinions so politely expressed by their courteous
advisers, or, as is more likely, they were to such an extent
intoxicated by the liquors they found in the wine-cellars of
the houses that had been destroyed that they did not feel
obliged to heed these admonitions.   At any rate, they did
not disperse until a body of militia appeared.[55]

The authorities took no more vigorous measures to punish
the offenders than they had taken to suppress the disorders.
Only nineteen of the thousands engaged in the riots were arrested.   These were men of the lowest character, and, since
the Riot Act had not been read as the law provided, it was
necessary to prove that they had taken part in the actual
pulling down of a house before they could be convicted.[56]
A few days before the trials the World announced: "It
may, indeed there can be no doubt that it will, be a happy
circumstance for the misguided rioters at Birmingham, that
the judges appointed for their trials are men not only of
extensive legal knowledge, but of admired humanity."[57]

---

[54] Morning Post, July 20, 1791.
[55] For accounts of the riots that have not been cited, see Morning Post, July 18, 19, 22, 30, 1791.   The World, July 18–22, 1791.
The Oracle, July 18, 19, 23, 1791.   Evening Mail, July 18–20, 1791.
The Star, July 16, 18, 20, 1791.
[56] For reports of the trials, see Authentic Account of the Riots
in Birmingham, etc.   The Star, August 1, 24, 1791.   The Diary;
or, Woodfall's Register, August 26, 1791.   Whitehall Evening Post,
August 25–27, 1791; September 1–3, 1791.   General Evening Post,
July 16–19, 1791.
[57] The World, August 9, 1791.

Of the five rioters who were finally convicted, only three were executed. The others were released by the clemency of the king. It was said that the juries at the trials, either accidentally or purposely, were composed entirely of persons who sympathized with the church party.[58] In any event, the circumstances were such that even the Evening Mail, a paper which was favorable though not extremely partizan in its attitude towards the administration, felt obliged to admit that " from the general complexion of the late trials at Warwick, it is tolerably evident that party prejudices, even in cases of life and death, can be carried too far, and that the dire course of national justice may be stopped by the political point of view in which conscience shall behold the nature of an oath. Compassion is, no doubt, a noble attribute, and nearly allied to mercy; but there are cases in which the exercise of either may be a high crime against the peace of society; and lenity to rioters comes under that description."[59] The World, on the other hand, announced to its readers that " the trials of the rioters at Birmingham were, perhaps, the most uninteresting thing which has taken place these ten years."[60] For this reason, no account of them whatever was given.

In forming conclusions concerning these disorders, it is important to consider that the majority of those who took part in them were from the lowest stratum of society, and, according to contemporary statements, ordinarily gave no attention to any church or sect. Yet, by some means, in the midst of riot and lawlessness, in the name of church and king, their efforts were so directed that they destroyed only the property of the members of the societies which were deemed hostile to the church and the constitution. While the troubles were in progress and after they had been quelled the influence of those who were in authority seems to have been exerted to shield the participants in the disorders. Though the partizans of the government were quick

[58] Hutton, Life of William Hutton, 275.
[59] Evening Mail, August 29–31, 1791.
[60] The World, August 31, 1791.

to seize on the riots at Birmingham as an additional argument to support their political purpose, nevertheless it must
be stated that sufficient evidence has not been adduced to
prove that any member of the administration had any direct
part in their instigation.   However, it should be noticed that
the papers which supported the minister were unanimous in
commending the spirit which had given rise to the disturbances, though they professed to regret the excesses that had
resulted.   They asserted that the troubles had been occasioned
by the handbills which had been distributed, and they ascribed these handbills to the same persons who had been
present at the dinner in the hotel.   The papers laid special
stress upon the fact that the fears expressed before the celebration had been realized, and that the subsequent riot had
been the work of the admirers of the French Revolution.[61]

---

[61] Such arguments and sentiments appeared in the papers already
cited.

The World said, July 18, 1791: "The populace of Birmingham,
conceiving that a commemoration of French anarchy in this country
was an insult to the majesty of the Constitution, and a design to
disturb the general and enviable tranquility of the State, assembled
on Thursday before Doadley's hotel, where about eighty persons
were met for the purpose of celebrating the *glorious* 14th of July.
We lament, however, that what certainly proceeded from so
laudable a principle should end in consequences so unjustifiable;
but their resentment being once warmed, soon became inflamed,
and the influence communicated to certain religious conventicles
where they conceived an opposite, though no less inflammable spirit
originated."

Same, July 20, 1791: "Such are the mischiefs of public meetings
which have for their objects revolutions of governments generally
approvable and approved. . . . Some very inflammatory bills dispersed by dissenters previous to the meeting of the 14th of July,
we fear, have all the late disturbances to answer for."

Same, July 21, 1791: "That the riots at Birmingham originated
in a well founded zeal of the people for the support of their government is evident.   Those only, therefore, are to blame who, by
the celebration of revolutions in other countries, and by publications
of an alarming and seditious tendency, impress upon the minds of
the people the idea of deep laid schemes for the overthrow of our
own happy and glorious constitution."

The Oracle, July 18, 1791: "Humanity will certainly regret the
injuries sustained by the dissenters of Birmingham; but the people
lately have been witnesses to a conduct highly reprehensible in the
pastors of such men.   They whose sacred functions it is at all
times to preach peace and to promote it, have latterly been fore-
most in the ranks of such as eulogize the miserable anarchy of a
neighbour nation.   Their publications too have endeavoured to

The evidence adduced shows that this statement of the papers was either a mistake or a wilful perversion of the truth to serve political interests. If the misrepresentation was intentional, it certainly does not tend to discredit the conclusion that the entire affair was but a part of the propaganda instituted by Pitt in self-defense immediately after the failure of the Russian armament.

incite the million to tear the vulnerable fabric of our Constitution to pieces, and frame one for themselves."

Same, July 19, 1791: "The outrages at Birmingham, though they are justly deplored by every good citizen, at least prove one theory which gives a salutary damp to the enthusiasm of the revolutionists. They prove that the mob is hostile to them, and that, therefore, all hope of popular aid in their revolutionary schemes are vain.   It will now be obvious that the policy of government has been cautious and secure in giving no check whatever to the factious proceedings of designing dangerous characters.   The insult offered by these men to the Constitution which is their protectress, has made itself so flagrantly visible, that the people themselves will need the temperate restraint of the ministry to prevent a general sacrifice to offended power."

CHAPTER III.

PARTY REALIGNMENT.

The chief question at issue between the English political parties in 1792 was whether Pitt or Fox should dominate the government. Aside from the advantages which possession gave, there were several other reasons why the former was confident of ultimate success. Whether his motive was ambition, patriotism, or a mixture of both, it is certainly true that Pitt, in meeting the problems which faced him in this and the following years, manifested the ability and the willingness to adapt his wishes and principles to existing opportunities whenever he was convinced of his inability to make circumstances conform to his will. Whether it be decided that his stake was the common good or the gratification of his own desires, it is undeniable that his political methods resembled those of a man who was playing a stupendous game, and who was too intent on winning to be over-scrupulous as to the means employed to attain the end in view. In appearance at least he sought to bind his associates to him by ties of self-interest rather than by sentiment or appeals to principle. But, if his political conduct during these seven years be compared to a game, it must be admitted that he played it with consummate skill and ability, and for a time at least with continued success. His appeal to the selfishness of those whom he wished to control was seldom in vain, and stamped him as a statesman able to estimate accurately the character of the men with whom he had to deal.

We should be slow to affirm that Fox was actuated by motives or employed methods that were on a higher plane than those of his eminent rival. The Whig leader was probably as capable as was Pitt of shaping his principles to meet the exigencies of his political ambition and of advocating reform because he believed that it would ultimately be the popular side. It may be that, if opportunity had offered, he would have hazarded public fortune to secure his private interest. But to his credit be it said he did not do so. He resisted the importunities of powerful and influential friends, severed ties which had endured for a generation, and faced the immediate destruction of cherished hopes, which but a few months before had seemed on the point of realization, in order to raise his voice on behalf of a cause which he professed to believe was in the interest of the public good. We do not imply that he was in advance of the school of politics in which he had been trained, or was above rewarding his followers with public spoils. Yet it is an eloquent testimony to the personal magnetism of the man that, at the hour of parting, he could claim the respect and admiration of those who could no longer agree with him politically, and that he was able to prevent the final dissolution of his party organization for more than a year after many of his aristocratic friends had withdrawn from him their support.[1]

The political situation in the spring of 1792, as it appeared to Pitt, seemed to present the following possibilities. He and Thurlow still found it difficult to work together in harmony, and an open breach between them was only a matter of time. Whenever that time should come, Pitt naturally wished to be in a position to dictate the dismissal of the lord chancellor. In the meantime, however, the Whigs appeared to have triumphed in the matter of the Russian imbroglio, and the prestige of the minister seemed to have been lessened accordingly. Again, the king had already been called on to consent to the retirement of the

---

[1] For evidence on the personal relations of Fox with the aristocratic members of the party, in addition to the citations that will be found in other parts of this study, see Carlisle Papers, 698. Lessons to a young Prince from an old Statesman, 6. This pamphlet was an anonymous publication which purported to instruct the Prince of Wales as to how he should read Burke's Reflections. It was published in 1791, and was probably written by Burke himself.

Duke of Leeds, and it was manifestly impolitic to request him to dismiss Thurlow without good reasons. Should the chancellor unite his forces with the aristocratic Whig leaders it was by no means certain that George III would not look with favor on such a combination even though Fox was not then in favor. Among the personal adherents of Pitt there was not a man of sufficient attainments to succeed to the chancellorship if Thurlow should be dismissed. In addition to this, the defection of Thurlow in the House of Lords would leave Grenville the only champion of the ministerial program, with the ex-chancellor as an adversary, and this possibility was an item of no mean consideration since, in spite of its ample voting strength, the administration was singularly destitute of leaders in the upper house.[2] Therefore, if the minister was to secure himself in the possession of the government, it was necessary for him not only to strengthen his hold on the leadership of his own party but also to weaken the Whigs. His efforts to divide and discredit the opposition, which he now maintained with renewed vigor, had a twofold purpose: he hoped to bring those who adhered to the party into such ill repute that the king would not intrust the government to them, and at the same time to detach a conservative element in order to add it to his own followers. Incidentally, he remembered that the woolsack might be useful to induce a reluctant Whig to desert his party. But the fear of the French Revolution was the effective weapon with which he expected to destroy the strong organization that opposed him. The reform element in the party itself, in the spring of 1792, had prepared the way for its own destruction. It only remained for Pitt to take advantage of the situation.

Singularly enough, the opportunity came with the organization of a society to support an issue of which Pitt himself had earlier been an enthusiastic champion. On April 11, 1792, one hundred and thirty-seven gentlemen, including

---

[2] For a discussion of this phase of the situation, see Burges to Auckland, Auckland MSS. XXXII, 308–310; also Dropmore Papers II, 272.

twenty-two members of Parliament, founded an association which they called " Friends of the People associated for the Purpose of obtaining a Parliamentary Reform." According to the statement which the charter members signed, this association was organized for the purpose of " promoting to the utmost of their power, the following constitutional objects, making the preservation of the Constitution, on its true principles, the foundation of all their proceedings." The first of these " constitutional objects " was " to restore the freedom of election, and a more equal representation of the people in Parliament." The second was to secure to the people a more frequent exercise of their right of electing their representatives."[3] Those who participated in this organization were largely of two classes. One consisted partly of the younger element among the Whigs and partly of older members, like Sir Philip Francis, who did not agree with the views of the conservative landowners. The remainder were such men as Major Cartwright and others who had been members of similar societies in the early eighties, when a more radical reform than was now proposed had been advocated by Pitt and the Duke of Richmond. The more prominent members of Parliament who signed the declaration were Charles Grey, Sheridan, and Thomas Erskine, the advocate.[4]

At a meeting of the society on April 26, 1792, an " Address to the People of Great Britain " was drafted for publication. As a further means for carrying on the propaganda, a motion for parliamentary reform was to be made in Parliament. Grey was selected to make and Erskine to second this motion. The address merely set forth the moderate aims of the society and the eminent precedents for advocating a reform such as the society favored.[5]

---

[3] Wyvill, Political Papers III, Appendix, 128. The proceedings of this society were published in several forms shortly after its organization. For titles see the appended bibliography. The proceedings also appeared in the contemporary newspapers. A convenient edition of them was published as an appendix to the third volume of the Political Papers of Rev. Christopher Wyvill. This edition will be used in the citations which follow.
[4] Wyvill, Political Papers III, Appendix, 129.
[5] Wyvill, Political Papers III, Appendix, 143.

As was pointed out at the time by a newspaper,[6] it was extremely unlikely that the aristocratic Whigs could be brought to support a reform that would lessen their own influence by eradicating the rotten boroughs, some of which they controlled. Fox recognized the nature of the situation and did not join the society. On the day before Grey was to announce his motion a meeting of prominent party leaders who were opposed to the movement was held to consider what attitude should be adopted. They knew that Fox would vote with his friends although he had not joined their club. Those who attended the meeting seem to have decided to follow their usual course in such cases, and to oppose the measures, though without any thought of deposing Fox from the leadership. However, the mere fact that a meeting was called showed that considerable feeling had been aroused. Pitt learned of the meeting through Lord Auckland, and immediately determined to put into effect a piece of political strategy.[7]

On April 30, 1792, Grey gave notice that in the next session he would submit for consideration a motion for parliamentary reform. He accompanied the announcement with a brief statement of the circumstances, and of the reasons for the proposed motion. Ordinarily this would have ended the matter until the motion was actually made. Pitt immediately rose, remarking that he believed that he was not strictly in order, but since no objection was made he would go on with his speech. He admitted in the beginning that he was not going to act consistently with his past record, but excused himself on the ground that " the question to be brought forward on this subject would involve something more than the character, the fortune, the connexion, the liberty, or the life of any individual." He was convinced that it would " affect the peace and tranquility which, under the favour of Providence, this country had, for a long time, enjoyed, in a superior degree perhaps to any part of the habitable globe." He argued that the time

---

[6] The Oracle, April 16, 1792.
[7] Auckland, Journal and Correspondence II, 401.

set for the motion was inopportune, and called attention to the situation in France. "He did not mean," he said, "to allude to the sentiments of any particular member of that house for the purpose of being severe; but when they came in the shape of advertisements in the newspapers, inviting the public as it were to repair to their standard and join them, they should be reprobated, and the tendency of their meetings exposed to the people in their true colours." He next urged the friends of the constitution to be particularly active against such men, because he had seen with concern "that those gentlemen of whom he spoke, who were members of that house, were connected with others, who professed not reform only, but direct hostility to the very form of our government. This afforded suspicion that the motion for a reform was nothing more than a preliminary to the overthrow of the whole system of our present government. . . . When he saw these opinions published, and knew them to be connected with opinions that were libels on the form of our government,—the hereditary succession to the throne—the hereditary titles of our men of rank,—and the total destruction of all subordination in the state, he confessed he felt no inclination to promise his support to the proposed motion for a parliamentary reform." Few men besides Pitt would have had the audacity to make such a speech. He was accusing a society of reputable men, organized to promote a less radical reform than he himself had championed, of something closely akin to treason, merely on the ground that they had been courteous enough to reply to the communications of another society which recommended that its members read Paine's Rights of Man; and he made this accusation in face of the fact that even the second society professed to favor no further change in the British constitution than a reform of the lower house of parliament.

Fox, who had not joined the Friends of the People, replied to this extraordinary speech. He admitted that he would not have advised the bringing forward of the pro-

posed motion at that time, but said that, since it had been
done, he would support it. He pointed out that Paine's
book was not designed as an argument for the reform of
the government, but " went the length of changing the form
of it." He asked, " Why, then, should those who professed
reverence for the constitution of this country be charged
with having taken up with sentiments contained in a book
that was a libel on it ? " Burke spoke next, and " ridiculed
the idea of a moderate or temperate reform as impossible."
Windham, Thomas Grenville, and other sympathizers with
the aristocratic Whigs also expressed themselves as opposed
to reform. But, in general, they agreed with the sentiment
of Lord North, who concluded his speech by saying, " He
hoped his differing in this particular instance from the
opinion of his honourable friend who had given notice would
make no alteration whatever in that friendship which had
hitherto subsisted between them."[8]

But this debate, which, it will be observed, had been started
by Pitt, served the purpose which the minister had in view.
It confirmed the impressions which he had received
from Auckland, that the question of reform as agitated by
Grey's society had already created a serious difference of
opinion in the opposition. He had now only to convince
prominent Whigs that the Friends of the People were such
a serious menace to the peace and safety of the country
that it was their duty to accept offices and support his administration for the purpose of counteracting the influences
of this society. With that purpose in view, he wrote to
Auckland on the day after the discussion in Parliament,
requesting him to obtain a list of the Whigs who had attended the party council two days before, and in the same
letter he made the following statement :—

" I wish also you would turn in your mind whether it
might not be useful to summon a Privy Council, at which
the Duke of Portland, Lord Guilford, Lord Fitzwilliam,
Lord Loughborough, and the leading persons might attend

---

[8] For this debate, see Hansard, Parliamentary History XXIX,
1300–1341.

for the express purpose of considering proper instructions to be given to the Lord Lieutenants and Magistrates in the different counties, and such other measures as the present circumstances may require."[9]

It was clearly Pitt's aim to cultivate, by means of a campaign against imaginary dangers, the fears which had already been aroused in the minds of some of the prominent Whigs and so to gain their support for his measures. His purpose was primarily to promote party defection among the Whigs, and only secondarily, if at all, to check the propaganda of the reformers. Probably he had no great fear at this time that this particular reform movement would become a matter of any considerable importance. James Bland Burges, who to a large extent shared the confidence of the ministers, writing May 4, 1792, with regard to the movement, concluded, "They [the reformers] have not, however, met with any success; on the contrary, the people are generally against them."[10] Sir Gilbert Elliot, a prominent Whig who had hitherto been much concerned for fear lest the reform movement would gain ground owing to the agitation, wrote to his wife on May 12, after he had gone to London, "On the whole, this affair seems less formidable than it might have been, and is likely enough by want of heartiness in many of the members and by divisions among themselves, to dwindle and expire pretty quietly."[11] No other evidence has been found which indicates that there existed at this time among the people at large any sufficient sympathy with this movement to warrant the measures now adopted by the administration.

However, two days after he had sent the above letter to his wife, Sir Gilbert Elliot had a conversation with the Duke of Portland "on the subject of these associations, which have come to be thought much more seriously of than one could so soon have imagined." And he reported

[9] Auckland, Journal and Correspondence II, 402.
[10] Hutton, Selections from the Letters and Correspondence of Sir James Bland Burges, 220.
[11] Life and Letters of Sir Gilbert Elliot II, 21.

that Pitt told the Duke of Portland he had the permission
of the king to take up the matter of the associations
with him, at the same time expressing satisfaction "at the
disposition which had been shown by the Duke and his
friends to preserve tranquility." In the conversation "Pitt
told the Duke that he had undoubted information of many
foreigners who are employed to raise sedition in England,
and that money is sent from France to assist in this attempt." He proposed that Portland and his friends should
attend the Privy Council for the purpose of taking steps
to avert these alleged dangers, and he even offered "to make
those Privy Councillors whom the Duke should recommend
for that purpose." The minister suggested also that a
proclamation should be issued "against seditious writings
and publications, and calling on the magistrates to be vigilant
in suppressing any appearance of tumult if it should be
necessary."[12] Portland refused to take part in the Privy
Council, but expressed his willingness to support the
minister in any measure necessary to secure the interests
of the country.

In spite of this partial miscarriage of their program, the
ministers decided to issue the proclamation and to prepare
addresses in both houses of Parliament. It was hoped that
by making the question one which concerned the safety of
the most cherished English institutions, the Whig aristocrats
would thereby be induced to support the ministers without
inquiring too closely into the nature of the alleged dangers.
But it is not improbable that the real occasion for so much
haste in carrying out this program grew out of an incident
in the House of Lords.[13]

That body was considering paragraph by paragraph a bill
" for appropriating a certain sum annually for paying off
the national debt," which was one of Pitt's own measures.
A discussion arose on the provision that "no future loan
shall be made without being provided for at the same time."

---

[12] Life and Letters of Sir Gilbert Elliot II, 23–25.
[13] Buckingham, Court and Cabinets II, 207.

Thurlow, while he supported the bill, ridiculed this feature, which, he said, " would only hand down to posterity aphorisms." The force of his argument was that the clause was useless, since no minister in the future would feel any obligation to comply with such a provision if it should interfere with his plans.[14] Now we know that Pitt was only awaiting a suitable opportunity to get rid of the lord chancellor, and that he had taken the precaution to commit the king to his program by informing him of the supposed dangers to the constitution from the Friends of the People and by securing his approval of the administrative measures which were designed to avert these dangers. Pitt, therefore, felt that the king would dismiss Thurlow if he should demand it. There was no immediate need of the services which the lord chancellor had been accustomed to render as a leader in the upper house. With the Great Seal added to other inducements which he had to offer, Pitt hoped to gain additional support from the Whigs in the upper house before Parliament should assemble again. Accordingly, he resolved to make Thurlow's speech on the sinking-fund paragraph the occasion of his dismissal. On May 16, 1792, he wrote to the king declaring that he would resign if the lord chancellor were not dismissed. George III did not hesitate, and on that same day Thurlow was asked to resign.[15]

The prospects for the success of Pitt's schemes now seemed bright. On May 31, 1792, he issued his proclamation against seditious writings, which he had previously submitted to the Duke of Portland for approval.[16] He proposed to increase the excitement which the proclamation would naturally arouse by discussions both in Parliament and throughout the kingdom, and accordingly he caused addresses to be brought forward in both houses, which became the subjects of long debates. He hoped that these

---

[14] Debrett, Parliamentary Register XXXIII, 418. Hansard omits this debate from the Parliamentary History.

[15] Stanhope, Life of William Pitt II, 149. Buckingham, Court and Cabinets II, 208. Dropmore Papers II, 271.

[16] Life and Letters of Sir Gilbert Elliot II, 26.

debates would mark the final separation of some of the
aristocratic Whigs from Fox and his friends, but, according
to the speech of Windham, the success was slight as the
Whigs merely adhered to their policy of differing on the
proposition at issue, and showed themselves unwilling to
sever their relations as yet with their leader.[17]   But the
value of the proclamation against seditious writings had
yet to be tested.   For two months after its publication addresses of thanks and professions of loyalty were sent from
almost every county and borough in the kingdom.[18]   Some
of these addresses were directly inspired by members of the
administration; others, perhaps, were the results of meetings called by the clergy or other officials or by partizans
of the government in the communities from which they
came.   When the wishes of the government became known
to its supporters it did not become necessary to make suggestions as directly as did Lord Grenville to his brother on
June 13: " Our addresses are going on swimmingly, and it
will, I think, soon be time for the loyal county of B——
to show itself."[19]   Nor is it probable that the ministers took
as much pains with the phraseology of all the addresses as
they did with this one.   When the first draft was presented
for his approval, Grenville wrote, " I think the address
perfectly unexceptionable as it now stands; but I should
wish to add a sentence somewhere, expressing the satisfaction and concurrence of the county in the sentiments
expressed by Parliament on this subject, because I think
it may not be indifferent to future debates to have to quote
expressions of this sort, in order to show that, on a great
occasion like this, the sense of the people was immediately
and completely expressed by Parliament."[20]   In order that
Buckingham might know more precisely the kind of address that was desired, a copy of one from Devonshire,

[17] Hansard, Parliamentary History XXIX, 1476–1534.
[18] London Gazette 1792, 372–769.   The addresses were published
in the order in which they were received.
[19] Buckingham, Court and Cabinets II, 209.
[20] Buckingham, Court and Cabinets II, 211.   For further particulars concerning this address: Dropmore Papers II, 282, 284, 285.

which had also been submitted for approval, was inclosed with this letter.

No sooner had the snare been set than the ministers became busy in their attempts to capture their prey. According to the plan, of which the proclamation of May 21 was a preliminary, the time had now come to begin negotiations with the aristocratic Whigs.[21] On the very day that the debate on the address took place in the House of Lords, Dundas made the first overtures.[22] On June 9, a few days later, Burke visited the Duke of Portland, and, in the presence of the duke, Lord Loughborough, Lord Fitzwilliam, and Lord Malmesbury, argued at great length, amidst the silence of his auditors, "that it was absolutely necessary to force Fox to a specific declaration." In addition, he contended that the times required "a union of all abilities, all the weight, and all the wealth of the country." After Burke had gone, Loughborough, for whom the Great Seal was intended[23] and who had already been approached, took up the argument and asserted that Burke had said "what was true, but that it should not be said."[24] On June 13 Loughborough called on Portland with a definite proposition which had been made to him by Dundas on behalf of the administration. The Whigs were offered the lord chancellorship, the secretarysnip of state for home affairs, the presidency of the council, and the privy seal, besides two or three members of the Privy Council in the House of Commons.[25] Portland imagined that this was a bona fide proposal for a union of parties, and immediately desired that Fox be consulted. He himself suggested that the most feasible solution would be for Pitt to resign the chancellorship of the exchequer in favor of a neutral man like the Duke of Leeds, under whom both Pitt and Fox would serve as secretaries of state.[26] Fox expressed a readiness to go into office if

---

[21] Dropmore Papers II, 272.
[22] Life and Letters of Sir Gilbert Elliot II, 35.
[23] Buckingham, Court and Cabinets II, 212.
[24] Malmesbury, Diaries and Correspondence II, 453.
[25] Malmesbury, Diaries and Correspondence II, 458.
[26] Malmesbury, Diaries and Correspondence II, 459.

his friends thought it best, provided he was given an equal
share of power with Pitt. At the same time he expressed
his belief that the minister had no other purpose than to
weaken the Whig party and strengthen his own.[27] Meanwhile, on June 15, Loughborough dined with Pitt and
Dundas. The minister said "that he did not come with the
command of the king to propose a coalition, but that he
would be responsible that it would please the king and queen,
and that the only difficulty at all likely to arise was about
Fox." The difficulty suggested was that the king would
have nothing to do with the Whig leader on account of his
approval of the French Revolution and parliamentary reform.[28] After further consultation with Portland and his
friends, in which he tried to convince them that it was un-
reasonable to expect the minister "to give up the Treasury,"[29] Loughborough again dined with Pitt and Dundas on
June 25. The minister now "declined going further with
the arrangement." But Loughborough told Malmesbury
that he "spoke in such a manner as to leave no doubt
whatever that he meant and wished it should come forward
again."[30]

In the meantime Burke was doing his utmost to convince
the friends of the Duke of Portland that "the principles
broached by Grey and others, and not disavowed by Fox,
had necessarily drawn a line of division in the party, and
that it was necessary to declare this distinctly and decidedly;
that for the better security, and in order to give a strong and
convincing mark of it to the public, Lord Loughborough
should, by being made Chancellor, represent the party in
the Cabinet."[31] Pitt had by no means given up the project;
he had merely changed his tactics. Lord Guilford, the
chancellor of Oxford, was critically ill, and the minister
proposed that on his decease the Duke of Portland should

---

[27] Malmesbury, Diaries and Correspondence II, 461.
[28] Malmesbury, Diaries and Correspondence II, 459.
[29] Malmesbury, Diaries and Correspondence II, 465.
[30] Malmesbury, Diaries and Correspondence II, 468.
[31] Malmesbury, Diaries and Correspondence II, 466.   Life and
Letters of Sir Gilbert Elliot II, 51–52.

be elected to succeed him, and with the permission of the
king should receive the garter.[32] With considerable effort
on the part of the ministers, Portland was elected to the
chancellorship of Oxford;[33] but he refused the "blue
ribbon."[34]

At this point it is well to recall another plan for a coalition between the parties, which did not originate with the
administration and had little to do with the final arrangement, but which historians have confused with the negotiations described above. We have already noted that when
the prospect of a coalition was first mentioned to the Duke
of Portland, he suggested the Duke of Leeds as chancellor
of the exchequer. Leeds seems to have heard of this through
some one of that group of personal hangers-on whom
Malmesbury not inaptly designated a "string of toad-
eaters."[35] A meeting was arranged between Portland
and Leeds, which took place on July 20, 1792.[36] At this
meeting Leeds offered to speak to "the King himself, or
Mr. Pitt, should any interference be thought expedient in
that quarter."[37] After receiving further communications
from his personal adherents, Sir Ralph Woodford and
Stephen Rolleston, who had really inspired the entire
scheme, Leeds wrote to Portland asking for permission to
relate the substance of their conversation to the king.[38]
With a view to granting this permission, Malmesbury was
assigned the task of consulting Fox in order to gain his
consent. In a conversation on July 30 the Whig leader
approved of the proposed step but insisted that Leeds speak
to the king before mentioning the matter to Pitt and
Dundas. He expected thereby to prove the truth of his

[32] Dropmore Papers II, 294.
[33] Dropmore Papers II, 300.
[34] Malmesbury, Diaries and Correspondence II, 471.
[35] Browning, Political Memoranda of the Duke of Leeds, 179.
[36] Browning, Political Memoranda of the Duke of Leeds, 175.
[37] Browning, Political Memoranda of the Duke of Leeds, 179.
Leeds MSS. VIII, 1–37. Malmesbury, Diaries and Correspondence
II, 470.
[38] Browning, Political Memoranda of the Duke of Leeds, 180–182.
Leeds MSS. VIII, 39–43.

contention that the minister had never had any other purpose than to divide the opposition.[39]   When, on August 14, Leeds visited the king and unbosomed himself, George III told him that he had heard nothing on the subject for a long time, but that Pitt had some months before spoken of "something like an opening on the part of the Duke of Portland and his friends," and that he had replied, "Anything complimentary to them, but no power."[40]

The negotiation now reached the ears of Pitt, who naturally resented such an interference in his relations with the king.   Therefore, when Leeds felt obliged to tell the minister of what he had done, he received "a very curt note from him," appointing an interview for August 22.[41]   After he had told his story, Pitt replied "that there had been no thoughts of any alteration in the government, that circumstances did not call for it, nor did the people wish it, and that no new arrangement either by change or coalition had ever been in contemplation."   Leeds recalled the conferences with Loughborough, which Pitt acknowledged, but said "that such meetings had not in view any change of administration."[42]   Naturally   these   assertions   surprised Leeds.   But, if allowance is made for the exaggerations in statement caused by Pitt's resentment and for the inaccuracies inevitable in reporting such a conversation from memory, it is probable that the minister told substantially the truth.   His purpose was merely to strengthen his hold on the government by dividing the opposition, and he was only holding out some vacant offices as a means to accomplish that end.   It was becoming increasingly necessary for Pitt to bring matters to an issue.   With Thurlow in opposition, he could not meet Parliament without the possibility of serious embarrassment unless he could win and hold considerable support from the aristocratic Whigs.   The very fact that they were likely to gain such a considerable ally

---

[39] Malmesbury, Diaries and Correspondence II, 472. Leeds MSS. VIII, 47.
[40] Browning, Political Memoranda of the Duke of Leeds, 188.
[41] Browning, Political Memoranda of the Duke of Leeds, 192.
[42] Browning, Political Memoranda of the Duke of Leeds, 194.

as the ex-chancellor seemed to make it necessary to use more extreme measures in order to induce a sufficient number of them to secede from their party.

At this juncture a new phase of policy began to develop for Pitt on the Continent, a phase that concerned the time-honored relations between England and France. His father had been obliged to leave the task unfinished, but now the trend of events in France seemed to be toward a situation which, should he be able to take advantage of it, would enable the son to carry the work to completion. If, in the latter months of 1792, Pitt was willing to hazard much on a single throw, he was no longer playing for a petty stake. He was already reasonably certain that in the end his government would come out of the struggle with Fox as strong as and perhaps stronger than at the beginning, and his only concern was as to whether it would be strong enough for him, at an opportune moment, to plunge England into the sea of continental strife for the purpose of obtaining territory which seemed at the time easy of capture. The precise moment at which Pitt ceased to be contented with the prospect of securing his own political position and began to strive for the larger prize is not easy to determine. The circumstances which attended this change of his program, as far as it pertained to continental affairs, will form the subject of the next chapter, but it has been necessary to note the change of purpose in order to understand the extraordinary measures which the minister used in the later months of 1792 for the purpose of making absolute his dominance in English politics.

According to a letter which George Rose, secretary of the treasury and one of Pitt's confidential subordinates, wrote to Auckland on July 13, 1792, the minister's first hope had been to induce a large number of the aristocratic Whigs to secede in a body and coalesce with his administration. To succeed in this plan, it was necessary to leave Fox with the reformers, since the Whig leader would certainly not agree to become as subservient as Pitt desired

that his associates should be. On the other hand, the noblemen whose support the minister wished to secure were exceedingly reluctant to sever their relations with Fox, though
they would readily have joined the administration party if
their talented leader had agreed to accompany them.[43] Consequently Rose was convinced as early as August 20 that
the best plan would be to induce prominent Whigs to accept
office as individuals.[44] Rose and Burges, both of whom had
the confidence of the ministers, were agreed that it was
imperative to find some solution of the matter before the
meeting of Parliament.[45] Lord Auckland desired one of
the vacancies in the cabinet, and on August 31 Pitt himself
authorized Rose to write to him, stating that he could do
nothing until after Parliament assembled, as he still hoped
to induce prominent members of the opposition to accept
office under his government.[46] That he would succeed in
his attempts in this direction was now reasonably certain.
The only doubt lay in the time required for Loughborough
and those of his type to make up their minds. That they
should come to a decision at once was imperative if Pitt
were to carry out his projects, and extreme measures therefore became necessary.

Parliament was summoned to meet on November 15, 1792.
Loughborough and Windham had already been offered
places.[47] Consequently they became active in their efforts
to persuade the adherents of Portland to unite with Pitt.
Even Burke wrote to his son in September, " Lord Loughborough and Windham are alarmed about the present state
of Europe in a different manner from that which is common, and they have a real desire of doing something."[48]
However, they would not accept office without the consent
of the Duke of Portland, and the duke persisted in his
decision that, while he was ready to support the adminis-

---

[43] Auckland MSS. XXXII, 326.
[44] Auckland MSS. XXXIII, 106.
[45] Auckland MSS. XXXII, 308–310.
[46] Auckland MSS. XXXIII, 183, 210.
[47] Baring, Diary of the Right Honourable William Windham, 257.
[48] Fitzwilliam, Correspondence of Burke III, 526.

tration in particular measures designed to secure the safety
of the country, he saw no need for making a public announcement that opposition was at an end.[49]   Under these
circumstances, on November 15, Parliament was further prorogued until January 3, 1793, and Pitt proceeded to take
more energetic steps to convince the aristocratic Whigs that
it was necessary for them to separate from Fox.

In addition to the addresses from the counties and boroughs, already mentioned, two other results of the proclamation of May 21, 1792, contributed to the spread of a fear
of sedition and French principles in the minds of the landed
class and the people generally.   One, at least, of these consequences had been anticipated in the original plan.   The
justices, in their charges to the grand juries at the regular
assizes, had included comments on these subjects.   Some
of these comments were afterwards published and distributed.[50]   At the same time, the clergy in their sermons
endeavored to impress similar warnings on the people.
Perhaps it did not require any direct suggestions from the
source from which preferment would come to induce a
would-be bishop to preach a political sermon.   Still, if pressure from above had been necessary, it is worth noting that
at another time Pitt, in directing his subordinate to notify
a new dean of Canterbury of his appointment, had also
requested him to contrive " at the same time to make sure
of the return we wish as far as you can with propriety."[51]
But the government's proclamation was probably all that
was needed in this case to urge the patriotic divines to
what they may easily have believed to be their duty.   However that may be, the fact remains that the ecclesiastics
became even more extreme in their loyalty than the minister
himself ever professed to be.   Take for example the views
of the chaplain of the Duke of York:—

---

[49] Carlisle Papers, 697.
[50] Dropmore Papers II, 284.   For titles of several that were published, see the appended bibliography.
[51] Harcourt, Diaries and Correspondence of Right Honourable
George Rose I, 107.

"As men have not in reason any right to govern themselves, or to be governed by their own consent, so neither do
there appear in the established order of nature any traces
of a plan by which they may enjoy that privilege. As soon
as man is born he is subject, by the ordinance of nature and
Providence, to the government of others."[52]

Another sermonizer on "Christian Politics" asserted:—

"Power belongs with God; and all power and authority
come from God. They are given and intrusted by Him for
the general good of his creatures. Power can no more
originate from the people than the soul can originate from
the body; or than heaven can originate from the earth: the
higher produces the lower; the greater produces the less;
and not the reverse of it."[53]

It should not be inferred that even a majority of the clergy
held these views, though it is clear that most of them inclined in that direction. "Let every soul be subject to the
higher powers" and "Meddle not with those who are given
to change" became favorite texts for sermons.[54] We should
remember that the clergy were often men of considerable
consequence. They were sometimes the younger sons of
the nobility and were, in many cases, prominent in the local
affairs of the community. Their sermons were frequently
published in pamphlet form, and it is only necessary to
examine the files of a contemporary review to understand
something of the estimation in which they were held.

Coincident with the warnings of the justices and the sermons of the clergy, neither of which were calculated to allay
the excitement that naturally resulted from the meetings
held for the purpose of approving the proclamation of May
21, the administration newspapers carried on a similar

---

[52] Nares, Principles of government deduced from Reason, 18.
[53] Agutter, Christian Politics, 5. Continuing, the preacher de-
nounced republican government as "the lowest and worst of all
forms of government. . . . Where the people are deluded with
the name of liberty, whilst they groan under severest tyranny of
licentiousness and are insulted by the lowest of the people."
[54] For titles of other sermons, etc., of this character which have
been examined, see the appended bibliography.

propaganda. Every local disturbance, arising from whatever cause, was heralded as sedition, or something worse.[55]
The country gentleman, who did not understand the ulterior
source of all these alarmist reports, naturally thought the
government neglectful of its duty in not taking more radical
steps to meet such impending dangers. The situation is
disclosed in a reply written by Grenville, November 14, to
a letter from his brother, urging measures of this kind:—

"It is not unnatural, nor is it an unfavourable symptom,
that people who are thoroughly frightened, as the body of
landed gentlemen in this country are, should exaggerate
these stories as they pass from one mouth to the other; but
you, who know the course of this sort of reports, ought not
too hastily to give credit to them."[56]

It is also apparent from the letters of Burges and Rose
to Auckland, as well as from the first part of the letter
noted above from Lord Grenville, that the ministers themselves were not seriously alarmed at the prospect of any
seditious outbreaks.[57] This conclusion is strengthened by
the fact that on November 15 they thought it proper to
delay the meeting of Parliament until the early days of the
next year.

Three days after the proclamation postponing the meeting
of Parliament was issued, Pitt summoned Loughborough
to a conference.[58] From the accounts which have been

---

[55] The only possible reference is to the files of the contemporary
papers. Few days passed on which a paragraph of this nature was
not published. The following from the Public Advertiser, October
2, 1792, will serve as an example:—
"Is this a time for the Blue and Buff to think of getting into
power, when they are known to be zealous patrons of the French
Revolution, and have been attempting to form societies in this
country similar to that of the detestable Jacobins, who seem to be
only actuated by ambition or love of mischief, and who care not
what blood is shed and what horrors prevail, so that their au.
thority is not diminished. Let the Blue and Buff make the *amende
honorable* before they presume to expect the public to place any
confidence in them, and fairly acknowledge that sedition is not
freedom nor subordination slavery."
[56] Buckingham, Court and Cabinets II, 227.
[57] Auckland MSS. XXXIII, 288, 327; XXXIV, 342.
[58] Leeds MSS. VIII, 83, 85. The personal agents of the Duke of
Leeds had been secretly continuing their efforts to convey to the

preserved of this interview, the minister seems to have proposed to Loughborough that if he still found it impossible to accept the Great Seal, he should, in any case, give the administration open support in the upper house. According to the report of the conversation which Pitt sent to Grenville on the same day, Loughborough replied that he had long been willing to accept the office "whenever the Duke of Portland and his friends thought it would be useful that he should. . . . He therefore declined (as we expected) giving his answer till he should have seen the Duke." But the would-be lord chancellor "confirmed the account of the disposition of the party to support without making terms," and "stated his own clear opinion that it was the only line for them to adopt." However, Loughborough promised to call on Pitt again, after a few days, to give him the result of the interview with Portland.[59] Three days after this conference, Loughborough and Malmesbury dined with the Duke of Portland. Regarding the conversation which took place at that time, Malmesbury told Sir Ralph Woodford that "they talked everything over, but that they were of opinion nothing was to be done at present, for fear of exposing too much the weakness of government, but to give their support spontaneously; all change to be deferred for the present."[60] The reply which Loughborough was thereby enabled to give to Pitt was of such a nature that Rose wrote to Auckland on November 27: "Your friend, Lord Loughborough, has acted in a manner that does him the most possible honour, and marks his judgement strongly as his disinterestedness. You will probably hear the particulars mod-

---

king suggestions of the necessity for a change in the ministry, with a view to securing some important office for the duke. As a consequence they were suspicious of any independent move on the part of the aristocratic Whigs. When Loughborough was summoned by Pitt, they immediately reported the fact to their patron, and even went so far as to inform him that the interview had lasted exactly one hour and ten minutes, and that immediately afterwards Pitt had written a note to Grenville, who, after considering it for three hours, replied on the same day.

[59] Dropmore Papers II, 335.
[60] Leeds MSS. VIII, 87.

estly told by himself. I am sure you will never drop a hint of what I mention to you till you hear the same matters from other channels. He declines any change of situation."[61] From this time forward Malmesbury and Loughborough were to be united with Burke in an open effort to persuade the Duke of Portland and others of his friends to separate from Fox and declare themselves as supporters of the administration. Without attributing improper motives, it should not be forgotten that each of these men knew that material advantages would accrue to him from alliance with the government.[62] It will also be seen later that Malmesbury and Loughborough could not even wait for their rewards until the Duke of Portland had been persuaded to agree with their views.

In spite of these successes, the ministers do not appear to have been satisfied with the situation. They seem still to have desired to bind their friends among the Whigs by some stronger tie than mere "spontaneous support." Grenville has explained in his letter to his brother of November 20, 1792, how they now tried to aid Loughborough and Malmesbury in affecting this result. He says:—

"Our hopes of anything really useful from opposition are, I am sorry to say, nearly vanished. In the meantime, the storm thickens. Lord Loughborough has declined, and Fox seems to govern the rest in just the same old way.

"In the meantime, we are preparing an association in London, which is to be declared in the course of next week. I enclose you the plan of their declaration, in which, you see, the great object is to confine it within the limits of regular government, and not to go beyond that point. A few persons of rank cannot be kept out of it, but we mean it

---

[61] Auckland MSS. XXXIV, 430.
[62] Fitzwilliam, Correspondence of Burke III, 430. Life and Letters of Sir Gilbert Elliot II, 115. Loughborough expected to become lord chancellor; Malmesbury hoped for a restoration of the diplomatic pension which had been taken away at the time of the Regency debate, while Burke, among other ambitions for his family, had parliamentary aspirations for his son, which could be satisfied only when a coalition had been effected.

chiefly to consist of merchants and lawyers, as a London
Society, and that the example should be followed by each
county or district—including then as many farmers or yeoman as possible."[63]

In addition, as we learn from another source, suggestions
were made by the ministry as to the proper time for organ-
izing such an association in the county of which the Marquis of Buckingham was lord lieutenant.   The advertisement was published, and as Grenville had indicated the
London association was formed on December 5.[64]   But, on
the very day on which Grenville had written to his brother,
the first rumors were heard from France of an event which
precipitated more strenuous measures on the part of the
English ministry.

Before considering these measures we must notice another
association which, discerning apparently by intuition the

---

[63] Buckingham, Court and Cabinets II, 228.
[64] London Gazette 1792, 957.   This declaration was signed by more
than eight thousand persons.   Accounts of it may be found in the
contemporary newspapers.   A convenient place to examine it is,
Debrett, Parliamentary Register XXXIV, 39.   The declaration
was as follows:—
"We, the Merchants, Bankers, Traders and other inhabitants of
London whose names are hereunto subscribed, perceiving with
deepest concern, that attempts are made to circulate opinions contrary to the dearest interests of Britons and subversive of those
principles which have produced and preserved our most invaluable
privileges, feel it a duty we owe our country, ourselves and our
posterity, to invite all our fellow subjects to join with us in the
expression of a sincere and firm attachment to the constitution of
these kingdoms, formed in remote and improved in succeeding ages,
and under which the glorious revolution of 1688 was effected: a
Constitution wisely framed for the diffusion of happiness and true
liberty, and which possesses the distinguished merit, that it has on
former occasions been, and we trust in the future will be found
competent to correct its errors and reform its abuses.   Our experience of the improvement of agriculture and manufactures, of the
flourishing state of navigation and commerce, and of increased
population, still further impels us to make this public declaration
of our determined resolution to support by every means in our
power the ancient and most excellent constitution of Great Britain,
and a government by King, Lords and Commons; and to exert
our best endeavours to impress, in the minds of those connected
with us, a reverence for, and a due submission to the laws of
their country, which have hitherto preserved the liberty, protected the prosperity and increased the enjoyments of a free and
prosperous people."

purposes of the administration, came into existence rather mysteriously at this opportune time. This new society called itself an "Association for preserving Liberty and Property against Republicans and Levellers." This organization, which soon came to be known as the "Crown and Anchor Association," gave notice of its existence by an announcement which began as follows: "At a Meeting of Gentlemen at the Crown and Anchor Tavern, November 20, 1792, John Reeves, Esq., in the chair, the following considerations and resolutions were entered into and agreed upon." Then followed a discussion at length of supposed "mischievous opinions" that were being circulated, and of the nature of such principles, in addition to an attempt to explain the true "rights of man." The document concluded:—

Impressed with these sentiments in favour of our happy establishment, and alarmed by the michievous endeavours, that are now using by wicked men, to mislead the uninformed, and to spirit up the discontented by furnishing them with plausible topics, tending to the subversion of the state, and incompatible with all government whatsoever:

We do, as private men, unconnected with any party or description of persons at home, taking no concern in the struggles at this moment making abroad, but most seriously anxious to preserve the true liberty, and unexampled prosperity we happily enjoy in this kingdom, think it expedient and necessary to form ourselves into an association for the purpose of discouraging, in every way that lies in our power, the progress of such nefarious designs as are meditated by the wicked and senseless reformers of the present time; and we do hereby resolve, and declare as follows:

First.—That the persons present at this meeting do become a society for discouraging and suppressing seditious publications, tending to disturb the peace of this kingdom, and for supporting a due execution of the laws made for the protection of persons and property.

Secondly.—That this society do use its best endeavours to explain those topics of public discussion which have been so perverted by evil designing men, and to show, by irrefiagable [sic] proof, that they are not applicable to the state of this country, that they can produce no good, and certainly must produce great evil.

Thirdly.—That this society will receive with great thanks all communications that shall be made to it for the above purposes.

Fourthly.—That it be recommended to all those, who are friends to the established law, and to peaceable society, to form themselves, in their different neighbourhoods, into similar societies for promoting the same laudable purposes.

Fifthly.—That this Society do meet at this place or elsewhere every Tuesday, Thursday, and Saturday.

Sixthly.—That these considerations and resolutions be printed in all the public papers and otherwise circulated in all parts of the Kingdom.

This statement was signed by " J. Moore, Secretary," to whom it was requested that all communications be addressed.[65] Concerning the number and character of those present at this initial meeting, it is only known that the name signed as that of the secretary was an alias of Reeves, the chairman. The gentleman thus doubly honored had only a few weeks before reached England after serving his second term as chief justice in the recently established court in Newfoundland. The professed purposes of his new venture, as stated above, were three: to promote the organization of similar associations throughout England and to give publicity to their efforts; to ferret out and suppress sedition and seditious publications; and to carry on a propaganda against sedition. Just why this newly returned justice should have developed on so short a notice so great a fervor of patriotic zeal it is impossible to say. The idea of combining in the same person under different names the offices of secretary and chairman was suggested to Reeves by Andrew Wilson, who, about this time, began to publish the True Briton, a paper which became the authentic vehicle for making public the opinions of the ministers.[66] The committee for the government of the society was appointed without warrant from those whose names were used, as is clear from the letter of Charles Townshend to the secretary, dated November 27, 1792:—

[65] A convenient place to examine this declaration is, Debrett, Parliamentary Register XXXIV, 26. It is also to be found in contemporary newspapers and pamphlets. The titles of some of the latter are indicated in the appended bibliography.

[66] Parliamentary Papers, 1795-6, Vol. XVIII, Nos. 130 and 130a. Hansard, Parliamentary History.

Sir, I received this evening a letter without any signature dated from the Crown and Anchor, and I send the earliest answer. When I set down my name, I was determined to go through the business, and I am not afraid of any obloquy thrown out upon me, but I submit to the consideration of the supporters of the society whether the circumstances of my being Deputy Teller of the Exchequer be not a sufficient reason for my name being not inserted in the list of the first committee upon the outset of this business.[67]

Others chosen as members of this body seem to have had the honor thrust upon them in the same manner. At least one other besides Townshend assigned as a reason for refusing to serve the fact that he was an official under the administration.[68] One of the gentlemen who did accept in good faith afterwards declined to take an active part in the work on the ground that the managers were accustomed to act upon anonymous letters, which he thought might be written by private enemies of those concerned, and therefore have no other purpose than to vent personal spite.[69] The conductors of this association, while it was still a useful instrument for accomplishing the purposes of the administration, thought it necessary in June, 1793, to make the following declaration: "It is due to the society, to the Ministers, and to the public, to make this declaration—That none of the King's Ministers knew or heard of this association till they saw the first advertisement in the public prints."[70] Since, however, this association appeared at the

---

[67] Reeves MSS. I, 71.
[68] Reeves MSS. I, 121, 127, 129, 130, 132.
[69] Reeves MSS. IV, 147, V, 162.
[70] Association Papers; containing the Publications of the Loyal Associations, Preface, IV.   This preface naïvely continued:—

"Most certainly the Minister had no more to do in the formation of this association than of the two thousand and more that were formed in other parts of the kingdom. They were all voluntary movements of persons, who thought it a crisis in which the country should declare itself, and strengthen the hands of government, for the preservation of the King and Constitution. When the nation had thus plainly declared its apprehension for our laws and liberty, the government could not do otherwise than concert measures for their preservation. Hence the calling out of the militia—the assembling of Parliament—the proceedings against seditious persons and writings. All these measures have been called for or approved by the nation as necessary for its safety both public and private."

precise moment when the members of the administration were planning associations of a similar character among the higher classes; since, as will be seen further, it was conducted with the sole aim of persuading the lower classes to support the measures which the ministers were contemplating; since something connected with its origin made it necessary for one person to serve as both chairman and secretary and to assume, at the same time, the obligation of appointing the governing committee; and finally, since the deception with regard to the chief executive officials of the society was suggested by one who was working under the auspices if not in the employ of the government, there is certainly some reason to doubt whether such statements by the officials of the association as to its origin are to be taken at their face value. It is possible of course that the purpose of this society was altered somewhat by the information which came from France almost contemporaneously with its birth.

Although the British government appears to have had in mind for several months the possibility of hostilities with France, the decree of the French Executive Council, on November 16, 1792, relative to the opening of the Scheldt, seems to have been the measure which finally determined the ministers to enter upon a war policy.[71] The first knowledge of the decree reached London on November 25.[72] The next day it was confirmed.[73] Manifestly, before embarking on a war policy, it was essential that Pitt assure himself of the hearty support not only of the hesitating aristocrats but also of the people at large. He therefore decided to issue a proclamation calling Parliament together about the middle of December. In order to do this, the militia was called out on December 1, which made it necessary, according to law, that the legislative body assemble within fourteen days thereafter.[74] The decision to call Parliament had

---

[71] The events relative to the outbreak of the war with France will be discussed in Chapter IV.
[72] Auckland MSS. XXXIV, 377.
[73] Auckland MSS. XXXIV, 393.
[74] 26 Geo. III, c. 10.

been reached as early as November 29. On that date Grenville wrote to his brother, who, it will be remembered, was one of the " frightened landed gentlemen," as follows: " We have, I think, determined that, in consequence of the situation of affairs, both at home and abroad, we cannot discharge our duty to the country, nor even answer for its security, without calling the whole, or a considerable part of the militia." However, he concluded: " You must not, from this measure, think the alarm is greater than it is. The step is principally founded on the total inadequacy of our military force to the necessary exertions." This letter was not written to explain the purpose of the ministers in taking the step, but to enable the recipient to hold himself " in readiness to take your measures; " and to suggest to the writer " any particular of importance that may occur to you respecting the mode of doing the thing."[75]

In order to justify the calling out of the militia under the statute, it was necessary to allege that " rebellion or insurrection " existed in England. As a fulfilment of this requirement the ministry made the following assertion in the proclamation issued on December 1: " We have received information, that in breach of the laws, and notwithstanding our royal proclamation of the twenty-first day of May last, the utmost industry is still employed by evil disposed persons within this Kingdom, acting in concert with persons in foreign parts, with a view to subvert the laws and established constitution of this realm, and to destroy all order and government therein; and that a spirit of tumult and disorder, thereby excited, has lately shown itself in acts of riot and insurrection."[76]

At any other time the ministers might have found it difficult to establish the truth of the last assertion, and when Fox heard of the measure on the day that the proclamation was published, he expressed a different opinion in no uncertain language in a letter to the Duke of Portland: " If

---

[75] Buckingham, Court and Cabinets II, 230.
[76] London Gazette 1792, 901. Also Debrett, Parliamentary Register XXXIV, 31.

they mention danger of insurrection, or rather, as they must do to legalize their proceedings, of rebellion, surely the first measure all honest men ought to take is to impeach them for so wicked and detestable a falsehood. I fairly own that if they have done this, I shall grow savage and not think a French lanterne too bad for them. Surely it is impossible— if anything is impossible for such monsters, who for the purpose of weakening or destroying the honourable connection of the Whigs, would not scruple to run the risk of a civil war."[77]

After Pitt had published the proclamation, it seems to have occurred to him that his opponents might require some evidence of an "insurrection" before assenting to his extraordinary measure. In spite of the fact that the militia had been called out in the vicinity of London and the Tower fortified, the decision was reached to locate the insurrection in Scotland. Referring to the expected criticisms, on December 4 Pitt wrote to Dundas, who was at that time in his native country: "I doubt whether we could from our present materials give as precise answer as we could wish to cavils of this nature. The proceedings at Yarmouth and Shields certainly both amounted to insurrections, but they were not on political questions, and therefore what passed at Dundee furnishes the specific ground which seems best to be relied on. After all there will be no difficulty in avowing that at any rate we thought it necessary for the public safety."[78]

If any further evidence were necessary to indicate the real nature of this supposed insurrection, the existence of which had to be demonstrated before suppression could take place, we find it in the opinion of a member of Parliament from Scotland. Sir Gilbert Elliot, a Whig of the Loughborough faction, wrote to his wife on December 13, immediately after his arrival in London, as follows:—

For my part, I am determined to support government in its measures for suppressing sedition and putting the country in a

---

[77] Russell, Memorials and Correspondence of Fox IV, 291.
[78] Stanhope, Life of William Pitt II, 177.

6

state of defence against the many dangers it is exposed to both at home and from abroad.   At the same time, the mismanagement of the Ministry has thrown great difficulties in our way in supporting their very first measure.   They thought it necessary that Parliament should meet immediately, and the only way which they had left themselves of calling it was calling out the militia, for it could not in any other case meet at so short a notice.   The militia cannot be called out during a recess of Parliament, except in the case of actual insurrection or imminent danger of invasion.   They are therefore obliged to justify it on the ground of insurrection; and as no insurrection has taken place in England, which seems, I think, rather more quiet than usual, they lay it all on the insurrections which have taken place in Scotland and, I believe, in Ireland.   The Scotch insurrections consist of the planting of the tree of Liberty at Perth, and the Dundee mob, and some others of less note.   This is certainly ridiculous to those who live in Scotland and know the truth.   This conduct of the Ministry imposes on those who wish to stand by government the heavy task of defending, or at least approving of, an unconstitutional act relating to the military, a subject on which it is easier to arouse jealousy than any other.[79]

It is evident that the militia was not called out because of any immediate domestic dangers which made it necessary for Parliament to meet before the expiration of the time to which it had been prorogued.   What the ministers seem to have desired was carte blanche to carry out an aggressive program on the Continent.   Pitt still remembered how he had been obliged to give up his Russian policy the year before because of opposition by the Whigs, and more particularly because of a lack of popular support.   He was resolved not to repeat that mistake.   The obvious method of securing popular approval for hostilities against France was to convince the people that the French were endeavoring to overthrow the existing English institutions. It was also evident that the disruption of the Whigs would be complete if the aristocratic element could be convinced that the danger from the French principles was real and immediate.   It has been seen that when, in the middle of November, the Whigs were still unconvinced, it was decided to postpone the meeting of Parliament until the first days

---

[79] Life and Letters of Sir Gilbert Elliot II, 80.

of the next year. Thus six weeks were given in which to
carry on a more aggressive propaganda for accomplishing
the purpose of the ministry. Up to November 15 nothing
had occurred which seemed to make it possible to bring
matters to a crisis on the Continent before the expiration of
that period. The associations were instituted and were naturally attended by discussions both in pamphlets and in
newspapers. But before the campaign had fairly begun, the
decree of the Executive Council furnished a plausible, if
not a valid, occasion for aggressive action against France.
It was therefore necessary to bring about immediately that
which the ministers had but a few days before given themselves six weeks to accomplish. The measure decided upon
to produce this result was bold almost to rashness. It is
probable that this boldness was one of the elements that
made the measure so effective. The mere fact that the ministers had taken such an extreme position gave a color of
truth to their assertions that their action had been based on
information which was not proper to divulge at that time,
but which made it necessary to give them complete confidence or condemn them in the most severe manner. It was
a dangerous game, and it is not probable that Pitt would
have dared to play it if he had not been confident that the
majority of the people had already been unduly excited by
the agitation which had been kept up since the spring of
1791. It required only a few days to convince the ministers
that they had estimated the public mind correctly. On
December 5 Lord Grenville wrote to his brother:—

We determined last night to call out, in addition to the regiments
already ordered, the militia of the maritime counties from Kent
to Cornwall inclusive, and those of Berks, Bucks, Herts and Surrey.
You will, in consequence, receive by this messenger the warrant
and letter for that purpose. The reason for the addition is partly
the increasing prospect of hostilities with France, and partly the
motives stated in your letter. Our object at first was to limit the
number in order not to give too great an alarm. The spirit of the
people is evidently rising, and I trust we shall have energy enough
in the country to enable the government to assert its true situation
in Europe and to maintain its dignity. We shall proceed to busi-

ness on Thursday; but how long we shall sit, it is impossible, as yet, to decide. I think the present idea is to bring forward bills immediately which are necessary for strengthening the hands of government. Hitherto, we have every reason to be satisfied with the impression our measure has made.[80]

In a letter written to Lord Auckland the day before, the same minister expressed his opinion that Holland was going "a great deal too far in its expressions of a disposition to recognize the present French government." He also said that with respect to "the comparative state of our preparations with those of France, . . . to you privately, I may say that our confidence on that head is very great indeed." He continued: "The spirit of this country seems rising, though there still prevails an apparent dread of the events which all the new circumstances of the present moment may bring forward. But every hour's exertion gives vigour to people's minds; which are dispirited when nothing is apparently done; and I trust the meeting of Parliament on which so much depends may be very satisfactory."[81]

The ministers did not await in idleness the assembling of Parliament. Partly by direct suggestions from themselves, and partly through the cooperation of the now thoroughly frightened aristocratic Whigs, loyal associations were organized throughout the country;[82] the ecclesiastical establishment, perhaps willingly enough, became an organ for propagating so-called constitutional principles; political sermons were preached:[83] and the Crown and Anchor Association

---

[80] Buckingham, Court and Cabinets II, 232. Dropmore Papers II, 348. Buckingham had advised the calling out of more militia in order to give a longer time for drilling it; in this way it might be more serviceable if it should be needed.

[81] Auckland MSS. XXXV, 32.

[82] Dropmore Papers II, 337, 344, 345, 352, 354–355. Auckland MSS. XXXV, 441. Prothero, Private Letters of Edward Gibbon II, 349. The newspapers almost daily contained announcements of the formation of such associations.

[83] Life and Letters of Sir Gilbert Elliot II, 77. Lady Malmesbury mentions a sermon written by George Ellis, a member of Parliament, who afterwards, in connection with Canning, conducted the Anti-Jacobin. This discourse was preached by the local clergyman. For the titles of some of the sermons which were published, see the appended bibliography.

sent to some person in each parish who was known to favor their cause a circular letter[84] accompanied by literature for distribution to ministers, churchwardens, and overseers.

Whether in response to these efforts or for other reasons, many local associations were organized.[85]   The Crown and Anchor Association issued also a broadside, published in the administration papers, announcing that they felt " it to be their duty to warn all good citizens to be watchful and on their guard, in order to detect and bring to justice such persons, whether foreigners or British subjects, who appear to plot and contrive against the peace and good order of this happy country."[86]   The chief immediate result of their agitation in this direction was the trial of Thomas Paine on December 18—a barren victory, since Paine, who had made, so far as we know, no converts to republicanism in England, was now a member of the National Assembly in France and had to be convicted in absentia.[87]   In carrying on a propaganda of discussion, Reeves and the association were more successful in using their " best endeavours to explain those topics of public discussion which have been so perverted by evil and designing men."   The first response to their advertisements was a flood of manuscripts from second-class preachers and cheap pamphleteers, who desired an opportunity to get their productions before the public.[88]   Many of these contributions were accepted and printed and some of them were widely distributed.   Songs were printed and sung on the streets.   The sentiments expressed were often of a nature little in harmony with

---

[84] Preserved in the British Museum in a volume of tracts and broadsides.

[85] For evidence that many of them were direct results of the efforts of the Crown and Anchor Association, see the correspondence with respect to them preserved in the Reeves Manuscripts in the British Museum.

[86] Preserved in the British Museum.   Also published in newspapers of that date.

[87] Howell, State Trials XXII, 357–472.

[88] Reeves MSS.   Letters which accompanied such offerings, and in some cases the manuscripts themselves, are scattered through these papers.

English traditions.[89]   The fictitious correspondence between Thomas Bull and his brother John, which appeared in broadsides supposed to contain "one penny-worth of truth," are representative examples of such literature.[90]

The spirit of the people must have been rising when such tracts as these could be received favorably. Yet Lady Malmesbury wrote of one of the broadsides as one of the cleverest things she had ever read.[91] Another loyal subject who had received a tract wrote to Reeves that it contained "so much clear information to the lower classes of people

[89] Association Papers; Containing the Publications, etc., of the Loyal Associations. Other titles not contained in this collection will be found in the appended bibliography.

[90] There are several of these broadsides preserved in the British Museum. The following quotation from "One Pennyworth More, or a second Letter from Thomas Bull to his Brother John," will show their character: "When we talk about Kings, it reminds me of what happened here very lately. A man, like a London Rider, thrust himself in amongst us at the public house. He talked at a high rate about French Liberty, and the tyranny we live under here at home; he laughed at the *nonsense* and *blasphemy* of Kings having authority from Providence. What, said he, are we such fools as to believe that Kings are sent down booted and spurred from the clouds to ride mankind?

"Some of our company stared at him and looked as if they felt the spurs in their sides; but, says I, hold a little Mr. Londoner, you don't put the case quite right. You know we must all be ridden by somebody, for we cannot ride upon ourselves. When a good horse carries a gentleman, he is as well pleased as his master; but suppose, Mr. Londoner, suppose he should take it into his head to throw the master that he might be ridden by his equals, then in that case you know, Mr. Londoner, he will have a horse on his back instead of a man; aye, twenty or a hundred horses, all clambering upon his back at once, till they break him down, and he is fit for nothing but the dogs. This is my way of understanding liberty and equality. And now go ask your Birmingham Doctor how much that horse will better himself. This is the way they have bettered themselves in France. They that will not carry a King, shall have the beasts of the people upon their backs; and the poor fools are pleased because they think it will be their turn to ride next. Everybody can see how bad it would be for horses to carry horses; and it is always the same thing where the people carrv the people. After this Londoner was gone, we found he was one of those fellows who was hired to go about with Tom Paine's books; but he did not think proper to produce them: if he had we should have put them into a pitch kettle and stirred them about well, and then burned the pitch and books together; this being the proper end of that black doctrine, which some men put into others to set the world on fire."

[91] Life and Letters of Sir Gilbert Elliot II. 77.

that I cannot say too much in its favour."[92]   But as Paine was the one man brought to account at this time, so his work, which was frankly republican, was the one source to which the agitators were obliged to have recourse for their specific instances of seditious utterance. For that reason, an attempt was made to confuse with Paine those who advocated reform, and to attribute to them the views of the author of the Rights of Man. Just as, in the spring of 1792, Pitt condemned the Friends of the People as dangerous because they replied to letters written by another society which, without adopting Paine's principles, recommended that his book be read, so, in the spring of 1794 he was destined to accuse the officials of still another society of high treason on the same grounds. Similarly, at this time all of the agitation in England against monarchy or any of the existing governmental institutions was contained between the covers of the Rights of Man. The best advertisement that this work received was the systematic exploitation of its contents carried on by those who professed to oppose its principles.[93] Nowhere is there any evidence of a party who desired to act on the suggestions which it contained. The Sheffield Society which recommended it to their members insisted that the sole purpose of their organization was to secure a reform of Parliament, and although the administration sent spies to their meetings no more serious offence was ever proved against them.[94]

In order to aid in this agitation two additional newspapers were founded, one of them having for its motto: "Nolumus leges Angliae mutari." These journals, according to the under-secretary for foreign affairs, now became the authoritative organs of the administration.[95]

---

[92] Reeves MSS. V, 142.

[93] Critical Review V, 583. The conductors of this review, who were, at this time, supporters of the administration, were very emphatic in expressing this idea.

[94] Howell, State Trials XXIV, 200–1408. In the trial of Thomas Hardy in 1794 an unsuccessful effort was made to prove that this society had treasonable intentions.

[95] Auckland MSS. XXXVI, 404. The papers were called " The

As a result of all these forces, set in motion to frustrate
a danger the very existence of which depended upon the
unsupported statements of the members of the administration, the excitement of the people reached a high pitch by
the middle of December, when Parliament came together.
It is not possible to describe the characteristic spirit of the
time without making quotations for which there is not space
here. It is almost incredible that such an extravagant
propaganda could have been carried on against an imaginary
danger with so great success. But it should be remembered
that events hitherto undreamed of were happening in
France, and that the mere suggestion of such happenings
in England was enough to arouse the English nobility and
clergy to an exaggerated sense of the danger of their posi-
tions. Again, it should not be forgotten that this Quixotic
campaign, which was destined to continue much longer, had
already lasted nearly two years. It was not a sudden conviction that influenced the aristocratic Whigs in Parliament and led to their eventual conversion to the policy of
the administration. This change of heart, as well as the
terrors of the people at large, was due to a systematic effort
on the part of the government to bring it about.

Parliament assembled on December 13, 1792. Two days
before, a meeting of prominent Whigs had been held at
Burlington House, the residence of the Duke of Portland.
The majority of those present expressed their intention of
supporting the government. But, according to Lord Malmesbury's report, " Fox treated the alarms as totally ground-
less—that they were raised for particular purposes by Ministers—that there was not only no insurrection, or imminent
danger of invasion, but no unusual symptoms of discontent,
or proneness to complain in the people; that the whole was
a trick, and as such, he should oppose it." Portland himself said little.[96] On the next day, at the same place, there
was a meeting of Whig lords to decide what line the party

True Briton " and " The Sun." The latter was published in the
afternoon. They immediately became important factors in the
political situation.
[96] Malmesbury, Diaries and Correspondence II, 473.

should pursue in the upper house. They determined, " after a good deal of very desultory talk, and a great many sour and very peevish things from Lord Derby towards Lord Loughborough," to support the address, and to permit it to pass without a division. But each member was to say what he might think proper on any part of it. There was no meeting of the Whig members of the Commons. Fox appeared at the conclusion of the meeting of the Lords at Burlington House and said " that he should certainly advise another line of conduct."[97] As a result, Sir Gilbert Elliot wrote to his wife, " It is now unavoidable that we should publicly go to the right and left."[98]

The speech from the throne[99] announced that : " Events have recently occurred which require our united vigilance and exertion, in order to preserve the advantages which we have hitherto enjoyed. The seditious practices which had been in great measure checked by your firm and explicit declaration in the last session, and by the general concurrence of my people in the same sentiments, have of late been more openly renewed, and with increased activity. A spirit of tumult and disorder (the natural consequence of such practices) has shown itself in acts of riot and insurrection, which required the interposition of a military force in support of the civil magistrate. The industry employed to excite discontent on various pretexts, and in different parts of the Kingdom, has appeared to proceed from a design to attempt the destruction of our happy constitution, and the subversion of all order and government; and this design has evidently been pursued in connection and concert with persons in foreign countries." Therefore, the speech continued, the king deemed it " right to take steps for making some augmentation of my naval and military force."[100]

---

[97] Malmesbury, Diaries and Correspondence II, 475.
[98] Life and Letters of Sir Gilbert Elliot II, 79.
[99] It is, perhaps, unnecessary to say that such speeches at this time were the work of the ministers, and were in no way representative of the personal views of the king.
[100] Hansard, Parliamentary History XXIX, 1556.

The lord mayor of London was selected to move the address in the House of Commons. He referred to the proclamation which had been issued in the spring, and asserted that "he was scarcely seated in the Mayoralty chair, before he became possessed of a variety of information, through different channels, which convinced him that the same mischievous attempts were renewed with augmented force, under a material change of affairs in another country." The sole evidence upon which he rested this assertion is his statement that numerous societies had been established "within the city of London, corresponding and confederating with other societies in different parts of the United Kingdom all formed under specious pretences, but actually tending to subvert the constitution of the country." Wallace, who seconded the address, repeated and expanded the statement of the mayor but carefully refrained from giving any facts. He declared that "publications had been circulated through the country, calculated to inflame the minds of the people, to render them dissatisfied with the present government, induce them to pull down our happy constitution, and establish in its stead another, formed on the model of the French Republic. That societies, by which these publications were circulated, must have had such a revolution for their object, could not be doubted by any man who considered that there was a close connection between them and the ruling powers in France." And again, instead of adducing some evidence that the connection which he had alleged existed, he continued in the same strain:—

"These societies sympathized with everything French; their countenances betrayed a dejection, when the Duke of Brunswick was on his march to Paris, which could be surpassed only by the extravagant joy which they expressed when he was obliged to retreat."

In replying to such statements as these, Fox, in the opinion of his former associates at least, fulfilled his promise to the Duke of Portland that he would become "savage." He certainly left no doubt as to which side he intended to take

in the discussion. He had hardly begun when he said:
"I state it, therefore, to be my firm opinion and belief,
that there is not one fact asserted in His Majesty's speech
which is not false—not one assertion or insinuation which is
not unfounded. Nay, I cannot be so uncandid as to believe,
that even the Ministers themselves think them true." Coming to the questions at issue, he continued:—

The next assertion is, that there exists at this moment an insurrection in this Kingdom. An insurrection!—Where is it? Where
has it reared its head? Good God! an insurrection in Great
Britain! No wonder that the militia were called out, and Parliament assembled in the extraordinary way in which they have been;
but where is it? Two gentlemen have delivered sentiments in
commendation and illustration of the speech, and yet, though this
insurrection has existed for fourteen days, they have given us no
light whatever, no clue, no information where to find it. The
right honourable Magistrate tells us, that, in his high municipal
position, he has received certain information which he does not
think it proper to communicate to us. This is really carrying the
doctrine of confidence to a length indeed. Not content with
Ministers leading the House of Commons into the most extravagant
and embarrassing situations, under the blind cover of confidence,
we are now told that a municipal Magistrate has information of an
insurrection, which he does not chuse to lay before the Commons
of England, but which he assures us is sufficient to justify the
alarm which has spread over the whole country! The honourable
gentleman who seconded the motion tells us that the insurrections
are "too notorious to be described." Such is the information which
we receive from the right honourable Magistrate, and the honourable gentleman, who are selected to move and second the address.
I will take it upon me to say, that it is not the notoriety of the
insurrections which prevents them from communicating to us the
particulars, but their non-existence.

The orator concluded his long speech, which was full of
such pertinent and angry comments, by moving an amendment to the address. Windham and Burke declared their
intention of supporting the measures of the administration.
Thomas Grenville, who had supported the proclamation of
May 21, and who was later to be instrumental in the negotiation that was to effect a final party coalition, was now
not able to find anything "equivalent to an insurrection."

He therefore supported the amendment, as, naturally, did Grey and Sheridan. Since Pitt had just been made warden of the Cinque Ports, and had not been reelected to Parliament, he was absent, and it fell to Dundas to reply to Fox. The secretary for home affairs summed up his case by saying, "The fact was that an universal and most serious alarm had been excited among the country gentlemen, farmers, etc., and some active measures were necessary on the part of government, in order to restore confidence to the country, and prevent the dangers which threatened its security." He then proceeded to enumerate the disorders mentioned by Pitt in the letter which has been cited. These he could consider "as nothing less than insurrection." However, if he was to be asked "what strictly constituted an insurrection, he must own that he should find it difficult to give any precise definition." He did not now wish to enter into the contest of words but would only remark "that a mob on one occasion, and in particular circumstances, might constitute an insurrection, which would not at another period and in different circumstances." But whether convincing or not, defence on the part of the government was unnecessary. Fox, as he said in concluding his speech, had merely opposed himself "to the furor of the day." The address was carried by a vote of 290 to 50. Yet, among the minority were several of those who were supposed to be most closely connected with the Duke of Portland.[101]

Two days later Fox moved that the king be requested to send a minister to Paris "to treat with those persons who exercise provisionally the functions of Executive government in France, touching such points as may be in discussion between His Majesty and the French Nation." He prefaced this motion by saying that he did not mean thereby to express any "approbation of the conduct of the existing French government, or the proceedings that had led to the present state of things in France. He meant simply to

---

[101] Hansard, Parliamentary History XXX, 1–60. Debrett, Parliamentary Register XXXIV, 1–74.

declare, and record his opinion, that it was the true policy
of every nation to treat with the existing government of
every other nation with which it had relative interests,
without inquiring or regarding how that government was
constituted, or by what means those who exercised it came
to power." Lord Sheffield, a former Whig, immediately
exclaimed: "It is impossible to be silent. Are we then in
that deplorable situation? Are we the vilest and most contemptible of nations? Are we to be the first to acknowledge, to cringe to these cut-throats and robbers, who have
not the recommendation of being able to control their own
banditti?" At the conclusion of a long debate the question was negatived, as the mover had expected, without a
division.[102]

Meanwhile, Loughborough and Malmesbury had not met
with the success for which they had hoped in their efforts
to persuade the Duke of Portland to sever entirely his party
relations with Fox. On December 16 Malmesbury and Sir
Gilbert Elliot called on the duke and endeavored to persuade him that the break was necessary. But Malmesbury
recorded that "the only word we could draw forth was,
that he was against anything that could widen the breach,
and put it out of Fox's power to return."[103] Two days
later, Loughborough called on Malmesbury and insisted on
further exertions. They decided that it was "absolutely
necessary for the Duke of Portland to declare his sentiments and ours in the House of Lords." Therefore, Malmesbury and Windham called on him, and induced him to agree
to speak on "a bill relative to the power of the crown over
aliens" which Grenville was to introduce the next day.
Lord Fitzwilliam left London on that day, "from difficulty
how to act, and distress of mind relative to Fox."[104]

On the nineteenth Portland excused himself for his failure
to speak by saying that he had not reached the house in

---

[102] Hansard, Parliamentary History XXX, 80–128. Debrett, Parliamentary Register XXXIV, 98–154.
[103] Malmesbury, Diaries and Correspondence II, 477.
[104] Malmesbury, Diaries and Correspondence II, 478.

time. However, he still "reprobated the idea of breaking with Fox," though he promised to speak on the twenty-first.[105] On the twentieth Lord Loughborough, tired of waiting, sent Elliot to ascertain whether the duke would consent that he should accept the Great Seal. The answer was an emphatic negative.[106] On the next day Portland complied with his promise. He expressed his approval of the Alien Bill, because he thought "some measure of this sort necessary to quiet the alarm that had been excited in the minds of the people." But he qualified his action by saying that it was not on account of any personal attachment to the present administration that he supported the measure; that he could not forget the manner in which they came into power, nor could he forget several other things which he proceeded to enumerate.[107] Naturally this did not satisfy those at whose request the statement had been made. On the next day there was a meeting of that faction at Malmesbury's house at which Lord Loughborough said that "it was become necessary to decide what was to be done, and how the Duke of Portland could be obliged to declare his sentiments to be contrary to those of Fox."[108] Sir Gilbert Elliot was sent to converse with the duke, and he brought word that Portland's excuse was that "from embarrassment in speaking in public, he had omitted to declare his general intention to support government under all the circumstances of the present crisis." Loughborough was therefore persuaded to give the duke another chance before taking more radical steps, and a delegation was sent to call on the Whig leader.[109] Malmesbury, Elliot, and Windham went, and, after putting the case, informed the duke of Loughborough's threat to call a meeting of the party in order to force action, if Portland did not comply with their wishes. According to Malmesbury's report, the much-

---

[105] Malmesbury, Diaries and Correspondence II, 479.
[106] Malmesbury, Diaries and Correspondence II, 480. Life and Letters of Sir Gilbert Elliot II, 89.
[107] Hansard, Parliamentary History XXX, 158.
[108] Malmesbury, Diaries and Correspondence II, 481.
[109] Malmesbury, Diaries and Correspondence II, 483.

harassed leader agreed to what they said, but confessed a
private affection for Fox. He further consented to make
another statement in the House of Lords, and also to
authorize Lord Titchfield to declare the same opinions in
the Commons. In addition, he said " that any friend of his
declaring these sentiments . . . may state himself to speak
his sentiments and be authorized to say so."[110]

On December 26, two days after the above interview, the
Alien Bill was brought to its third reading in the House of
Lords.[111] Pitt wrote on the same day to Grenville, who
was absent on account of illness, describing the debate which
ensued :—

Lord Guilford, Lord Lauderdale, Lord Lansdowne opposed the
third reading of the bill.   Lord Hawkesbury made a very good
speech; Lord Carlisle a very fair and explicit one, not only in support of the bill but on general grounds; and Lord Loughborough
made one of the best speeches I ever heard, which concluded with
a decided declaration of *full support* in the strongest terms we could
wish.   Lord Carlisle, Lord Bute, Lord Malmesbury seemed by their
manner to concur in the full extent.   The Duke of Portland said
nothing and looked embarrassed.   Lord Rawdon said a few words
only to declare himself in favour of the bill and disposed to give
support to government, but in terms that seemed to be against his
inclination.   Of course there was no division.   I look upon the
day to be a very important and useful one.[112]

But Malmesbury did not take such a hopeful view. He
said that " the Duke of Portland, to the great concern and
grief of his friends, did not say a word. I urged him repeatedly to get up, but he said he could not, he felt it was
impossible; that Lord Loughborough had said all that could
be said, and that it was impossible to speak after so fine a
speech. I pressed him to say those very words and nothing
more, but without effect."[113]

Portland's friends now decided to overcome his embarrassment by speaking in his stead. On December 28, in the

[110] Malmesbury, Diaries and Correspondence II, 485.   Life and
Letters of Sir Gilbert Elliot II, 90.
[111] Hansard, Parliamentary History XXX, 161–170.
[112] Dropmore Papers II, 360.
[113] Malmesbury, Diaries and Correspondence II, 488.

House of Commons, Elliot rose to speak on the Alien Bill.
He expressed regret that he differed from Fox and could
no longer act with him, but he considered it as " the duty
of every man to stand forward in support of His Majesty's
government, and thus to maintain the Constitution and save
the country." He declared that he expressed " the same
sentiments with many other honourable friends with whom
he had been accustomed to act, and who still continued to
act upon their ancient principles, and under their ancient
leader (the Duke of Portland)—that illustrious personage
whose character was so highly respected, and whose sentiments could never fail to have the greatest weight." He
concluded by saying that he gave " his entire approbation to
the precautions which had been taken by ministers as highly
necessary and proper in the present situation of affairs."
Fox very naturally resented this implication that Portland
had separated from him, and he explained that, as he understood the situation, the duke had agreed to maintain his
former party relations; that the Alien Bill and other similar
measures were to be regarded as subjects on which they held
different opinions, but that the opposition to the administration was to be maintained.[114] This assertion raised a question of veracity between Elliot and Fox, and on December
31 the former made an explanation. He asserted that he
had been misunderstood, that all he had intended to present
was the opinion which he had formerly expressed, though
in his own mind he had no doubt it was a sentiment which
had the approval of that noble person. Immediately after
the speaker took his seat, Lord Titchfield rose to make the
statement which Portland had promised. He asserted that
his " opinion of the gentlemen who compose the present
administration was in no respect altered. . . . His political
sentiments and attachments remained the same that they
had ever been. . . . But he felt the dangers which sur-
rounded us, and the necessity, in that case, of giving to gov-

---

[114] Hansard, Parliamentary History XXX, 176–180.   Life and
Letters of Sir Gilbert Elliot II, 96–98.

ernment such support as might enable it to act with effect; a support, therefore, directed to that effect, and governed by those considerations would be given."[115]

But Pitt had now decided to bring relations with France to an immediate crisis, and he pressed Loughborough to take the Seal. But Loughborough still hoped to win over the Duke of Portland, and requested a further delay. By January 18, 1793, however, Loughborough told Malmesbury that he had decided to accept the office, but was only doubtful as to the time.[116] Lord Grenville wrote to his brother the next day that the time was to be the following Wednesday, and added, "It is as yet very difficult to say what proportion of the ci-devant Opposition will follow Lord Loughborough's example, and join government avowably, but I am inclined to hope a pretty large one."[117] On January 20 Loughborough called on the minister, and returned to Malmesbury's house. He informed his host that Pitt had decided on war, and ended, according to Malmesbury's diary, by telling him "in Pitt's name and from him, that Pitt wished everything that had passed between him and me at the time of the Regency to be forgotten; and that he wished to have my support, that I would consider myself as much connected with him as ever. He likewise offered office through me to Sir Gilbert Elliot."[118]

Three days later, Malmesbury accepted Pitt's offer and notified both Pitt and the Duke of Portland of that fact.[119] He also informed Sir Gilbert Elliot of the minister's proposition.[120] A few days afterward Windham was also offered a place.[121] Thus Fox was able for the time being to pre-

---

[115] Hansard, Parliamentary History XXX, 191–192. Life and Letters of Sir Gilbert Elliot II, 100. Sir Gilbert wrote to his wife that Windham had written Titchfield's speech and submitted it to Portland. The duke had made the addition nullifying the sentiment which the Loughborough faction desired to have expressed.
[116] Malmesbury, Diaries and Correspondence II, 498–501.
[117] Buckingham, Court and Cabinets II, 236.
[118] Malmesbury, Diaries and Correspondence II, 501.
[119] Malmesbury, Diaries and Correspondence II, 501–504.
[120] Life and Letters of Sir Gilbert Elliot II, 106.
[121] Life and Letters of Sir Gilbert Elliot II, 112.

serve his party from final dissolution by sheer force of his own personality, and the attempt to separate himself and the Duke of Portland ceased for a while to be agitated.[122]

---

[122] Life and Letters of Sir Gilbert Elliot II, 115.   Elliot wrote to his wife February 16, 1793:—

"Nothing has happened in politics, nor seems likely to happen. One reason of this calm, I think, is Lord Loughborough's having attained his own point.   Lord Malmesbury is now equally still on the subject; we neither meet, nor converse, nor bustle with him as we did a few months ago.   The fact is that he has also settled his point, and will accept the first foreign mission that is offered him.   One strong, and indeed just and reasonable inducement for his taking this line is, that it will restore him to a claim to his pension—£2000 a year.   He was, in fact, entitled to it before in point of professional claims.   All this, however, being settled in his own mind, a comfortable apathy and quietness has taken the place of his former animation."

CHAPTER IV.

The Outbreak of the War with France.

The first inquiry which it is necessary to make in a discussion of the French declaration of war against England in February, 1793, is the extent to which the English ministers were instrumental in creating the conditions which brought about that result. We may readily adopt the generally accepted view that the English government was pursuing a pacific policy until the events of August and September, 1792, had taken place in France, but it is less easy to understand the purposes of Pitt's administration from that time. The domestic situation in English politics must be kept constantly in mind. It may have been true, as was said by a paper which supported him, that as early as October 16, 1792, Pitt contemplated taking part in the continental war as soon as any other state should be involved by France.[1] It may also have been true at the same time that Pitt told the truth when he wrote to Lord Auckland, the day before, that the meeting of Parliament, which he had fixed for November, did not imply war. Yet the writer of that letter explained that it was impossible to take such measures as had been taken in that direction without " an early communication to Parliament."[2] Remembering the failure of his Russian program of less than two years

---

[1] The Oracle, October 16, 1792.

[2] Auckland MSS. XXXIV, 85. It is probable that Pitt expressed his real attitude toward France at this time in a letter to Grenville which was written on October 16; in it he explained some changes made by him in one of the despatches of the foreign secretary relative to the French situation:—

"In substance, my reason for changing it was to make the declaration more general and leave it clearly to ourselves to determine what consequences are too important to let us remain spectators. The French retaining Savoy, or any other acquisition great or small, might be argued to come within the description *un nouvel ordre de choses.*" Dropmore Papers II, 332.

before, Pitt would certainly make sure of two things before embarking on a second hostile project, however tempting the opportunity might be. He would not interfere in the French troubles without a pretext sufficient to justify such an action to the English people; and he would make sure of his majority in Parliament. For though a majority in both houses of Parliament were supporters of the administration, the opposition party, particularly in the upper house, contained a great number of men of ability, and was strong enough to oppose successfully any measure which did not meet with popular approval. Therefore, if the ministers had desired to take part in the continental struggle at this time, it would have been unwise for them to do so, since it would have placed the existence of their administration in jeopardy. Moreover, it was manifestly to the interest of the French that England and Holland should remain neutral.

In view of these circumstances, we are not surprised to know that on November 6, 1792, Lord Grenville told Lord Auckland that England and Holland " ought to remain quiet as long as it was possible to do so." In answer to Auckland's inquiry with regard to the recognition of the French Republic, Grenville replied that England would probably decline such a request at that time, but in terms which would leave her free to act differently if a republican form of government should be permanently established.[3] Even as late as November 23 Grenville was " strongly inclined to believe that it is the present intention of the prevailing party in France to respect the rights of this country and the Republic."[4] Before this, and immediately after the evacuation of Brussels, practically the same sentiments were expressed in the declaration which England made to her ally through Lord Auckland.[5] In other words, up to this time the English ministers had refused to commit themselves, but had

---

[3] Auckland, Journal and Correspondence II, 465. Auckland MSS. XXXIV, 197.
[4] Auckland MSS. XXXIV, 350.
[5] Auckland MSS. XXXIV, 342. Debrett, State Papers I, 217.

been careful to leave the way clear for any action they might afterward desire to take.

On November 25, 1792, rumors of the French decree relative to the opening of the Scheldt reached London. At first, Grenville was inclined to discredit them.[6] On the next day, before the report was confirmed, in reply to a question which had been asked by Lord Auckland several days before, an official despatch was prepared which stated that England would follow the policy adopted by the Dutch with respect to any French boats entering the Scheldt. In the same despatch Grenville suggested that if the French were determined to force a rupture, it seemed of little moment what was the particular occasion taken for it. The chief consideration, he thought, was to determine, in that case, " to what degree it would be more or less advantageous to us or the French in point of our respective state of preparation, that things should come to a crisis now, or sometime hence." He added, " Such preparatory steps as were judged advisable, and not likely to attract too much notice, have already been taken, with a view to enabling us to proceed with more expedition in case of any sudden necessity for augmenting our naval force." Before this despatch was sent, the news of the decree was confirmed, and Grenville inquired in a postscript whether, if Dumouriez should take any steps to follow it up, " it would be more advantageous that this point should immediately be brought to its issue, or that by representations time should be given for further preparations." At the same time, the English minister objected to the request of the Dutch that several vessels be sent to Flushing or the Downs in order to assure Holland that she would be protected by her ally. The reason given for not complying with this request was that such a step would impede the naval preparations then in progress; but it was suggested to Auckland that the season of the year might be " ostensibly used as a reason for declining what is asked of us in this respect."[7] In the " most secret and con-

[6] Auckland MSS. XXXIV, 377, 382.
[7] Auckland MSS. XXXIV, 392–395.

fidential " letter which accompanied this despatch Grenville
confessed that he was afraid that there was "too much
reason to believe that the French were determined to drive
England to extremities."[8]   In considering the significance
of such a statement we are impressed with the fact that it
was addressed to a man who believed that England was
sincerely desirous of peace, and who, ten days before, had
suggested that Grenville make inquiries in order to ascertain
whether he could not by mediation secure a cessation of
hostilities between the powers which were at war.[9]   Nor
should we forget that immediately after this despatch was
sent to Holland the English ministers decided, by mobilizing
the militia and calling Parliament together, to force a
decision from the aristocratic Whigs and at the same time
create a popular desire for hostilities against France.

But, for some reason, the Dutch failed to appreciate the
English point of view, and refused to proceed to extreme
measures.   On November 23, the day on which Auckland
had written to ask for instructions on the subject, a French
commandant had requested from the States General permission to take his boats through the Scheldt.   It was
decided to refuse permission, but if, in spite of this, the
passage should be made, the French were not to be fired on,
and measures were to be taken to obtain a disavowal and
recall of the application.[10]   However, the Dutch still declined
to attach too great significance to the situation, and Auckland wrote to the English ministers that, while the right of
navigation contended for might serve to arouse the people,
he did not think the question was of much real importance,
since the navigation of the river could at any time be ob-
structed by the Dutch.[11]

In the meantime the English ministers were endeavoring
to remedy their lamentable lack of information concerning
the intentions of the French.   Chauvelin had been sent to

---

[8] Auckland MSS. XXXIV, 396. Dropmore Papers II, 341, Grenville to Auckland, November 26, 1792.
[9] Dropmore Papers II, 334.
[10] Auckland, Journal and Correspondence II, 469.
[11] Auckland MSS. XXXIV, 432. Dropmore Papers II, 346.

London before the fall of the monarchy in France, and had been received as the representative of the king. The Republic had retained him as its minister, but as yet he had not officially presented to the English court the credentials of his new office. In this anomalous situation he wrote to Grenville, November 19, 1792, requesting an interview.[12] Two days later the English minister replied that, before he could give an answer, " he must, under the present circumstances, request that Monsieur Chauvelin will be pleased to explain the object of the conference which he has desired."[13] Chauvelin replied on the following day that he thought the " private conversation " which he had proposed would have produced advantageous effects, and he regretted that Lord Grenville thought otherwise.[14] Grenville waited six days before he replied to this note, then, having received news of the decree concerning the Scheldt, he replied favorably requesting Chauvelin to call on him for an interview.[15] According to the report of the conversation which Grenville sent to Auckland, Chauvelin prefaced his statement by saying that he could communicate only that which he had been authorized to say when his first note was written. Since that time he had heard of the declaration of the English ambassador at The Hague, and had had reports of French boats entering the Scheldt. He could not say what difference these things might make as to the attitude of the French, but he could assure the minister that before these events took place France was sincerely desirous of cultivating peace with England. He contended that the opening of the Scheldt was not intended as a hostile measure, and that the French had no intention of attacking Holland. He added, further, that the Executive Council was willing to communicate at present in this informal manner, and to leave to the judgment of England the time when the Republic should be recognized. Grenville excused himself from a pertinent reply on the ground of Chauvelin's confession that

---

[12] Debrett, State Papers I, 218.   [14] Debrett, State Papers I, 219.
[13] Debrett, State Papers I, 218.   [15] Debrett, State Papers I, 219.

what he had said had been based on instructions received before the latest developments in the case. When Chauvelin offered to convey to the French any assurances of a friendly disposition on the part of England, Grenville replied that he did not feel that the government could send any such assurances, especially as Chauvelin had no other instructions than those which he might have presented several days before, but he assured him that "the King was resolved to maintain inviolate all the rights of this country and those of its allies." Finally, he added that he would be glad to hear other communications from Chauvelin *"dans la même forme."*[16]

This interview, which, so far as it pertained to the subject, indicated a desire for peace on the part of the French, did not cause the English ministers to delay for a moment their proposed measures for preparing the public mind for the approaching hostilities. On December 1, two days later, the proclamation calling out the militia was issued. On December 2, through the intervention of W. A. Miles, one of his former diplomatic employees, Pitt had a conversation with Maret, who was an agent of the French foreign office, the purpose of which seems to have been much the same as that of Grenville with Chauvelin, that is, to gain information concerning the intentions of the French. Two reports, which differ in several particulars, have been preserved of this interview. One was sent by Pitt to Lord Auckland;[17] the other by Maret to Le Brun, the French minister of foreign affairs.[18] Maret came to meet Pitt believing that the English minister desired to preserve peace, and he interpreted the conversation in that light. He had received this impression from Miles, who knew little of the real intentions of Pitt, but who was a friend of Le Brun and was sincerely desirous of promoting the purpose of Maret. Indeed, so persistent was Miles in his efforts to

[16] Auckland MSS. XXXIV, 441.
[17] Auckland MSS. XXXV, 28.
[18] Debrett, State Papers I, 220. See also, for a minute of the report which Maret gave Miles of the interview the next day, Miles, Correspondence of W. A. Miles I, 368.

secure peace at this time that he besought Pitt to allow him to go to Paris in order to treat with Le Brun in person.[19] According to Pitt's report to Auckland, Maret began by saying that the French government " would be glad if means could be found, by private agents, with no official character, to set on foot a negociation." The English minister replied that he was willing to converse freely in order to " learn whether it was possible to avoid those extremities which we would very much regret, but which seemed from what we saw of the conduct and doings of France to be fast approaching." " I then mentioned to him distinctly," says Pitt, " that the resolution announced respecting the Scheldt was considered as a proof of an intention to proceed to a rupture with Holland ; that a rupture with Holland on this ground or any other injurious to their rights must also lead to an immediate rupture with this country." Maret thereupon expressed a belief that the French government had no intention of proceeding to hostilities with the Dutch, but that it wished to be on good terms with both that nation and the English. He said that those were the sentiments of Le Brun when he left Paris, and that from the despatches since received by Chauvelin, which he had seen, he believed that they were unchanged and that Dumouriez shared in them also. Maret hinted that public opinion in France might force the Executive Council to ask the English court to receive some person in a formal character, but this proposition Pitt naturally refused to consider. When Maret in conclusion expressed his confidence in a satisfactory settlement of all difficulties, even including that of an envoy, the minister remarked that there was still " another point, namely, the decree of France to assist revolution." And when Maret replied to this that it was passed in a " moment of fermentation, and went beyond what was actually intended," that it referred only to nations with which France was at war, and that the Executive Council might find some means of revising it if it was objectionable,

---

[19] Miles, Correspondence of W. A. Miles I, 347–369, 397, 401–402.

Pitt still answered " that whatever were the sentiments of the *Conseil Executif,* the decree as it stood might justly be considered by any neutral nation as an act of hostility."

From these extracts it appears that Pitt in his report emphasized his justifications for war rather than the desires for peace, upon which Maret laid stress in his note to Le Brun. At any rate, it is quite certain that the official despatch of Lord Grenville to Auckland at The Hague which accompanied Pitt's minute offered no encouragement to pacific measures on the part of England's ally. Its contents were chiefly a recitation of the grounds which Holland had for a rupture with France. One paragraph, which was inclosed in brackets and to which attention was directed by an. index finger, read: " Our general preparations will be proceeded in with as much vigour and despatch as circumstances will admit; and I trust that the Republic [Holland] will not be remiss, on her part, to take every possible means of putting her forces, both naval and military, in the most respectable state."[20] In order that he might not be misunderstood, in his " private and secret " letter to the English ambassador Grenville gave further emphasis to his purpose. He wrote, " The tenour of my dispatch will sufficiently show you that I think the Pensionary's government goes a great deal too far in its expressions of a disposition to recognize the present French government, under all the circumstances of insult and offence of which the Republic has to complain." Continuing, he said: " I have not expressed in my dispatch all the security which we feel respecting the comparative state of our preparations with those of France, because it is unwise in a public paper to commit one's self. But to you privately, I may say, that our confidence on that head is very great indeed."[21]

There was certainly no room for doubt that England was bound by the treaty of alliance to give aid to Holland if the latter country should be attacked.[22] But, to say the least, it seems unusual that the succor should have been proffered

---

[20] Auckland MSS. XXXV, 38.   [21] Auckland MSS. XXXV, 32.
[22] Martens, Recueil de Traités IV, 373.

unasked, and at a time when the Dutch still refused to admit that they had been attacked. It is easy to believe that Grenville stated a truth when he wrote to Auckland on January 6, 1793, "We are awkwardly situated about the Scheldt till we hear something officially and formally from the Republic on the subject."[23] That no such declaration had been made before had not been the fault of the English ministers. On December 29, 1792, Auckland had been notified that the ships, which had been promised a month before,[24] would be sent immediately to Flushing. But Grenville added that he was particularly requested to insist that the vessels might not be detained "longer than was found really necessary," since their absence delayed the English naval preparations. He concluded by urging that the Dutch prepare for war, and that they consider the least aggression an act of hostility.[25] On December 18, immediately after the assembling of Parliament and in the midst of the propaganda which attended that event, Grenville had also written to inform Auckland that "nothing could exceed the good disposition" of the people of England. He continued, "If we can maintain the present spirit it will enable us to talk to France in the tone which British ministers ought to use under such circumstances as the present." He added, "Everything now depends on vigourous preparations in Holland, and even what cannot be done in fact should be done in appearance."[26]

Meanwhile, the French were making another attempt to ascertain what conditions the English ministers would impose before consenting to remain at peace. On December 23, 1792, in a letter to Lord Fortescue, with which was a letter from Paris that was to be shown to Grenville, Miles complained: "I have been asked what are the conditions this country exacts from France, and am assured that, if they are not too hard, they will be acceded to. If ministers would explain themselves—for the French are ignorant of what is meant to be exacted of them—I am of opinion that

---

[23] Auckland MSS. XXXV, 469.   [25] Auckland MSS. XXXV, 281.
[24] Auckland MSS. XXXIV, 439.   [26] Auckland MSS. XXXV, 160.

a satisfactory *éclaircissement* would almost instantly ensue, and the peace of Europe be obtained and preserved. But if no hints are thrown out, no communications made, directly or indirectly, how in the name of common sense are the differences to be adjusted? "[27]

On December 27, following the instructions of the Executive Council, Chauvelin, styling himself minister plenipotentiary of France, sent a note to Lord Grenville the day after he had requested an interview with Pitt himself. He declared that the Executive Council wished to know whether France ought to consider England as a neutral power or as an enemy. He insisted that Holland would not be attacked, and made an attempt to explain the decree of November 19. On this point he said that "the National Convention never meant that the French Republic should favour insurrections, should espouse the quarrels of a few seditious persons, or, in a word, should endeavour to excite disturbances in any neutral or friendly power whatever." He concluded his reference to this topic by adding, "This decree, then, is applicable only to those people, who after having acquired their liberty by conquest, may have demanded the fraternity, the assistance of the [French] Republic, by the solemn and unequivocal expression of the general will." He further argued that the opening of the Scheldt was "a question irrevocably decided by reason and justice, of small importance in itself, and on which the opinion of England, and perhaps of Holland itself, is sufficiently known, to render it difficult seriously to make it the single subject of a war." On these grounds, an explanation of the intentions of England was demanded.[28]

On the day after Grenville received this note he wrote to Auckland saying that he would tell the French envoy that the explanations were entirely unsatisfactory. He then proceeded to urge that the Dutch prepare for immediate war, and concluded with these words: "It is evident that the present intentions of France are those of aggression.

---

[27] Miles, Correspondence of W. A. Miles I, 416.
[28] Debrett, State Papers I, 224.

Whichever of the allies is first attacked, there can be no
doubt, under the present circumstances, that they must make
common cause to render the calamity of war short, if it is
unavoidable."[29]   The reply which Grenville sent to Chauvelin on December 21 had been written with two purposes
in view: first, as a declaration by the English ministers of
a hostile policy toward France, and it was so understood in
England; and secondly, to serve as a defence of that policy
to the English people.[30]   The reply, which was immediately
made public, began by reminding Chauvelin that since
August 10 the king had suspended all official communications with France, and that the French minister himself was
accredited only to Louis XVI.   Chauvelin had asked for no
other recognition, but Grenville thought it necessary to
assert that he could not treat with him as a representative
of the French Republic.   Nevertheless, he deemed it wise to
answer the explanations which had been offered.   With regard to the decree of November 19, he insinuated but did
not state expressly that the French had belied their professions by promoting sedition in Great Britain.   He charged
the French with " violating the territory and neutrality " of
Holland by sending a boat up the Scheldt.   Regarding the
question of the Scheldt itself, he urged that France had no
right to set aside treaties.   Then followed this statement :—

England never will consent that France shall arrogate the power
of annulling at her pleasure, and under the pretence of a pretended
natural right, of which she makes herself the only judge, the political system of Europe, established by solemn treaties, and guaranteed
by the consent of all the powers. This government, adhering to

[29] Auckland MSS. XXXV, 270.
[30] Auckland MSS. XXXV, 588. Grenville gave an account of the
affair in a cipher despatch to Trevor, the British minister at Turin,
on January 10, 1793. Public Advertiser, January 19, 1793. This paper,
which supported the administration, said, " Lord Grenville's answer
to the would be Ambassador is a decisive proof that Administration
neither hold out an idea of the probability nor the wish for peace
with modern France." In a letter to Gibbon, January 23, Lord
Sheffield said: " But war between this country and France is more
certain than you seem to think. You cannot have read Lord Grenville's notice of Chauvelin's paper. I like it much, it seems to show
that war is inevitable." Prothero, Private Letters of Edward Gibbon
II, 362.

maxims which it has followed for more than a century, will also never see with indifference, that France shall make herself, either directly or indirectly, sovereign of the Low Countries, or general arbitress of the rights and liberties of Europe. If France is really desirous of maintaining friendship and peace with England, she must show herself disposed to renounce her views of aggression and aggrandizement, and to confine herself within her own territory, without insulting other governments, without disturbing their tranquility, without violating their rights.[31]

In other words, Grenville implied that England reserved to herself alone the office of " general arbitress of the rights and liberties of Europe," at least as far as the relations of other nations with France were concerned.

But the other nations did not seem to regard their rights with the same degree of sensitiveness as did the English ministers, and on the next day after this note was sent Grenville wrote privately to Auckland: " As so many circumstances seem to point at the great probability of things being speedily brought to a crisis with France, it seems extremely desirable that the Dutch government should come to some determination which they may formally communicate to his majesty's ministers, either for advice or simply as a notification, respecting the line which they mean to follow on the subject of the Scheldt."[32]

It now appeared that both parties had charges to bring concerning the breach of treaties. The commercial treaty between France and England in 1786 had provided that subjects of one of the realms travelling in the other should

---

[31] Debrett, State Papers I, 227.

[32] Auckland MSS. XXXV, 383. The letter continued:—
" I have already in my public dispatches intimated the opinion of this government that further infractions or violations of the rights and territory of the Republic ought not to be permitted. But the precise mode and time of bringing forward a question which in the first instance at least concerns the Republic most directly should, as you will easily see, be suggested from thence, and not originate here. The King's determination to fulfil his treaties has been so clearly expressed as to admit of no doubt. The opinion which this government entertains of the political expediency of the Republic giving up to violence or intimidation any of its unquestionable rights has also been unequivocally stated. The rest must depend, at least in the first instance, on the Dutch Ministers—but every consideration makes it important to know their resolution, as it may be material for the regulation of many points of our conduct."

not be obliged to obtain special permission or safe-conduct.[33] Lord Grenville's Alien Bill, to which we have already referred, was confessedly intended to enable the government to prevent any Frenchmen from coming into the country except such as might be considered desirable.[34] It was, therefore, but natural that, on January 7, 1793, the Executive Council, through Chauvelin, should remind the English ministers that " it is at the very moment when France is accused in the British Parliament of violating treaties, that the public conduct of the two governments offers a contrast so proper to justify the retorting the accusation."[35] In this note Chauvelin acquiesced in the fact that his official position had not been recognized, but he remarked that this could not " alter or destroy the quality of delegate from the French government with which the undersigned is evidently invested." Grenville had implicitly conceded as much to him in the reply which had been made to the explanations sent by the French minister on December 27. But in this case the note was returned immediately " as being totally inadmissable, Monsieur Chauvelin assuming therein a character which is not acknowledged."[36] Apparently thinking that he had not acted in a sufficiently inconsistent manner, Grenville, on receiving a second note which Chauvelin sent to him on January 7, sent a reply two days later acknowledging receipt of the note and reminding Chauvelin that in the conversation on November 29 the English ministers had agreed to receive non-official communications. He begged him to remember that a reply to the note of December 27 had been sent, and as a reason for not returning an answer to the one under consideration he made the following statement: " I do not know in what capacity you address me the letter which I have just received; but in every case it would be necessary to know the resolutions which shall have been

---

[33] Martens, Recueil de Traités IV, 157.
It was further provided that such persons should conduct themselves conformably to the laws of the states in which they were sojourning.
[34] 33 Geo. III, c. 4.   [35] Debrett, State Papers I, 232.
[36] Debrett, State Papers I, 233.

taken in France, in consequence of what has already passed, before I can enter into any new explanations, especially with respect to measures founded in a great degree on those motives of jealousy and uneasiness which I have already detailed to you."[37]

On January 11 Chauvelin notified Grenville that on account of its violation by the English and the absence of any adequate explanation therefor the French would consider the commercial treaty annulled. Again the English minister ordered that the letter be returned.[38] On the next day Le Brun's reply to Grenville's note of December 31 reached London. Chauvelin immediately requested an interview with the English minister, and assured him that he would "not attach any importance to the form of this private conversation."[39] Grenville consented, and requested that Chauvelin make his communications in writing.[40] According to the minute of this interview which Grenville sent to Auckland, Chauvelin began by saying that since the end of December he had been acting according to explicit instructions from the Executive Council. He then presented Le Brun's note, and in addition to this, he requested permission to have more frequent conversations with Grenville privately, if he could not be recognized officially. The English minister took both this request and Le Brun's note under consideration, and promised to give his answers later.[41]

Le Brun's note, after assurances of a continued desire for peace on the part of France, took up the questions which Grenville had raised in his paper of December 31. With regard to the decree of November 19, the former arguments used by Chauvelin were repeated and amplified, and then Le Brun continued :—

---

[37] Debrett, State Papers I, 235. The note to which this was a reply alleged an unfair treatment of the French by the English officials in the enforcement of the proclamation relating to the export of grain.
[38] Debrett, State Papers I, 236.   [40] Debrett, State Papers I, 237.
[39] Debrett, State Papers I, 236.   [41] Auckland MSS. XXXVI, 25.

We have said, and we desire to repeat it, that the decree of the 19th of November could not have, any application, unless to the single case in which the general will of a nation, clearly and unequivocally expressed, should call the French nation to its assistance and fraternity. Sedition can certainly never be construed into the general will. These two ideas mutually repel each other, since a sedition is not, and cannot be any other than the movement of a small number against the nation at large; and this movement would cease to be seditious, provided all the members of a society should at once rise, either to correct their government, or change its form *in toto,* or for any other object.

Thus, when by this natural interpretation the decree of the 19th of November is reduced to what it truly implies, it will be found that it announces nothing more than an act of general will, and that beyond any doubt, and so effectually founded on right, that it is scarcely worth the trouble to express it.

Concerning the general issue, Le Brun denied that France had any desire to become a universal arbitress of treaties, or that she desired to impose laws on any one. "She has renounced," he wrote, "and again renounces every contest; and her occupation of the Low Countries shall only continue through the war, and the time which may be necessary to the Belgians to insure and consolidate their liberty." As to the question of the Scheldt, he argued that it was a matter of little importance to either England or Holland, but of considerable importance to Belgium. The river had been closed without the consent of the Belgians, and this action was therefore contrary to the rights of nature and of nations. Still: "When that nation [the Belgians] shall be found in full enjoyment of liberty, when its general will can lawfully declare itself without shackles, then if England and Holland still attach some importance to the opening of the Scheldt, France will not oppose it; she will know how to respect their independence even in their errors."[42]

In his reply Grenville professed to find all of these explanations unsatisfactory. In answer to Le Brun's assertion that the French would be obliged to proceed to hostili-

---

[42] Debrett, State Papers I, 237.

8

ties if England maintained her haughty attitude and hostile preparations, he said that England would not cease in her efforts " to protect the security, the tranquility, and the rights of this country, to support those of our allies, and to oppose a barrier to views of ambition and aggrandizement, always dangerous to the rest of Europe ; but which become much more so when they are supported by the propagation of principles destructive of all order and society."[43]

Manifestly now, in order to force France into hostilities, the English ministry must take another line. From Le Brun's note it was apparent that the Executive Council, if given an opportunity, would make even further concessions with reference to the points in dispute. Such concessions, as will be seen, were afterwards made. But the English administration had already begun to search for a more general ground for war. In his private letter accompanying a copy of Le Brun's note which he termed " Chauvelin's last humble paper," Grenville stated as much to Auckland. The circumstances were these. Auckland had at last received from the Dutch a definite note favorable to the preservation of peace and neutrality, and in despatching it to Grenville he recommended that it be printed in the English papers.[44] To this suggestion Grenville replied on January 15, 1793, as follows :—

I had given directions for publishing the Greiffiers letter to you, but upon reconsidering that paper I am afraid the publication would do more harm than good here. It is, I doubt not, adapted to the present temper of the Republic, but the expressions of still hoping to preserve peace by adhering to neutrality would be construed here to exclude all measures to be taken on the general view of affairs, and for the object of restraining the progress of French arms and French principles, even though we should not be the immediate objects of attack. In truth, the Republic ought to convince herself of the impossibility of our acquiescing in all that has happened, with no better security against its recurring than a tacit disavowal, or even an express assurance.[45]

If this was a correct statement of the attitude of the Eng-

---

[43] Debrett, State Papers I, 241.   [44] Dropmore Papers II, 365.
[45] Auckland MSS. XXXVI, 37.

lish ministers, it is evident that the French would have found it difficult to maintain peace under the circumstances which then existed.

Lord Grenville soon had an opportunity to give further evidence of his intention. On January 17, the day before he sent his reply to Le Brun's paper, he received a second note from Chauvelin. The latter first asked whether the king of England would receive his letters of credence as minister of the French Republic, or whether he was to be classed with other foreigners under the regulations imposed by the Alien Bill.[46] Three days later Grenville informed him that he would be received in no other capacity than as "Minister from His Most Christian Majesty," and therefore that he could be recognized "but as a private person," and as such would "return to the general mass of foreigners resident in England."[47] The meaning of such a communication required no explanation. It only remained now to force France, if possible, to make a specific declaration. An occasion for accomplishing this end was already approaching.

On January 12, 1793, Brissot, of the Committee of General Defence, made a report to the National Convention on the relations with England. As a result, the convention passed a decree instructing the Executive Council to communicate four points to England: first, to assure the English government that the French desired peace and would respect the independence of Great Britain and her allies as long as they did not attack France; second, to request England to enforce the commercial treaty of 1786 with respect to Frenchmen travelling freely in the country; third, to uphold the treaty regulations touching the exportation of grain and provisions; and fourth, to explain the meaning of the hostile preparations which were being made. If satisfaction was not given on all these points, immediate measures for defence were to be taken.[48] The news of the condemnation of the French king had now reached England,

---

[46] Debrett, State Papers I, 243.   [47] Debrett, State Papers I, 244.
[48] Le Moniteur, January 15, 1793.

and both of these actions were considered by the ministers
as admirably fitted to advance their plans.   Lord Grenville,
in a letter to his brother on January 19, said:—

"The first question, of guilty, decided almost unani-
mously; the third, that punishment should be inflicted, was
deferred to the 16th.   Brissot's report, which you will see
in the French papers, seems well enough calculated for our
purpose.   The thing must now come to its point in a few
days; and we shall, I trust, have appeared to the public here
to have put the French completely *dans leur tort.*"[49]

It was evident that, under the circumstances, the popular
feeling against France would reach its height when Louis
was executed.   Pitt decided to take advantage of this fact
for the action which he expected would finally induce the
French to declare war.   He accordingly arranged to hold
a meeting of the Privy Council immediately after the news
of the execution should reach London that an order might
be issued requiring Chauvelin to leave England.[50]   On January 24 the news was received, and Chauvelin was ordered
to retire from the kingdom within eight days.[51]   On the
same day Grenville wrote to Auckland:—

"The business is now brought to its crisis, and I imagine
that the next dispatch to you, or the next but one, will
announce the commencement of hostilities.   Probably the
French will commence them; but if not, after all lines of
communication are interrupted of necessity, and after all
hope of satisfactory explanation is over, I do not see how
we can remain any longer *les bras croisés,* with a great force
ready for action, that force avowedly meant against France,
and the language and conduct of that power giving every
day more instead of less ground of offence to us and all the
world."[52]

Before the news of Chauvelin's dismissal reached France,
Le Brun had decided to make a final effort to preserve

---

[49] Buckingham, Court and Cabinets II, 237.
[50] Dropmore Papers II, 271–272, Pitt to Grenville, January 23, 1793.
Grenville's correspondence with the king is also published.
[51] Debrett, State Papers I, 245.   [52] Dropmore Papers II, 372.

peace. Maret, who had described himself rather too confidently as persona grata to the English ministers, was sent as chargé d'affaires to London to make the proposals. If Miles reported Maret's statements correctly, he was authorized to give England practically every assurance that had been asked. In addition, he was to suggest that Dumouriez come to London as a special minister for negotiating a treaty. When Maret reached London and heard of Chauvelin's dismissal, he decided to await further instructions from Paris before attempting any formal communications. In the meantime, the English ministers were informed by both Talleyrand and Miles of the nature of the proposals which were to be offered, but instead of giving Maret an opportunity for communicating the purpose of his mission, they made haste to order him, on February 4, to leave the kingdom within three days.[53]

For the avowed purpose of delaying the outbreak of hostilities in that quarter until Holland should be in a better position to defend herself, the English ministers had consented that Auckland should conduct a negotiation with Dumouriez. On the very day that Maret was ordered to leave London, instructions were sent to Auckland to guide him in managing his negotiations. According to these instructions, if the French general should submit to all the conditions that were to be offered—a thing certainly improbable from the nature of them—the English ambassador was merely to enter into discussions without reaching definite conclusions.[54] But before the negotiations were begun, war had been declared, and the news had reached England. As a result, on February 13, Auckland was instructed to listen to what Dumouriez had to offer, without entering into any discussion whatever of terms,[55] though in fact England for several weeks had already been acting

---

[53] For Talleyrand's letter to Grenville, see Dropmore Papers II, 374. For other details as to the mission of Maret, see Miles, Correspondence of W. A. Miles II, 50–65.

[54] Auckland MSS. XXXVI, 426–435. Dropmore Papers II, 377–379.

[55] Auckland MSS. XXXVII, 47.

as though hostilities had begun.   For example, on January 18 Lord Auckland had been authorized to furnish "Monsieur and the Comte d'Artois" with six thousand pounds in order to enable them to visit the courts of Europe for the purpose of furthering the royalist cause;[56] six days later, Grenville wrote that the king had ordered thirteen thousand of his electoral troops to be assembled for use in defence of the Dutch, to be paid by them;[57] on January 28 Parliament had been asked by the king "to make a further augmentation of his forces by sea and land," on the ground that it was necessary "for maintaining the security and rights of his own dominions; for supporting his allies; and for opposing views of aggrandizement and ambition on the part of France."[58]

From the negotiations which have been considered it is apparent that there were three issues involved in the attending diplomatic discussions, each of which was offered as a justification of England's hostile attitude toward France: the opening of the Scheldt; the decree of November 19; and the progress of French arms and principles.   In order to ascertain whether these issues were the real causes of this hostile policy, or were convenient pretexts for its justification, it will be necessary to examine them more closely.   In the view of the English administration, the provisional French government existed, in the sense that it could be bound by treaties and could have hostile measures directed against it.   On the other hand, it had no official existence, and therefore was not able to conduct negotiations for settling diplomatic disputes or making peace.   It is not necessary to criticize the English ministers for declining to recognize the French Republic, though the situation was unique and decidedly illogical, but it is reasonable to assume that if the administration had possessed amicable intentions it would have been disposed to wait for overt acts before proceeding to hostile measures against a government which,

---

[56] Auckland MSS. XXXVI, 108.
[57] Auckland MSS. XXXVI, 237.
[58] Hansard, Parliamentary History XXX, 238.

from its nature, could not be expected to observe the niceties of political etiquette.   In any case, England could at any time have demanded explanations from France, while the French were never able to make an official communication to the English government.   As a result, to use the expression of Fox, England became engaged in a war with a nation which she could not whip and with which she could not treat.

The opening of the Scheldt seems to have been the event to which the ministers were at first inclined to give emphasis as a provocation.   There can be no question as to England's obligation in regard to that point, if the Dutch had considered themselves aggrieved and had called for aid.   Instead of this, immediately after they heard of the French decree the English ministers began and persisted in their efforts to convince the Dutch that the question required the arbitrament of war.   This was done in spite of the fact that before the specific incident occurred Lord Auckland had assured the States General that England was ready to aid her ally whenever there was need.   Therefore it is apparent that if the English ministers desired a continuation of peace, and were liable to be involved in hostilities by the opening of the Scheldt, they had, to use Lord Grenville's expression, become involved in an extremely " awkward situation."

As regards the decree of November 19, if the ministers had possessed any evidence that the French were carrying on a republican propaganda in England, they might have had just grounds for a breach, even though it was quite apparent that the movement had made no serious headway. It has been seen that those who were responsible for the official expressions of opinion in proclamations and other public documents freely made such assertions.   The obvious thing for the ministers to do would have been to produce some concrete evidence to substantiate their allegations.   In the latter part of December, 1792, and the earlier days of January, 1793, when an effort was being made to

convince prominent Whigs that the country was threatened
by serious dangers, some evidence of this kind might have
been very useful. That it would probably have been
brought forward if it existed is apparent from a letter which
Grenville wrote to Auckland on January 1 :—

" We have some idea of laying before a secret committee
of the two houses (very small in number) some particulars
of the designs which have been in agitation here, enough to
enable them without reporting particular facts, and still less
names or papers (names indeed, they need not know) to
say that they are satisfied that such plans have been in
agitation. Could you supply us with anything that might
tend to the same object; it might be very useful in the view
of embarking the nation heartily in the support of a war if
unavoidable."[59]

The third consideration, which was brought forward by
Grenville as early as January 15, and made public three
days later in the king's speech, was the general issue of
restraining the progress of French arms and principles.
Indeed, this may be said to have been proposed as an ultimatum in the note to Chauvelin on December 31. No
attempt will be made here to decide whether a nation which
desired to remain neutral and had not been attacked was
justified in taking part in the contest because of the success
of the combatant which it was less disposed to favor.
However great may have been the conceivable danger to the
traditional balance of power, the time had not yet arrived
for facing that issue. The French had promised that they
would not retain their conquests, and, though their sincerity
might have been doubted, it is hardly reasonable that
ministers who desired to preserve peace would have made
such doubts the grounds for a war, especially when that
war would have been against a powerful nation flushed with
conquests. Such a conclusion becomes more difficult to
accept when we consider that the English ministers began
the contest with the confident belief that the French had

---

[59] Auckland MSS. XXXV, 381.

almost reached the limit of their resources, and with the
expectation that they would be able to bring the hostilities to
an early and successful termination.[60]

In view of these circumstances, it does not seem to admit
of doubt that the English ministers deliberately sought to
provoke the declaration of war which was made by the
French. It is almost equally apparent that the reasons
which have been considered do not afford a satisfactory
explanation of the purposes of the English administration.
Therefore, it is proper to inquire whether there is evidence
of other motives for such a war than those which were
assigned at the time it was begun. From the discussions in
the succeeding chapters we shall hope to show that England's chief purpose in the contest which followed was to
reduce the power of her ancient rival and to obtain possession of its colonies. In the negotiations for peace in 1796
and 1797 it will be found that the English ministers insisted
on retaining the more valuable of their conquests as a
sine qua non of the pacification, until they were forced by
internal difficulties to become less pretentious in their

---

[60] Several occasions have already been indicated on which Lord
Grenville expressed to Lord Auckland his confidence in the superiority of the preparations which England had made for war to those
of the French.

When Pitt, on January 20, 1793, told Loughborough that he had
decided to go to war, he proceeded, according to Malmesbury's
record of Loughborough's statement, to add:—

"That the nation was now disposed for war, which might not be
the case six weeks hence. That we were in much greater forward-
ness than the French. They had only six ships of line in the
Mediterranean—we upwards of twenty; that he had two millions
ready, and that he trusted the surplus of his permanent revenue would
be £600,000 a year. That the Dutch were quite right, and in earnest;
that Russia was willing to go all lengths; that Spain was ready to
join, and that all the little powers only waited on our giving the
signal." Malmesbury, Diaries and Correspondence II, 502.

In a letter to Westmoreland, on December 9, 1792, the minister
said, apropos of the prospective outbreak of hostilities, "The spirit
of the country seems within the last ten days to have taken so favourable a turn that I think we may look with great confidence to the
event, especially as our revenues in point of finance are such as will
exceed expectations." Salomon, William Pitt I, 599. See also,
Wilberforce, Life of William Wilberforce II, 10; Hansard, Parliamentary History XXX, 557.

claims. Taken together, these facts are, to say the least, significant.

In this connection it is well to observe the state of mind of a supporter of the administration after the events of August, 1792, in France. On the twenty-eighth of that month a newspaper which supported the minister made this suggestion: " The consequence of a war at this time between France and Great Britain would be that the former would be dispossessed of all its possessions both in the East and West Indies; that the works of Cherbourg would be destroyed; and that our quondam rival would be unable again to lift her head as a maritime power for at least a century—perhaps two."[61] The same paper concluded on the following day: " If the mind of Mr. Pitt were not as generous as it is confessed to be enlightened, France, for a perfidy that has been constant, might receive such a check as would humble her for ages. From India the French might be driven at once by the army of Cornwallis; and the West Indies might also be freed from a people which has become the natural enemy of Britain."[62]

These quotations indicate a state of mind which at that time was natural to a patriotic Briton. The French government seemed to be entirely disorganized; the country had been wasted by several years of continuous internal disorders. It was, therefore, not strange that, to an Englishman, France appeared to have lost the chief elements of her former greatness and to lie helpless at the feet of Great Britain.

It is not possible to indicate a specific moment when the mind of the English minister ceased to be as enlightened as it was stated to be by his editorial partizan. We have already pointed out that there were several reasons why, under the existing conditions, the war could not have been begun immediately, even if it had been thought desirable. A pretext had to be found by which it could be justified to other nations, and more especially to the English Parlia-

---

[61] The Oracle, August 28, 1792.   [62] The Oracle, August 29, 1792.

ment and people. A strong opposition party, which had
already thwarted one of the hostile projects of the minister,
had to be divided and weakened. At the same time, the
popular mind had to be excited to such a sense of danger
from the French that hostile measures against them would
receive general support.

By October 15, 1792, Pitt wrote to Auckland that his
preparations for war had already been carried to such an
extent that it was necessary to call Parliament at an early
date.[63] The efforts to divide the Whigs, which had been
begun for other reasons, were persisted in with vigor, and
the propaganda of opposition to French principles was also
continued. But up to this time no pretext existed which
could justify an interference in continental affairs. When
the news reached England that the French had officially
determined to open the Scheldt, that want, as we have
seen, was supplied. No time was spent in ascertaining
the wishes of the Dutch. On the other hand, the communications which were immediately sent to the ambassador
at The Hague implied that hostilities had been decided upon.
In the meantime, within less than a week after this news
was received, an extraordinary measure was put into effect
which was intended to have the double result of forcing the
division of the Whigs and inciting in the minds of the
people a hostile attitude toward the French. Organizations sprang up immediately to carry on this movement.
Enmity to France was preached from the pulpit, heralded
in the press, and distributed in tracts upon the streets. At
the time of the execution of the French king the excitement in England had reached its height. By December 18,
1792, Burges wrote to Auckland: " The spirits of our people
are higher than you can imagine. There appears to be but
one sentiment throughout the country—that of loyalty to
the king—affection to the existing constitution—ardour
to support it—and an earnest desire to go to war with
France."[64] We are therefore not surprised that, with

---

[63] Auckland MSS. XXXIV, 85.   [64] Auckland MSS. XXXV, 161.

reference to the execution of Louis, Grenville could write on January 24, 1793, the day that the news was received, " I cannot describe to you the universal indignation it has excited here."[65]

The ministerial correspondence and the editorials have the appearance of a premeditated program, with which certain diplomatic activities are in accord. In the early days of December, 1792, at least two members of the British cabinet were intriguing with a loyalist sympathizer from Guadalupe to provoke resistance to the authority of the National Convention in the French West Indies, with the understanding that England would send assistance in the probable case of the outbreak of hostilities between that power and France.[66] When Loughborough, on January 20, 1793, was finally induced by Pitt to take the Great Seal, the latter mentioned as one of the advantages which he anticipated from the war the conquest of the French colonies.[67] An editorial which appeared on the day before the news of the French declaration of war reached England in a paper that supported the policies of the administration, concluded with these significant words:—

France is the only power whose maritime force has hitherto been a balance to that of Great Britain, and whose commerce has rivaled ours in the two worlds; whose intrigues have fomented and kept alive ruinous wars in India. Could England succeed in destroying the naval strength of her rival; could she turn the tide of that rich commerce, which has so often excited her jealousy, in favour of her own country; could she connect herself with the French establishments in either India, the degree of commercial prosperity to which these kingdoms would then be elevated would exceed all calculations. It would not be the work of a few years only, but would require

[65] Dropmore Papers II, 373.
[66] A minute of the interview from which these facts are taken is preserved in the Public Record Office.   The interview took place on December 5, 1792, between Lord Hawkesbury and Mons. de Curt. It may be found in Foreign Office Papers, France, Vol. 40.
[67] Malmesbury, Diaries and Correspondence II, 501. Malmesbury recorded that Loughborough told him " that war was a decided measure; that Pitt saw it was inevitable, and that the sooner it was begun the better.   That we might possess ourselves of the French islands, that the nation was now disposed for war, etc."   Loughborough came from a conversation with Pitt directly to Malmesbury.

ages for France to recover to the political balance of Europe that preponderancy which she enjoyed previous to the Revolution. Such is the point of view under which government ought to consider the commercial interests! The indispensable necessity of extinguishing the wide spreading fire, whose devouring flames will sooner or later extend over all Europe; and the well grounded confidence of disembarrassing the commerce of Great Britain from those impediments which have so often clogged its wheels; these reasons, added to the prospect of annihilating the French marine, ought to determine us to immediate war.[68]

Such was, probably, the twofold motive which led William Pitt to launch England on a war which he erroneously believed would be of short duration. He desired to prevent the further spread of French arms and French ideas; but he also desired, and it was a matter of far greater significance, to complete the task which had been begun by his father. He expected to wrench from France both her conquests and her colonies, and to leave to the remnant of her population, in a reduced territory, the apparently impossible task of rebuilding the institutions and power which had been destroyed.

One of the first measures taken by the new European league against France points to the same conclusion. In the early days of April, 1793, the nations which were engaged in hostilities against the French sent representatives to a conference at Antwerp. Auckland announced that England was in favor of retaining conquests that might be made. As her share, he mentioned Dunkirk and the French possessions in the East and West Indies as desirable and appropriate.[69] The war went on and, if the newspaper which was said to be an authentic source of the views of the ministry is to be believed, the British demands were " indemnity for the past and security for the future."[70] In-

---

[68] The Times, February 8, 1793.

[69] For accounts of this conference see Auckland's despatches in the Public Record Office, F. O. Holland, Vol. 47. Also a despatch of Tauenzien on April 23, 1793, as quoted by Sorel, L'Europe et la Révolution Française III, 366–367; Sybel, Geschichte der Revolutionzeit II, 220; Häusser, Deutsche Geschichte vom Tode Friedrichs des Grossen I, 491.

[70] True Briton, December 25, 1794.

deed, Pitt himself expressed the same view on the floor of the house as early as June, 1793.[71]   So persistent were the ministers in their demand for indemnity that, when in the autumn of 1793 they issued a manifesto for the purpose of enlisting the aid of royalists in France, the right to such a return was insisted upon.[72]   How consistently this purpose was pursued and the circumstances that finally dictated its partial abandonment will appear in the following pages. Pitt had begun an undertaking which proved to be far more difficult than he had supposed.

---

[71] Hansard, Parliamentary History XXX, 1013.
[72] London Gazette 1793, 947.

CHAPTER V.

The Union of Parties.

Not until July, 1794, did Pitt finally persuade the Duke of Portland to sever his relations with Fox. This consummation of the efforts of the minister was not without significance for the success of his plans, but it should not be imagined that the coalition was so persistently urged because the ministers were fearful for the safety of the nation. It would be equally incorrect to conclude that this remnant of the aristocratic party which now joined the administration had experienced any change of principles. It requires only a brief recapitulation of the circumstances which have been described to make this apparent.

The old Whig party never acted together again after the meeting of Parliament in December, 1792. The schism had been growing since the discussions on the subject of parliamentary reform in the spring of the same year, and before the outbreak of the war with France there had been a realignment which had left little more than the names of the former Whigs and Tories. There were now two parties under the respective leadership of William Pitt and Charles James Fox. In neither was there marked solidarity, either of principles or of purposes. The party which supported the administration favored a war with France and were opposed to parliamentary reform, but the motives assigned for these views were by no means the same in all cases. The aristocratic members, who had recently been added, were opposed to reform on principle or from interest, and favored the war because they believed that the existing institutions were in danger. Those who were more nearly in accord with the views of the minister professed to oppose reform because they deemed it inexpedient under the existing conditions. They favored the war, in part at least, because they believed that England could obtain by it certain coveted commercial and colonial advantages. The remnant of the aristocratic Whigs, who under the leadership of the Duke of Portland still adhered to Fox, really had few views in common with him. They were like those who had formally joined the ministerial party in opposing reform and supporting the war. In everything except name they were members of Pitt's party. The real opposition was composed of Fox and the half hundred Commoners and half dozen Lords who consistently favored reform and opposed the war. But since the early months of 1792 a third party, which as yet had taken no part in the government, had begun to make its appearance. Its membership was chiefly among the non free-holding class in the cities and towns, and it could give expression to its desires only through addresses, petitions, and public appeals. Singularly enough, its platform had been formulated a decade before by the Duke of Richmond and tolerated, if not assented to, by William Pitt. The most significant political changes which occurred in the next few years were the growth of this third party and the final separation of the friends of the Duke of Portland from Fox and those who advocated a conservative reform.

The ministers kept up their efforts to gain other individual members of the opposition after Loughborough accepted the Great Seal in January, 1793, and Sir Gilbert Elliot and Malmesbury gave favorable replies shortly afterward. Lord Carlisle became a knight of the garter in June.[1] Gradually others accepted honors or offices from the administration.[2] The Duke of Portland still continued steadfast, though supporting the immediate measures which the ministers proposed. On September 29, 1793, Burke sent him an elaborate paper in an effort to convince him that Fox was a traitor and to persuade him to join the

---

[1] Carlisle Papers, 701.

[2] Morning Chronicle, December 2, 1793. A list was given of those who had received honors and emoluments up to this time, and their offices were named.

administration.[3] The duke replied that he would continue
to support the government as long as he believed that the
condition of the country made it necessary, but that he was
still unable to see sufficient reason for doing more. He
concluded: "Farther than this I cannot go; and so far
seems to me to be advancing no farther than I have done,
and should consider it my duty to do, in any occasion of
peril or importance to my country. In this I may be mistaken, as I may have been in other instances; but I must
acknowledge, that when I have been in long habits of inti-
macy and friendship, when I have observed many and strik-
ing instances of very superior talents and judgment, the
most incomparable integrity, the most perfect disinterestedness, I am much disinclined to impute to bad motives a conduct, however different and opposite it may be to that which
I feel myself obliged to hold. This may be a great weakness, but it is a weakness I am not ashamed of confessing."[4]
Windham, though still refusing to withdraw from the duke's
party, confessed that he found it difficult to meet the arguments with which Pitt importuned him.[5]

The propaganda which had been begun among the lower
classes in 1792 was kept up with considerable vigor along
the same lines. As a natural result of the system of spies
and informers which had been inaugurated, several acts of
injustice were committed on the pretext of punishing sedition. On May 27, 1793, John Frost was convicted for
seditious words, said to have been uttered on November 27,
1792. He was charged with having said, in a coffee-house,
when half intoxicated, that he was in favor of equality and
no king.[6] In the course of the year several others were
convicted on less substantial evidence. Perhaps the most
flagrant case was that of William Winterbotham, a dissent-

---

[3] Observations on the Conduct of the Ministry, Particularly in the
last session of Parliament: addressed to the Duke of Portland and
Lord Fitzwilliam. Burke brought fifty-four charges against Fox.'
[4] Fitzwilliam, Correspondence of Burke IV, 165.
[5] Baring, Diary of the Right Honourable William Windham, 277-
278.
[6] Howell, State Trials XXII, 471-522.

9

ing minister. He was accused of having made seditious
utterances in a sermon which was preached on November
5, 1792, in commemoration of the Revolution of 1688. No
complaint had been made to the authorities until a month
after the sermon was delivered. The statements with which
he was charged had been written down from memory by
the witnesses for the crown, who had also waited a month
before making their notes. Winterbotham, as well as others
who had heard him, denied that he had used such expressions. Yet he was convicted and sentenced to fine and
imprisonment.[7] Under the more rigorous procedure of
the Scottish courts, Muir and Palmer had already received
even heavier sentences for similar offences.

In the meantime, since the events of December, 1792, the
papers which supported the administration had made almost
daily attacks on both the public and private character of
Fox. The Morning Chronicle did not exaggerate when it

---

[7] Howell, State Trials XXII, 823–876. The more important of the
statements of the preacher which had fixed themselves so firmly in
the memories of his hearers were given as follows in the indictment:—
"The laws made at that time [1688] have been since abused and
brought into disuse; and it behooves me to speak of the present
times."
"Why are your streets and poor houses crowded with poor, but
because of oppressive laws and taxes? I am astonished that you
are quiet under these grievances, and do not stand forth in defence
of your rights."
"You fancy that you are under a good government and mild laws,
but it is no such thing."
"When there is a demand made to the House of Commons for a
supply, they deny it at first, and on a second demand, there are two
thirds or three fourths will grant it, and they will share it among
them."
"We have as much right to stand up as they did in France for
our liberty."
"His Majesty was placed upon the throne upon condition of keeping certain laws and rules; and if he does not observe them he has
no more right to the throne than the Stuarts had."
"Under these grievances 'tis time to stand forth in defence of
your rights."
As an enlightening commentary on the ability of these witnesses
to remember so accurately, one of them thought that "Stuart"
meant "some office under the crown."
For other sources of information concerning these and the other
trials which will be referred to, see the pamphlets the titles of which
will be found in the appended bibliography.

said on January 2, 1794: " Mr. Fox, for more than twelve months past, has been most violently attacked in a continued series of ministerial libels, without the least proof of any mismanagement in office, or dishonourable practice in opposition. Thus unblemished in his public conduct, indefatigable pains have been taken to blacken his private character; and when facts are wanting to support the attempt, bad intentions are alleged against him as a positive charge."[8]

In January, 1793, Fox had written a justification of his conduct in his Letter to the Electors of Westminster.[9] On February 20 the Whig Club, from which the seceding members of the party had not yet withdrawn, formally assured the discredited leader of its confidence.[10] In consequence of this action, Elliot, Windham, Sheffield, Burke, and forty other members sent a public letter of resignation from the organization.[11] But as late as January 15, 1793, the club had drunk the regular toast, " The Duke of Portland and the Whig interests," while his grace was present and had a share in the festivities.[12] The duke had also continued to maintain his former attitude toward Fox.

During the early months of 1794 other circumstances arose which caused the ministers to continue their efforts to induce the Duke of Portland himself to withdraw from his relations with Fox. The campaigns in the East and West Indies had been successful, but the results on the Continent had not been so satisfactory. The failure of the siege of Dunkirk and the evacuation of Toulon left many things to be desired, since it was largely in the continental

---

[8] For confirmation of the facts which are stated in this paragraph, it is only necessary to examine the columns of any of the papers which were supporting the administration. Few days passed that they did not contain some reference of this kind.

[9] A Letter from the Rt. Hon. Charles James Fox to the worthy and independent Electors of the City and Liberty of Westminster, January 26, 1793.

[10] True Briton, February 23, 1793. A copy of the resolution which was sent to Fox was published at the expense of the club, in all the papers.

[11] True Briton, March 6, 1793.

[12] Morning Chronicle, January 16, 1793.

struggle that the French had to be reduced to the necessity
of acceding to the English conquests in other quarters. It
began to look as though Fox might find additional supporters of his proposed motion for peace. The Duke of
Leeds was half inclined to take some step in that direction.[13]
Lord Sheffield, who had been active in support of the
measures which the ministers had taken in December, 1792,
wrote to Auckland as early as September 12, 1793:—

" I am by no means edified by the state of things at Dunkirk. I fear there is no ground for supposing Toulon in
our possession except that of Pitt's luck. If something
very extraordinary does not happen, he and the war will
be in a damned hobble."[14]   Again, the same nobleman wrote
on January 5, 1794, " You would all be kicked out before
the end of the session if there was a suitable man to put in
the place of Pitt."[15]

To make matters more embarrassing for the ministry,
the king of Prussia was asking for financial assistance to
carry on the war. Malmesbury had been sent to Berlin in
the latter part of 1793. On January 9, 1794, he wrote to
Pitt: " The question reduces itself to a very narrow compass. Can we do without the King of Prussia, or can we
not? If we can, he is not worth giving a guinea for; if we
cannot I am afraid we cannot give too many. We must only
look to making the best and quickest bargain possible, to
purchasing him as reasonably and binding as fast and securely as we can."[16]   Such demand involved additional ex-
penditure, and would darken still more the fair financial
prospect with which the ministry had embarked on the war.

Hostilities had hardly begun before the country entered
upon a serious financial crisis. Almost every gazette in the
spring of 1793 announced a number of bankruptcies.[17]   The
effects of this crisis were felt in the manufacturing as well

---

[13] Leeds MSS. VIII, 108.   Leeds wrote to Loughborough, and
therefore his intentions were known to the ministers.
[14] Auckland MSS. XLI, 68.
[15] Auckland, Journal and Correspondence III, 168.
[16] Dropmore Papers II, 494.
[17] London Gazette, 1793.

as the commercial towns.[18] If the statement of the Morning
Chronicle may be accepted, the gazettes did not tell the
entire story. "Alarming as is the catalogue of ruin in every
gazette, it does not exhibit a tenth part of the distresses of
the day; every man in an extensive trade receives hourly
information of unpaid bills, and houses on which he has
claims praying for time."[19] On the same day that this
statement was published, the minister suggested in the House
of Commons a select committee " to take into consideration
the present state of commercial credit."[20] Four days later
a report was made, after much discussion and consultation
with men who had extensive commercial and financial interests. According to this report, there had been an excessive issue of notes by banks which did not have sufficient
capital to provide for their redemption. The run on these
banks had extended to financial institutions which had no
part in this issue, but which, as a result of it, were unable
to realize a sufficient amount on their securities to meet
the demands which were made on them. When these notes
were suddenly either redeemed or discredited, an insuffi-
cient circulating medium was the result. This difficulty was
increased because of the fact that bankers were obliged to
keep on hand a larger reserve fund than was customary, and
the amount of circulation was thereby further diminished.
Consequently, the merchants had goods which they could
neither dispose of nor use as a security for borrowing the
money which they needed. The manufacturers were likewise affected, since they were not only deprived of their
usual orders from the merchants, but were also unable to
secure the loans which were necessary to make their regular
payments. The committee did not believe that the situation

---

[18] The Oracle, March 1, 1793:—
" Since the resolution for war the manufacturers at Birmingham,
Sheffield, Manchester, etc., experience a stagnation of trade. In the
uncertainty of affairs, the merchants are afraid to fulfil their com-
missions, and have consequently, for the present, abandoned all
thoughts of exportation, when so much is to be hazarded and so
little gained." This paper supported the administration.
[19] Morning Chronicle, April 25, 1793.
[20] Hansard, Parliamentary History XXX, 739.

could be remedied without extraordinary measures. Therefore it was recommended that five million pounds of exchequer bills be issued bearing interest at a rate of slightly
more than three per cent. These bills were to be distributed
to those who were in need of them, and were to be secured
by the goods of those to whom they were issued, which in
their turn had to be placed in one of several towns which
were designated. This suggestion was incorporated in a
bill which was passed on May 3, 1793,[21] but needless to say
the industrial and financial activities of the kingdom did
not immediately recover from such a depression. Toward
the end of the year relief had to be sent from London to
workmen who had been deprived of employment.[22]

In view of these circumstances, we are not surprised
that Grenville found a general indisposition in the House
of Lords to come forward and take an active part in support of the administration. As a consequence, he was obliged to ask Auckland to second the address in reply to the
king's speech at the opening of Parliament in January,
1794.[23] The former ambassador had been elevated to the
English peerage as a reward for his services at The Hague
in 1792.[24]

On March 7, 1794, Grenville expressed his regret to Mal-

---

[21] Hansard, Parliamentary History XXX, 740–766.

[22] Morning Chronicle, December 14, 1793. Critical Review IX, 584,
December, 1793 :—

"The arguments of opposition writers have received some additional force from the alarming and affecting distresses of the
manufacturing poor. It has been alleged with a colour of truth
that the miseries of the Spitalfield weavers could not be altogether
the effect of the war, but though this assertion be admitted in its
fullest extent, still it will not apply to the cotton and other manufacturers which have certainly been greatly distressed and nearly
ruined by the war; nay we have good authority to affirm that the
manufacturers out of employment at Manchester and other places
have been reduced to the sad necessity of applying to neighbouring
breweries for an article which had been usually set apart for the
nourishment of quadrupeds; and that the grains have been latterly
the food of those who had formerly lived with decency and
comfort."

[23] Auckland MSS. XLI, 347, Grenville to Auckland, January 16,
1794.

[24] Auckland MSS. XXXIX, 436. Eden had been raised to the
Irish peerage as Baron Auckland in September, 1789.

mesbury that the king of Prussia seemed disinclined to fulfil his engagements;[25] four days later, Sir Morton Eden wrote from Vienna lamenting the "want of decision" on the part of the Austrian court.[26] There was, therefore, no lack of reasons why the ministers should desire to destroy, as far as possible, any nucleus for an opposition party. As long as the support which the Duke of Portland gave to their measures was voluntary, this had not been done, and his grace was considered free to withdraw his support whenever he liked. Hitherto the duke had resisted the seductions of office to which some of his former partizans had proved themselves susceptible. Manifestly, then, he had to be persuaded that the country was in some immediate danger before he would yield to the importunities of his friends who were pleading the cause of his former political enemies. The fertile mind of the minister seldom failed to take advantage of circumstances, and the reign of terror which had been inaugurated in December, 1792, had succeeded admirably in aiding his policy. What was more natural then than that he should make use again of a similar scheme? The reform societies, which, as organizations, had so far escaped any public opposition from the government, furnished a sufficient basis for agitation, and these now became objects of attack.

We do not propose to describe in detail the organizations for promoting reform which existed in England at this time. Perhaps it is no longer necessary to point out that they were not the bodies of discontented men associated for treasonable purposes which they were alleged to be, but were societies composed of persons who believed that there was need of reform in the existing system of parliamentary representation. Their avowed purpose was to influence public opinion in favor of these reforms. They endeavored, therefore, to give the widest possible publicity to their proceedings. In spite of this, they were accused of having secret intentions, and strenuous efforts were made by the

---

[25] Dropmore Papers II, 516.   [26] Dropmore Papers II, 525.

ministry to prove that such was the case. Spies and informers were introduced into their councils as members,
and the records of their proceedings were given to juries,
accompanied by all the testimony which it was possible to
adduce against them. Despite these efforts, it proved impossible to demonstrate to the satisfaction of an English
jury that these men had been guilty of doing more than
advocating in an extravagant manner the reforms which
they favored. This failure is the more remarkable when
we realize that the persons so charged were members of a
class of English society unaccustomed to any part in public
life. The English administration soon began to interfere
with portions of their proceedings which were regarded as
cherished rights, yet they never professed, publicly or
secretly, to desire to do more than reform the representation
in the House of Commons. Such was the character of the
societies which will be presently considered, and a careful
search has failed to disclose any associations in England at
this time with more radical intentions.

How far the revolutionary movement in France gave
rise to or encouraged these associations is an interesting,
if not very fruitful, subject for speculation. It does not
seem capable of definite demonstration. In order to make
this conclusion clear, it will be necessary to examine briefly
the circumstances attending the origin of these societies.
The Friends of the People have been referred to already.
Among the other organizations, which deserve consideration
and were typical of the rest, stand the Society for Constitutional Information and the London Corresponding
Society.

The Society for Constitutional Information was instituted in 1780, and therefore was hardly inspired by the
French Revolution. It had some of the same members in
1794 who had been present at its organization, but it was
not at this time as flourishing as it had been formerly and
was by no means, in point of numbers, one of the most im-

portant reform societies which existed in London.[27] In the
spring of 1790 Henry Flood, an old-time opponent of the
government, had revived the subject of reform by his motion in the House of Commons.[28] The measure was lost,
but it served to increase the amount of attention given to its
consideration outside of Parliament. In some instances the
societies which had been founded in the early eighties took
on new life, and other organizations of a similar nature
came into existence. The Manchester Constitutional Society had its beginning in October of the same year.[29] In
the next year the Society for Constitutional Information in
Sheffield had its birth. In view of the discussions which
followed, the declaration to which the members of this
organization had to subscribe is not without interest :—

I solemnly declare myself an enemy to all conspiracies, tumults,
and riotous proceedings, or maliciously surmising any attempt that
tends to overturn, or in any wise injure or disturb the peace of
the people, or the laws of the realm: And that my only wish and
design is, to concur in sentiment with every peaceable and good
citizen of this nation, in giving my voice for application to be made
to parliament, praying for a speedy reformation and an equal representation in the House of Commons.[30]

The society which attained the most considerable membership did not originate until the latter days of 1791 or
the early part of 1792. It was conceived and instituted by
Thomas Hardy, a shoemaker, who became its first secretary. If the statements of the founder may be credited,
this project was suggested to him by the earlier tracts of
those who had established the Society for Constitutional
Information and had carried on the earlier reform agitation.[31]

---

[27] Wyvill, Political Papers II, 463. The three volumes of this
collection form a convenient source for reference as to the nature
of these societies and as to the reform movement which was begun
before the end of the American war. Other publications are noted
in the appended bibliography.
[28] Hansard, Parliamentary History XXVIII, 452–479.
[29] Wyvill, Political Papers II, 570.
[30] Wyvill, Political Papers II, 578.
[31] Francis Place MSS. IV, 18. Hardy wrote in a letter in 1799:—
" In the months of November and December 1791 my leisure hours

Hardy drew up a plan for his proposed society modeled largely upon the existing organizations of that kind. The preamble to this plan was as follows: " It has been a long and very just complaint that the people of this country are not equally represented in Parliament. Many large and populous towns have not a single representative." Details were added to substantiate this assertion, and the following conclusion was stated in the words of a public letter written by the Duke of Richmond: " We are more and more convinced from every day's experience that the restoring the right of voting universally to every man not in-

---

were employed in looking over and reading some political tracts which I had formerly perused with much pleasure during the American war: Among them were a great variety published gratis by the Society for Constitutional Information at that time, and some excellent pamphlets written by Granville Sharpe, Major Cartwright, Dr. Jebb, Dr. Price, Thomas Day, Rev. Mr. Stone, Capel Lofft, John Horne Tooke, Thomas Goodend, Lord Somers, Duke of Richmond, Sir William Jones, Davenant, etc. From the small tracts and pamphlets written by these really great men, much political information was diffused throughout the nation at that period by their benevolent exertions. The sphere of life in which I was necessarily placed allowed me no time to read larger books, therefore those smaller ones were preferred which were within the compass of my ability to purchase and time to peruse, and I believe they are the most useful to any class of readers. Dr. Price's celebrated treatise on Civil Liberty was the first that confirmed me in the opinion that the American war was both impolitic and unjust. After reading and attentively considering the short statement of the representation which was published by the Society for Constitutional Information, although it was an imperfect statement, yet it was very evident that a radical reform in Parliament was quite necessary. I at first imagined that it might be possible to begin a society in London of those who had no vote for a member to represent them in Parliament, such as the populous parishes of St. Giles, Mary-le-Bone, Bloomsbury, and all those of every parish in London, Westminster and Southwark, who were not housekeepers, but who were arrived at the years of maturity, and who had an inherent right to vote, but were unconstitutionally deprived of it by an arbitrary statute enacted in the eighth year of Henry VI. I supposed that such a laudable scheme only wanted a beginning, and by persevering to obtain it. Upon farther investigation of the subject I found that it was impossible to establish a society to have any effect upon so narrow a scale. For it is as clear as a mathematical axiom that the whole mass of the people are unrepresented or misrepresented. Therefore I relinquished that ideal plan and formed another on a larger scale which included all classes and descriptions of men (criminals, insane and infants alone excepted) agreeable to the plan of the Duke of Richmond, Major Cartwright, Dr. Jebb, etc."

capacitated by nature, for want of reason, or by law for the commission of crimes, together with annual elections, is the only reform that can be effectual and permanent."

Following this preamble were eight simple rules, which constituted the basis for the organization. It was to be a self-governing society composed of persons who did not have the right of suffrage and had been residents of Great Britain for at least one year. Each new member was to be recommended and seconded by other members, and his name and address were to be recorded. The purpose of the association was to be the realization of the platform suggested in the quotation from the Duke of Richmond's letter. The means to be used were organization, discussion, and correspondence with other societies which had been instituted for a similar purpose. When the membership exceeded twenty, the association was to be separated into two bodies, and this process was to be kept up as the divisions grew, thus enabling the membership to multiply without increasing the size of each body beyond the point favorable for discussion.[32] This plan was submitted to a small number of Hardy's acquaintances, and, on January 25, 1792, the first meeting was held. In the declaration of their intentions, which was made shortly afterward, reasons for a reform were urged with the concluding resolution: " That this society do express their abhorrence of tumult and violence and threat, as they aim at reform; not anarchy, but reason, firmness, and unanimity are the only arms they themselves will employ or persuade their fellow citizens to exert against the abuse of power."[33] In spite of repressive measures which might reasonably have been made the pretext for a different procedure, the London Corresponding Society adhered to the letter of this promise, at least until after the measures taken in 1796, which is as far as this inquiry has been concerned.

Whether this society would have come into existence, or the others would have continued their organization, if the

---

[32] Francis Place MSS. IV, 20.   [33] Francis Place MSS. II, 4.

French Revolution had not occurred, it is impossible to say. There is no evidence to show that the leaders of these associations ever proposed anything more than a reformation of the House of Commons. They invariably offered such reform as a panacea for all the political ills of which they complained. It had not required the French Revolution to call attention to the abuses which they desired to remedy, or to suggest the methods of organization and the propaganda which they adopted. It is more probable that the chief impetus was given by the circumstances which attended the war for American independence.

We do not imply by this statement that these societies did not take cognizance of the French Revolution or regard it with sympathy. They but followed the course of the radical Whigs in Parliament. On several occasions they sent felicitous addresses to the legislative bodies of the French, after the precedent set by the Revolution Society in 1789. Perhaps the most extravagant of these addresses was that prepared in the autumn of 1792 by the London Corresponding Society, and sent by that association in conjunction with several others. Yet even this address contained no stronger words than the following: "Warm as are our wishes for your success, eager as we are to behold freedom triumphant, and man everywhere restored to the enjoyment of his just rights, a sense of our duty as orderly citizens forbids our flying in arms to your assistance. Our government has pledged the national faith to remain neutral. In a struggle for liberty against despotism, Britons remain neutral. O Shame! But we have entrusted our king with discretionary powers, we therefore must obey. Our hands are bound, but our hearts are free, and they are with you."[34]

There was no attempt to conceal their sympathy with what they believed was an effort on the part of the French to improve their government. But toward the conditions in England the societies took a different attitude, and threaded their way through the intricate maze of political theories

---

[34] Francis Place MSS. IV, 46.

with remarkable precision for men with untrained minds. They consistently maintained that England needed reform and not revolution.[35]

Beginning October 29, 1793, an attempt was made to hold at Edinburgh a general convention of representatives from the societies in Great Britain which were organized for promoting parliamentary reform. The London Corresponding Society and several others from the English manufacturing towns sent delegates, but the majority were naturally from Scotland. The "British Convention of Delegates of the People, associated to obtain universal Suffrage and annual Parliaments," as this body styled itself, held fourteen sessions, in which the chief point at issue seems to have been whether it would be more proper to petition the king or the Parliament for the reforms which were desired. On December 5, the day appointed for the fifteenth sitting, the secretary of the convention and several other members, including the delegates from the London Corresponding Society, were arrested, and the papers of the convention confiscated. On the same day the lord provost of the city ordered the assembly to disperse. On the next day the sheriff broke up the meeting, though it was not

[35] A broadside addressed to Parliament and the people of Great Britain, published in the excitement of the closing days of 1795, gave a statement of the general views of the society which accorded with what had been its practice:—

"With respect to particular forms and modifications of government, this Society conceive, and ever have conceived, that the disputes and contentions about these, which have so often distracted the universe (like bigoted attachments to particular forms of worship) are marks only of weak and inconsiderate minds that in the pursuit of fleeting shadows forget the substance. Their attention has been uniformly addressed to more essential objects—to the peace—the social order—and the happiness of mankind; and these they have always been ready to acknowledge and believe might be sufficiently secured by the genuine spirit of the British Constitution. They have laboured, therefore, with incessant application, not to overthrow, but to restore and realize that constitution; to give practical effect to those excellencies that have been theoretically acknowledged; and to reform those corruptions and abuses, which, while some have attempted to justify, no one has had the hardihood to deny."

The numerous resolutions, tracts, petitions, broadsides, etc., which the society published agreed with what has been said of it.

necessary to use force, as the members readily submitted to the authority of the law. Skirving, the secretary of the convention, and Gerrald and Margarot, the delegates from the London Corresponding Society, were tried for seditious practices before the High Court of Justiciary at Edinburgh in January, 1794, and they were all transported to Botany Bay for fourteen years. The minutes of this convention are published as a preface to the report of the trial of Skirving, and give no indication that these delegates were engaged in more than fruitless discussions of the questions which they believed were involved in a reform of parliament. The style of the debates was such as would be expected from a body of men who felt their importance, and who lacked the mental balance of education. It is not necessary to agree with the later advocates of reform, who characterized as martyrs these men who were here convicted, but it is difficult to discover in the testimony which was adduced any justification for the sentences which were imposed.[36]

---

[36] For the trials of Skirving, Margarot and Gerrald, see Howell, State Trials XXIII, 391–1012. These reports naturally contain a considerable part of the materials for the history of the British Convention. Other extracts from the papers which had been seized were included in the reports of the secret committee of the House of Commons, which will be described later. The accounts in the contemporary newspapers add nothing that is new, and it has not seemed worth while to give specific citations. The titles of several pamphlets concerning the subject will be found in the appended bibliography. Some additional papers relating to the part which the London Corresponding Society had in the convention may be found in the Francis Place Manuscripts in the British Museum. An interesting example of these is the instructions which were given to Margarot and Gerrald by the society:—

"I. He shall on no account whatever depart from the original object and principles, viz. the obtaining annual Parliaments and universal suffrage by rational and lawful means.

"II. He is directed to support the opinion that representatives in Parliament ought to be paid by their constituents.

"III. That the election of Sheriffs ought to be restored to the people.

"IV. That juries ought to be chosen by lot.

"V. That active means ought to be used to render every man acquainted with the duty and rights of jurymen.

"VI. That the liberty of the press must at all events be supported, and that the publication of political truths can never be criminal.

On February 28, 1793, Sheridan moved in Parliament
that the " house constitute itself a committee to inquire into
the truth of the reports of seditious practices in this
country."[37]   On the day before he had called on Hardy,
who offered to show him all the papers and correspondence
of the society of which he was secretary.[38]   It was but little
more than two months previous to this time that Parliament
had been summoned on account of an alleged insurrection.
Obviously, Sheridan's purpose was to call attention to the
excuses which the ministers could offer to support their
action on that occasion.   In the hurry of events at that time,
all inquiry into the nature and extent of the alleged insurrection had been omitted, and it was only reasonable that
those who had not agreed with the measures which had
been taken then should now desire to investigate the assertions on which such measures had been based.   But the
motion which Sheridan brought forward was negatived
after a warm opposition by the supporters of the government.   The proposals and methods of the societies were
well known, and any dangers which might result from them
were already apparent, yet they were permitted to carry on
their propaganda until the next year.

If the diary of an interested person may be relied on, the
ministers had not ceased their proposals for a political
arrangement which would include the adherents of the
Duke of Portland.   In April or early in May, 1794, Dundas
called on Windham for the professed purpose of conferring
as to the growth of the political clubs, which were alleged

"VII. That it is the duty of the people to resist any act of
Parliament repugnant to the original principles of the constitution;
as would be every attempt to prohibit associations for the purpose
of reform.
   "VIII. That this Society, considering all party names and distinctions as hostile to the general welfare, do absolutely restrict
their delegates from assuming or accepting of that nature.
   "IX. This society do further require their delegates to be punc-
tual and frequent in their correspondence with this society."
Francis Place MSS. II, 75.
   [37] Hansard, Parliamentary History XXX, 523.
   [38] Howell, State Trials XXIV, 1100. Sheridan testified to this
fact in the trial of Hardy.

to be seditious. But this lieutenant, whom Pitt found so useful, contrived to turn the conversation to the proposed alliance. Windham answered that he would ascertain the sentiments of the duke.[39]

On May 12, a few days after this conference, Dundas presented to the House of Commons a message from the king, which gave information of the seizure of the papers of the London Corresponding Society and of the Society for Constitutional Information. Several of their leaders had been arrested at the same time. On the following day the papers which had been seized were presented to the house under seal. Pitt immediately moved that they be referred to a committee of secrecy. In reply to a criticism by Fox, Dundas justified the seizure on the ground that treasonable practices had been alleged. On the fifteenth the committee was chosen by ballot, and naturally, although Windham became a member, none of the friends of Fox were selected. On the next day the minister, as chairman of the committee, made a preliminary report, in which the societies were charged with " uniformly and systematically pursuing a settled design which appears to your committee to tend to the subversion of the established constitution." This charge was based in part on the assertions that as early as the spring of 1792 one of the societies applauded the proposal to publish a cheap edition of Thomas Paine's Rights of Man. The report stated that " this single circumstance would in the judgement of your committee, leave little doubt of the real nature of the designs entertained by this society." It further asserted that proposals had been made to assemble, under the color of advocating reform, a convention intended " to supersede the House of Commons in its representative capacity, and to assume to itself all the functions and powers of a national legislature ;" and it alleged, in conclusion, that although the committee had not " yet had the opportunity of investigating as fully as they could wish," still, " it appears to your committee,

---

[39] Baring, Diary of the Right Honourable William Windham, 308.

that in some of the societies referred to, proposals have been received, and that measures have recently been taken, for providing arms to be distributed among the members of the societies." With the same qualification, the committee reported that there had been "some indications of a disposition to concert means for forcibly resisting such measures as may be taken for defeating" the accomplishment of the treasonable purposes. Excerpts and quotations from the papers which had been seized accompanied the report. From these extracts it is apparent that, in spite of the purpose for which the selections had been made, the proposed convention had no other object than to obtain "in a constitutional and legal method" a "full and fair representation of the people of Great Britain."[40] At the conclusion of his speech, in which he perverted and misinterpreted the evidence presented in order to make it support his contention, Pitt moved for leave to bring in a bill to suspend the Habeas Corpus Act so far as it related to persons who were conspiring against the person and government of the king. Fox, in his reply, ridiculed the arguments of the minister, and pointed out that no evidence had been produced of intentions on the part of the societies which had not been publicly known before. But Pitt was certain of his power, and the bill was finally passed at three o'clock on the morning of May 18, in spite of a filibuster by the supporters of Fox. On May 22 the measure was approved by the Lords, though Thurlow said that, in his opinion, the evidence submitted would probably support no more serious charge than sedition.[41]

In the meantime, the negotiations with the Duke of Portland were temporarily interrupted by the illness of his wife.[42] On June 6, 1794, Pitt made to the house a second report from the committee of secrecy. This report attempted to justify the hints, which had been thrown out in

---

[40] Parliamentary Papers XIV, No. 112. Hansard, Parliamentary History XXXI, 471–497.
[41] Hansard, Parliamentary History XXXI, 497–606.
[42] Baring, Diary of the Right Honourable William Windham, 311.

10

the first report, of evidence sufficient to show that the societies were arming their members. The further suggestion, that the societies were preparing to oppose by force the measures of the administration, had to be omitted, since there was no evidence to support such a charge. As proof of the first statement, a letter was introduced, said to have been found unopened among the papers of Hardy,[43] which purported to be from an individual at Sheffield, offering to furnish pike blades of a good quality for a shilling each to those who would send the "money with the order." Although the report did not mention that the letter was found unopened, the ministers apparently believed that this fact alone was not sufficient to support the charge which they had made. Accordingly, they brought forward a series of letters bearing dates from May 19 to June 2, 1794, supposed to have been written from Whitehall by Dundas to Pitt, and professing to contain information that evidence had been discovered in Scotland of a treasonable conspiracy which had been undertaken by persons who had been prominent in the British Convention. An appendix contained numerous papers of the societies which had been omitted from the first report.[44] As a result of this report and of a briefer one by the committee of the Lords, addresses to the king were proposed in both houses, in the upper house on June 13 and in the Commons three days later. Naturally they were carried without difficulty.[45]

Whether moved by his fear for the safety of the country, by the seductions of place, or by the persuasions of his friends, the Duke of Portland was now on the point of yielding to the insistent efforts of the ministers. The negotiations had been renewed, and the only question that remained to be settled was the price of the alliance. It was proposed that a third secretary of state should be appointed. Pitt's original intention seems to have been that the Duke

---

[43] Howell, State Trials XXIV, 667, 1005.
[44] Parliamentary Papers XIV, No. 115. Hansard, Parliamentary History XXXI, 688–879.
[45] Hansard, Parliamentary History XXXI, 909–931.

of Portland should ostensibly succeed Dundas as home secretary and should have charge of the correspondence relating strictly to the affairs of Great Britain and Ireland. Dundas in turn was to become secretary of state for war, and to retain the management of the colonies and the war.[46] After accepting the offer, the duke professed to have misunderstood the proposition, and expressed a determination to withdraw from the arrangement. Thereupon, on July 5, the minister wrote to Grenville suggesting that Portland be given the foreign department, since he did not feel disposed to leave the management of the war to the former Whig nobleman. Grenville, in exchange, was to have the position that Portland had refused.[47] The minister received on the same day a favorable response to his request, and resumed his negotiations with the duke.[48] In a conversation on July 7 Pitt offered to take the colonies from Dundas and add them to the office which had been proposed for Portland.[49] This was a satisfactory solution to all of those concerned except Dundas, who did not quite justify the minister's confident belief in his pliability. On July 9 he wrote to Loughborough that he intended to resign that portion of his duties which would be left to him under the proposed arrangement. The chancellor immediately sent the letter to Pitt, who lost no time in writing to persuade Dundas to retain his position,[50] and even asked the king to unite with him in his plea.[51] A satisfactory understanding was eventually reached.

A week after this had been done, the True Briton, the "authentic vehicle" of the views of the ministers, announced that the internal circumstances of the country had happily, of late, "very considerably improved;" that the union of all good men for the preservation of the con-

---

[46] Stanhope, Life of William Pitt II, 252.
[47] Dropmore Papers II, 595.
[48] Dropmore Papers II, 596.
[49] Dropmore Papers II, 597. Baring, Diary of the Right Honourable William Windham, 314.
[50] Stanhope, Life of William Pitt II, 253.
[51] Stanhope, Life of William Pitt II, 254.

stitution, added to the energy of government, had tended
" to crush the spirit of treason and sedition that had begun
to manifest itself, and which created such just alarm in the
breasts of all truly and sincerely interested in the welfare of
the country;" that the additions made to the ministry, " by
the accession of those respectable noblemen and gentlemen
who no longer think it prudent to preserve the distinction
of party," was such as to give " the most solid satisfaction
to the country at large, as the most unequivocal proof, not
only that the former measures of ministers, from conviction
of their propriety, have produced unanimity, but that the
same powerful principle will actuate all future deliberations
and resolves of the executive government."[52]

In other words, now that the result which the ministers
desired had been attained, the sedition had vanished. Yet
the London Corresponding Society was still engaged in its
propaganda in favor of annual parliaments and universal
suffrage, and was collecting funds for the defence of the
prisoners who were confined in the Tower to await trial
on the charge of treason. But so far as the ministry was
concerned the society had served its purpose. The energetic measures which had been adopted were as effective in
arousing new zeal in the supporters of the government as
they would have been if a real danger had been disclosed.
There was now little prospect that the Duke of Portland
and his friends would ever join with Fox in successful
opposition to the policies of the government. Pitt was
therefore free to carry out his plans on the Continent without fear of hindrances in domestic politics. This was no
mean consideration, for it was now apparent that the war
would last longer and cost more than he had imagined when
he began it.

On July 15, the same day on which the True Briton an-

---

[52] True Briton, July 15, 1794. On July 29 the same paper said:—
" We heartily wish that our affairs on the Continent had as
favourable an aspect as our affairs at home.—For here we have a
union of all that is respectable in politics against a very few discontented; etc."

nounced that the dangers from treason had vanished, Pitt
set down in the form of a minute his plans for the future.
These plans had to do in part with military operations to
come and in part with measures for securing the conquests
which had been made.[53]   They only serve to confirm the
opinion presented in an earlier chapter of this study as to
the purpose of the English minister in promoting the war.

While arrangements were being made for carrying out
these plans for foreign conquest, which were destined to
meet with indifferent success, delayed justice was being

---

[53] Dropmore Papers II, 599. This document is described as a
"Minute of Mr. Pitt in reference to military Operations against
France."

AUSTRIA.

" To represent the necessity of concerting vigourous measures for
the protection of the Dutch frontier, and for keeping up the communication with Condé, Valenciennes, Quesnoy, and Landrecies, and
to state the force applicable to those purposes.
" To insist on a change of commanders.
" To concert further measures for increasing the Austrian force
on the side of Flanders, if possible, in the course of this campaign, and at all events, before the opening of the next, to at least
100,000 effective.
" To agree on the acquisitions to be made by Austria, without
which no peace shall be made but by their consent, provided they
agree to keep up the stipulated force, and not to make peace without our consent, or without our retaining the acquisitions which we
have now or shall have made in the East and West Indies, and
provided they also agree to the cession desired by the Dutch.
" If these points are settled, to offer either to conclude immediately a treaty of defensive alliance, or to agree to conclude it
at the end of the war.
" To agree on a concert of measures with the Princes, and on
taking steps to assist the levies of French troops, as well as on
the recognition of the French King, and the Regent, as soon as
any footing shall be gained in the interior of France.
" To ascertain whether any pecuniary arrangements are necessary and practicable to enable Austria to prosecute the war vigour-
ously for at least two campaigns after the present.

PRUSSIA.

" To insist on the immediate march to Flanders of the army
under M. Möllendorf; and on its being completed, without loss of
time, to the number stipulated by the treaty.
" To express a readiness to enter into a full explanation as to
the acquisitions to be made by Austria and to engage to form a
mutual guarantee of our respective possessions as they may stand
at the peace.
" To propose, as soon as the present force is completed to its
stipulated amount, to subsidize an additional body of 30,000 men."

meted out to those who had been accused of treason.   On
October 8, 1794, Hardy, Tooke, and Thelwall, three of the
prisoners who had been confined in the Tower, were tried
before a Commission of Oyer and Terminer on the charge
of high treason.   They were acquitted, and consequently
the remaining prisoners were dismissed without trial.   Those
who had been charged with the same offence in Scotland
had a different fate.   Robert Watt seems to have been an
ignorant, ambitious, religious enthusiast.   He had connected
himself with the reform societies as early as 1791, and, with
a view of securing advancement for himself, had communicated with Dundas for the purpose of giving him information concerning them.   These communications had continued until August or September, 1793, according to Watt's
confession.   He had taken part in the British Convention,
and, subsequent to the dispersal of that body, had, on his
own initiative, organized a small committee which proceeded
to take several curious measures.   He had caused a few
pikes to be made, which, he said, were both for sale and for
distribution.   Forty-seven of them were found.   With these
arms, and the five or six men who were involved, he proposed to take Edinburgh, and afterwards London and Dub-
lin.   He affected to have believed that as soon as his program was begun, " persons in various ranks of society would
carry it on."   The only defence which he offered on his
trial was his correspondence with Dundas and the lord
advocate in 1792 and 1793.   Watt and David Downie, who
had been engaged with him, were convicted and received
the rigorous sentence of the Scotch law.[54]   Downie was

---

[54] True Briton, September 12, 1794. The following sentence was
pronounced:—
  " You, and each of you, prisoners at the bar, are to be taken from
the bar to the place from which you came, from thence to be
drawn upon a hurdle to the place, there to be hanged by the neck,
but not till you are dead; for you are then to be taken down, your
hearts to be cut out, and your bowels burned before your face,
your heads and limbs severed from your bodies and held up to
public view, and your bodies shall remain at the disposal of his
Majesty; and the Lord have mercy on your souls !"
  The king ordered that the sentence be mitigated, and that the
severing of the head be the only mutilation.
  Morning Post, October 11, 1794.

afterwards pardoned, and the only one to suffer was he who, though from questionable motives, had formerly been zealous in behalf of the government. Perhaps his punishment was just, yet it is impossible not to remember that he had previously been in communication with the ministers, and that his harmless plot came to light at an opportune moment for assisting them in producing the evidence which they sadly needed. It was also alleged that he had been urged by a visitor to change his confession after he had written it.[55]

---

[55] Morning Chronicle, November 28, 1794.
    For information concerning all of these trials, see Howell, State Trials XXIII, XXIV, XXV. See also numerous pamphlets of which the titles will be found in the appended bibliography. Full reports and numerous paragraphs of comment appeared in the contemporary newspapers.

CHAPTER VI.

PITT AT HIS ZENITH.

Since 1792 William Pitt had been ruling England according to the dictates of his own will. He had not obtained
his power by any usurpation of functions which did not
properly belong to his office. He did not retain it by opposing his wishes to the desires of a majority of the governing body. His method was to manipulate the men on the
political chess-board in a manner that would give him the
appearance of acting in accordance with the popular wish
while in reality he was carrying out his own plans. From
this distance it may be difficult to agree with the wisdom of
his policy of attacking France in 1792, though the attendant
circumstances probably made his estimate of his prospective
enemy a natural one. His conduct of the war after it was
begun may be open to serious criticisms, but it is easier
to form judgments after events have occurred than it was
to make plans for situations of which history afforded no
previous examples. Yet even under adverse conditions Pitt
maintained the government of England during a most critical period of European affairs. In 1797 he admitted that
his plans abroad had been defeated, and yet there was no
other person thought of to take his place. From the point
of view of the people and the nation, his measures had resulted in little but ill. In the maintenance of his own power,
he had proved himself a master hand at the political game.

In May, 1793, George Rose, his secretary of the treasury,
had told Pitt that the attack upon France would not be
received in England as favorably as would his defending of
Holland unless it should be attended with brilliant success.[1]
The minister was now confronted with the danger against

---

[1] Auckland MSS. XXXIX, 437, Rose to Auckland, May 10, 1793.

which Rose had warned him. From the beginning of the
war the government had resorted to loans to finance the
operations, but it had also been compelled to impose new
taxes, and, in February, 1795, the True Briton announced
that "there never was in this country so large a sum raised
in one year by taxes as that which is intended in the present."[2] Obviously, it was necessary to maintain the enthusiasm of the people in order to gain their support for
projects which required such impositions. The problems
confronting Pitt were as follows: to conduct a continental
war, relying for support on powers which were kept in the
struggle chiefly by the force of English subsidies; to devise
loans and taxes sufficient to provide the funds for satisfying
the demands of his allies, in addition to the expenses which
attended his own operations on the Continent and in England's more peculiar domain; and lastly, to convince the
people who must provide these funds that there were any
good and sufficient reasons for such an extensive outlay.
Any one of these obligations was sufficient to overtax the
ability of an ordinary man. The object of this chapter is to
explain the means which he used for accomplishing the last
of these undertakings. Never does the minister seem to
have lost sight of the fact that, if he was to play successfully
the rôle which he had attempted, he must keep the people
firm in the belief that they were opposing real dangers,
against which they ought to bring all of their strength.
Furthermore, none of his other measures met with as great
success as those which he instituted for the purpose of preventing complaints from the taxpayers on whom the burdens of the war rested most heavily.

After 1792 the clergy of the established church were
among the most active agents for indoctrinating the people
with a belief in the necessity of the governmental measures.
Their part in the events of that year has been mentioned.
After the war began, fast days were appointed on which
they were expected to discourse on political topics, and the

---

[2] True Briton, February 26, 1795.

celebration of the martyrdom of Charles I was also revived.[3] But, in many cases, the clergy did not await an
appointed day for discussion of the political situation. The
doctrines of these patriotic divines were in harmony with
the principles of the British constitution which they believed
to be divinely inspired and were wholly antagonistic to the
principles of the corresponding French institutions which
they viewed as proceeding from a radically different source.
Consequently to them the war was almost a holy contest,
and the measures of the ministers were deserving of their
loyal support.[4] Such views were not, of course, the results

---

[3] True Briton, January 30, 1793:—
"It has not been very customary of late years for much
observance to be paid to the anniversary of the 30th of January; but we are inclined to believe that this day will be more
particularly distinguished, from the peculiarly afflicting circumstances of the present times. We understand, and we hear it with
satisfaction, that there will be a very full attendance of both Houses
of Parliament."
The date was also celebrated at other places. The titles of some
of the sermons preached will be found in the appended bibliography.
In view of this celebration, it is interesting to observe the attitude
that had sometimes been taken toward the celebration previous to
the discussions which arose subsequent to the French Revolution.
It was related that one humorous divine took as an appropriate
text the passage: "O give thanks unto the Lord, to Him who hath
smote great Kings." Another, still bolder, chose the suggestive
statement: "By this time he stinketh."
Public Advertiser, February 1, 1790.
[4] It will be possible to cite only a few passages from some of
these sermons. The titles of others will be found in the appended
bibliography.
"Blessings Enjoyed by Englishmen," etc. "Sermon preached
in Greenwich Church April 19, 1793, by Andrew Burnaby." After
reciting the blessings of the British constitution, the preacher continued:—
"France, a prodigy of every crime and enormity under heaven—
after overturning the altars of her god;—after imbruing her hands
in the innocent blood of her sovereign;—after trampling upon
the most sacred rights;—after violating every principle of virtue,
truth, justice and humanity; and after devastating every city and
province in her own territories;—France, after exhibiting the most
dreadful spectacle to the world, which must strike horror and dis-
may into every, both present and future generation, is endeavouring
in defiance of repeated professions, and in open violation of the
most solemn treaties, to rob and despoil us of the blessings here
enumerated."
On the same date, W. Gilbank, in his sermon on the "Duties of
Man," said among other things:—

of any direct injunctions or requests of the ministers. The
appeal to the clergy was of a more subtle character. Their ✓
fears were excited and their ambitions ministered to under
the cloak of inspiring them to patriotic exertions.[5]   The

"We have, therefore, most sincerely to beg of God to continue
us in the possession of a constitution, which in its principles, at
least, seems to be at the summit of political perfection." Further
on he concluded: "The time would fail me to enumerate all the
blessings which the lower orders of this kingdom possess and the
numerous causes which they have to be quiet and mind their own
business."

James Scott, D.D., in a sermon preached at Park Street Chapel
on the same day, spoke of the reform party, which he described in
this way:—

"That unnatural faction, who openly declare themselves the advocates for Gallic anarchy, and under the plausible pretence of reform would introduce here the same scenes of confusion, blood and
horror. Influenced by motives equally sordid and dangerous, have
we not seen them conspire against the honour of their sovereign,
the majesty of the constitution, and the happiness, and I had
almost said the very existence of the country. It is a fortunate
circumstance, however, that in all their agonies and contentions
for power, they have betrayed such a shameless contempt of
character, such a bare-faced and profligate prostitution of principle,
that they are become the detestation and horror of all good men."

Rev. John Gardiner on the same day preached a sermon at St.
Mary Magdalen, Taunton. He concluded his description of the
French with these words:—

"Such then are the characters—barbarous regicides, infidels and
atheists, plunderers and assassins, monsters in philosophy—savages
in cruelty—such are the characters against whom Great Britain has
been compelled to unsheath the sword."

That the enthusiasm did not wane as the war went on, witness
a quotation from a sermon preached in the same church in 1795:—

"Alas, if the Ministers of God were to be silent on this subject—
if they did not again and again resound in your ears, that in the
present extraordinary war the interests of religion, as well as
humanity, are at stake—the stones of these walls, the vaults from
under your feet would cry out."

Finally, in 1796, Alexander Hewatt, D.D. (the author of a history
of South Carolina), in discoursing on "Religion essential to the
Being and Happiness of Society," found occasion to say:—

"Times were, when we were taught to believe that the Rulers of
the people could do no wrong. Now the case is reversed, and the
doctrine of the new school is, that the people can do no wrong.
Their voice is blasphemously pronounced to be the voice of God.
But woe to that nation, where the people's voice is the supreme law;
and to that individual whose life is at the mercy of a popular
tribunal."

[5] The case was well stated by the Rev. J. H. Williams, vicar of
Wellsbourne, in his introduction to the two sermons which he
preached on the fast days of 1793 and 1794. These sermons had
been unfavorably criticized by the supporters of the administra-

effects of these pulpit discourses and of subsequent publications were of too complicated a character to admit of satisfactory analysis here.   The general attitude of the people toward the church, the esteem in which the individual clergymen were held in their respective communities, the political functions which they were accustomed to assume, and many other similar conditions would have to be ascertained before a rational estimate could be made.   Therefore, it is only possible to say that, to a considerable degree, the ecclesiastical organization seems to have been a factor

---

tion, and were published as a justification of the preacher. In his introduction he said:—

"Though some of us may think that we are more properly at our post, when we are standing upon the watch-tower and giving notice of the approach of moral or religious foes; yet a crafty statesman soon contrives methods to bring us down into the field. By the allurements of honour and reward, by the delicate operation of character, by an artful and delusive connection of his own ambitious measures with the order of civil society, which our conscience tells us we are bound to support, he leaves us no neutral point to stand upon; he makes us combatants, often without our knowledge, and sometimes against our will. But there is nothing more mortifying to an ingenious spirit, than to feel the supernal pressure, in matters which belong more peculiarly to ourselves; or in plainer words,—the not being suffered to do our own business in our own way. Now the whole and sole business of a parish priest is this, by the influence of his example, and by the frequency and soundness of his instruction, to promote the general cause of virtue and religion, and to increase the number of real Christians and good men. This is the vineyard that he is hired to labour in, and this labour is worthy of its hire; for a real Christian and a good man can never make a bad citizen. But in this even path of his vocation he is not always suffered to proceed. It is not sufficient, in the opinion of his secular masters, that he strive to make men good Christians, and by consequence, good citizens and good subjects; he must form his flock into good politicians also; he must teach them that secular orthodoxy, to which he himself has never subscribed; he must show them those signs of the times which he himself is unable to discern. For this purpose the trumpet is blown in Sion, and a War-fast is proclaimed. Thus the infallible authority of fallible men which the church had once so shamelessly enforced, is in her turn retorted upon herself, at a period when her reason is less able to acquiesce in it, and she is required to persuade a pious assent to the justice and necessity of a war by the united voices of all her ministers; some of whom may possibly object to its justice, many of whom may be unconvinced of its necessity, and almost all of them, by being happily excluded from the cabals of the factions and the cabinets of the authorities, must be deprived of all solid judgement, either as to the actual grounds of its provocation, or the real objects of its prosecution."

in keeping before the people a favorable view of the measures of the government.

Meanwhile, events had been occurring which made it
more necessary than ever that the ministers should continue
their efforts to preserve good feeling among the people. It
had become impracticable to defend the Dutch any longer,
and, on November 18, 1794, it was decided at a cabinet
meeting to inform the stadtholder that England would not
object if Holland should accept the French proposals for
peace.[6] On April 17, 1795, news reached England that
peace had been made with France by Prussia.[7] In August
of the same year came information of a similar action on
the part of Spain.[8] The aid given to the loyalists in France
had been productive of no apparent results, except to impose additional burdens of expense upon England. The
expedition to Quiberon, which had promised so much, had
been a failure. Though treaties were concluded with
Russia in February, 1795,[9] and with Austria in May of
the same year,[10] the latter carried a provision for a loan of
four million six hundred thousand pounds, which the
ministers had to provide for and at the same time defend
in Parliament. The ministerial measures were certainly
not prospering as well as might be wished.

In the spring of 1795 a difference of opinion came
perilously near causing a serious breach in the cabinet.
Pitt, though he had refused to pay the subsidy promised
to Prussia in the treaty made in 1794, on the ground that
the conditions had not been complied with, now came forward with a proposal to do so. Grenville thought that such
a proposal would endanger the negotiations then in progress
with Russia and Austria, and would bring no real benefit
to England, even if successful. He believed that the attempt to make such a treaty would "weaken if not destroy

---

[6] Dropmore Papers II, 646. The treaty with Holland was signed
May 16, 1795. Martens, Recueil de Traités VI, 92.
[7] Dropmore Papers III, 57.
[8] Dropmore Papers III, 93.
[9] Martens, Recueil de Traités VI, 10–23.
[10] Martens, Recueil de Traités VI, 64–87.

any hope of obtaining the support of Parliament for another campaign." Therefore he refused to agree to the measure, and tendered his resignation. In spite of this embarrassing circumstance, Pitt proposed to go ahead with his own plans, when the conclusion of the treaty between France and Prussia, at Basle, put an end to the project, and made it unnecessary that the disagreement between the ministers should become public.[11]

The administration was able to derive as little satisfaction from the internal affairs of England as from those abroad. There had been a serious drouth in 1794.[12] Supplies from the Continent had been interfered with by war, and as a consequence the price of corn in the summer of 1795 was double what it had been in the previous year.[13] Meetings were held and remedies for the scarcity discussed. Sometimes agreements were made to abstain from certain varieties of food, and instructions for preparing palatable dishes without the use of corn were published. A considerable tax was imposed on the use of hair-powder, which, it was supposed, would lessen the quantity of flour used for that purpose.[14]

---

[11] Dropmore Papers III, 25–31, 50. For a more detailed discussion of this incident, though from a somewhat different point of view, see E. D. Adams, Influence of Grenville on Pitt's Foreign Policy, 31–36.

[12] Morning Post, July 19, 1794:—
"From every part of the Kingdom we hear of the uncommon heat, and the want of grass for cattle; many thousand farmers in Devonshire, Oxfordshire, Warwickshire, and other highlands have turned them into the hay fields instead of mowing the grass."
Morning Chronicle, June 23, 1795:—
"To such a degree is the scarcity real, that according to the opinions of the persons best acquainted with the subject, if the rains had been but a fortnight later in setting in, London must have been in absolute want for bread; for such would have been the melancholy prospect of a general failure of a crop, that no man who had wheat in his possession would have thought it safe to part with it at any price."

[13] London Gazette 1794, 1795, contains regular quotations of the price of grain. On September 27, 1794, the average price of wheat in England and Wales was given as 50s. 10d. per quarter. By August 15, 1795, it had risen to 115s. 7d.

[14] Gentleman's Magazine LXV, 523. This is an account of a Court of Common Council of London held June 17, 1795, at which a committee was appointed to look into the means for reducing

When Parliament met in the autumn of 1795, the
minister himself moved that a select committee be appointed
to take into consideration the high price of corn.[15] The
Privy Council had previously taken steps to ascertain the
cause and extent of the scarcity and to alleviate it.[16] The
situation was clearly the result of circumstances that could
not be immediately remedied; but hungry people do not stop
to reason, and there were serious bread riots in a number
of towns.[17]

These conditions, which seemed to be in part a result
of the war, did not serve to render less obnoxious the
burdens of taxation which had to be borne. The public
mass-meetings of the London Corresponding Society were
attended by increasingly large numbers. At several of these

the high price of provisions, and to take into consideration means
for relieving the poor from the hardships resulting from the high
price of bread.

Gentleman's Magazine LXV, 542. Some persons at Birmingham
agreed to abstain from the use of wheat bread at any meal except
breakfast, and to use only a moderate quantity at that time. Vege-
tables were to be substituted for it. This was to be done in order
that the poor might have more bread.

Gentleman's Magazine LXV, 563. It was suggested that the
government prohibit the making of biscuits, rolls, cakes, or pastry,
or any other bread except household bread, etc.

Gentleman's Magazine LXV, 697. The members of the Privy
Council signed an agreement to use in their families no bread of
a greater fineness than the standard wheaten bread, and recommended that others do the same.

Morning Chronicle, July 15, 1795. The merchants, bankers, and
traders of London, in a meeting, suggested that steps be taken "to
promote the general use of that sort of bread which is made of
the whole produce of the wheat," and to set on foot other remedies of a similar nature.

See the appended bibliography for the titles of pamphlets relating to this subject.

[15] Hansard, Parliamentary History XXXII, 235.

[16] Morning Chronicle, March 18, 1795. Gentleman's Magazine
LXV, 611.

[17] Gentleman's Magazine LXV, 343. London Packet, June 24–26,
1795. Morning Chronicle, July 11, 1795; August 12, 1795. The
Oracle, June 26, 1795; July 1, 1795; July 10, 1795. The Telegraph,
June 25, 1795.

The Oracle, which supported the administration, said on July 1:—

"The tumults which prevail in the interior parts of the country,
on account of the dearness of provisions, are much more general
and alarming than the public are at present aware of."

The remedy proposed was that the people eat less.

meetings food was distributed, a feature which probably served to swell the attendance. The petitions to Parliament and the king and the addresses to the nation at large now included a prayer for peace, as well as appeals for "annual parliaments and universal suffrage." The high price of food was attributed to the war, and was urged as a reason why the petition should be granted. Yet, in spite of these circumstances, even the papers which supported the administration were obliged to admit that these immense meetings were conducted in an orderly manner, and broke up without any disturbance of the peace. It would seem to be a significant comment on the character of those who were the leaders of this popular movement that they were able to conduct assemblies estimated as numbering from ten to one hundred thousand men in such a manner that no disorders resulted. As there were ample reasons for asserting that the affairs of the nation were being mismanaged, and as a scarcity of food does not tend to increase the affections of a people toward their government, such moderation bears eloquent witness to the loyalty of the mass of the common people toward the existing constitution.[18]

The London Corresponding Society was not the only organization of this character favoring a peace. Meetings were held at other places under different auspices, and resolutions were adopted which signified the same desire.[19] But the ministers, through their newspapers, still insisted that, "by a little perseverance, we shall ultimately obtain our great objects—indemnity for the past and security for the future; without both of which, peace, we should dread,

[18] Morning Chronicle, June 30, 1795; July 1, 17, 1795. The Oracle, June 30, 1795; October 27, 1795. The Telegraph, July 1, 1795. The Times, June 30, 1795; October 27, 1795. Gentleman's Magazine LXV, 609, 874.

Much information concerning these meetings may also be found in the Francis Place Manuscripts in the British Museum. The titles of broadsides, pamphlets, etc., will be found in the appended bibliography. The meetings were held after public advertisement, and the proceedings were given as wide publicity as was practicable.

[19] Morning Chronicle, January 31, 1795; July 14, 30, 1795; September 12, 1795. Debrett, State Papers III, 340–347.

would be the certain death blow of the independence of the British nation."[20] It was, however, evident that if the administration was to stem the growing popular disapproval of its measures and to obtain sufficient funds wherewith to preserve its aggressive attitude, other expedients must be devised for arousing the people at large to a proper pitch of indiscriminating enthusiasm.

Accordingly, it was arranged that, in the king's speech at the opening of Parliament on October 29, 1795, the hope should be expressed that the existing situation in France might terminate in " an order of things compatible with the tranquility of other countries; " but that at the same time it should be clearly stated that the best way to accelerate that end was to prepare for prosecuting the war, and that, therefore, exertions were being made to improve England's naval superiority, and to carry on vigorous operations in the West Indies.[21] In reply to criticisms from the supporters of Fox, Pitt asserted that, " on a general review of the state of the country ten months ago, and at the moment he was speaking he felt no small degree of satisfaction." The argument which he put forward to sustain this contention was that by the depreciation of the assignats France had been reduced to such a condition as to render it almost impossible for her to continue the war. He believed, therefore, that the proper course for England to pursue was to continue the war for a short time longer, thus forcing the French to sue for peace.[22]

But, on the day that Parliament assembled, before the king's speech was discussed in the House of Lords, Grenville brought forward another matter which for the moment served to distract the attention of the people from the financial burdens of the war. This new distraction was an alleged attack upon the person of the king. We need not charge the ministers with instigating such an act in

---

[20] True Briton, December 25, 1794; January 26, 1795. The Sun. November 3, 1795.

[21] Hansard, Parliamentary History XXXII, 143.

[22] Hansard, Parliamentary History XXXII, 182.

11

pointing out that they used it to serve their policy, but the circumstances deserve careful consideration. That feature of the attack which received the greatest attention occurred while the king was on his way to attend the opening of Parliament. It seems that a somewhat larger crowd than usual had assembled to witness the progress of the king as he went to perform his official duty. While on his way, a missile of some description, directed from an unknown source by an undiscovered hand, struck the glass door of the coach. This missile was described by one of the attendants as a marble thrown with considerable violence, and by another as a half-penny the force of whose flight had been spent before it struck the glass. Others suggested that it might have been a shot from an airgun. Further report said that persons in the crowd which had assembled cried out, " Peace! " " No War! " " Bread! " One witness professed to have heard in addition the cry " No George! " but another, with an equal opportunity for observation, insisted that he had not heard such an exclamation. It is interesting to note that in the afternoon of the same day the king was permitted to return from St. James without any guards. Four persons were taken into custody at the time of these disorders. One of them was afterwards convicted of saying, " No George." Although a reward was offered, no record has been found of any further information as to the person who threw the treasonable missile.[23]

---

[23] For accounts of these events see: The Oracle, October 30, 31, 1795. Morning Chronicle, October 30, 31, 1795. The Times, October 30, 31, 1795. History of Two Acts, 12. Hansard, Parliamentary History XXXII, 145–154.

While the Oracle, which had changed owners a short time before, still supported the administration, it was perhaps less likely to color its report of such an occurrence in order to make it conform to a political purpose than either of the other papers which have been examined. Therefore a quotation will be given from the account which it contained on the day after the attack:—

" His Majesty's procession to the House of Peers was yesterday through the greatest concourse of people ever remembered on a similar occasion. The Park, from the Stable-yard to the Horse Guards, was completely filled, as were also the streets from thence to the House of Lords. His Majesty was insulted with groans and hisses, and with a cry of ' No War!' ' Bread!' ' Bread!' ' Peace!'

When the Lords reassembled at five o'clock in the afternoon of the day of the attack on his majesty, they postponed a consideration of the king's speech, and proceeded immediately to examine witnesses with regard to the events which had taken place a few hours before. If the contradictions in this testimony be overlooked and the statements interpreted in the least favorable manner, no evidence was produced which could justify very serious measures. Out of a multitude, many of whom had suffered because of a lack of food, it was alleged that several had been found who gave utterance to seditious exclamations. By some

---

At the end of Great George Street, Westminster, some deluded person had the audacity to throw a marble or bullet through the door-glass of the carriage. On his Majesty's return, stones were repeatedly flying from the mob towards the carriage, many of which bruised the yeoman attendants around it. About the middle of the Park another side glass was broken. At the stable-yard-gate, the carriage turning out into the Park, an elderly man, one of the grooms, attendant upon the near wheel horse, was by pressure of the people thrown down, and, shocking to relate, both wheels of that heavy carriage went over him at the upper part of his thighs, before he could be taken up; he was alive when dragged from that horrid situation. At St. James Gate, entering the court yard, another stone passed through the door glass, the splinters from which flew in his Majesty's face. The carriage returning empty to the Mews, was pelted with mud and stones, and every glass in it broke; the coachmen, grooms and horses, received many violent blows with large stones, aimed probably at the carriage. His Majesty, returning about four o'clock from St. James's in his private coach, *without any guards,* was followed by a mob, and assailed with a shower of stones. A party of horse, returning to the Horse Guards, luckily within sight down the Park, were sent for and arrived fortunately in time to protect the King from personal injury."

This report should be compared with the evidence before the House of Lords, which is given in the Parliamentary History. A witness who was in attendance near the carriage testified as follows concerning the return:—

"Anything on the return?—On returning, I heard several somethings come against the state coach.

"What things?—I do not know. I did see one stone, and that about as big as a large walnut.

"Did you go with the coach till it got back to the palace?—Yes.

"Was there a glass broke then?—Entering the stable-yard, I heard something come against the glass."

It will be observed that, subsequent to the pelting which the coach was said to have received after the king had left it, there was no possible way to determine the nature of the damage which it was supposed to have received while he occupied it.

person or persons ineffective missiles had been hurled at the royal equipage. There was not the slightest evidence that any one had conspired to harm the king. Certainly, if such a project had been planned, there could hardly have been a more inane method chosen for putting it into execution. Yet, at the conclusion of the testimony, Grenville moved an address to the king, and invited the Commons to join the Lords in presenting it. He expressed abhorrence of the " daring outrages " which had been offered, and stated, very significantly, that Parliament was confident it would be joined in its address by " all descriptions of your Majesty's subjects." On its face, this address seemed harmless enough, though Lord Lansdowne said in a speech at the time that he believed that " it was no more than a counterpart of their [the ministers'] own plot; the alarm-bell to terrify the people into weak compliances."[24]

On November 4, 1795, the day on which the reward was offered for the apprehension of the persons who had attacked the king, a proclamation was published against seditious writings and practices.[25] In all respects this proclamation was similar to that of May 21, 1792, and similar results followed. Meetings were held in almost every county and borough in the kingdom, and addresses were sent to the king congratulating him on his escape and expressing abhorrence of the attack.[26]

But mere professions of loyalty by people who had never given expression to different sentiments were not sufficient for the purposes of the ministry. It was necessary that there be a specific remedy directed against a tangible danger. The large attendance at the meetings of the London Corresponding Society undoubtedly gave the ministers concern and justly aroused in their minds a desire to curb the growth of a power which might in time threaten the existence of their administration. Therefore it was not strange that Pitt, following the plan which he had formerly found so

---

[24] Hansard, Parliamentary History XXXII, 154.
[25] London Gazette 1795, 1204.
[26] London Gazette 1795, 1179–1479.

useful, should again make terror the "order of the day," and, that he might increase the popular excitement, should propose regulations which would enable him to repress at his will the proceedings of the societies that advocated reform.

On the day before the publication of the proclamation against sedition, a newspaper which represented the government asserted that the London Corresponding Society had inspired the attack on the king. To support this charge, it appealed to the intuition of its readers, who had been fed daily on highly colored misrepresentations of the purposes of the reformers. On the basis of such evidence, the paper urged that the exigencies of the occasion demanded harsher laws,[27] and in this it spoke for the ministers who had no other excuses or arguments to give in defense of the bills, which they immediately brought forward.

On November 6 Grenville proposed in the House of Lords "An Act for the Safety and Preservation of his Majesty's Person and Government against treasonable and seditious Practices and Attempts." Four days later Pitt moved for leave to bring into the lower house a bill entitled "An Act for the more effectually preventing seditious Meetings and Assemblies." Both bills became statutes, on December 18, 1795, after warm and elaborate discussions both in and out of Parliament. The Treasonable Practices Bill was chiefly designed to give statutory form to the common law practice of interpreting the clauses in former statutes in such a way as to extend widely and often very unjustly the meaning of treason. One section, to remain in force for three years, made it a high misdemeanor to publish or speak anything to incite hatred or contempt of the king, the government, or the constitution.[28] The Seditious Meetings Bill was designed to prevent public assemblies of more than fifty persons unless they were held under the supervision of the government. In order to accomplish this result, the following categories of regulations were provided.

---

[27] The Sun, November 3, 1795.   [28] 36 Geo. III, c. 7.

Before any meeting of more than fifty persons could be held, " for the purpose or on the pretext of considering of or preparing any petition, complaint, remonstrance or declaration or other addresses to the King, or to both houses, or either house of Parliament, for alteration of matters established in Church or State, or for the purpose or on the pretext of deliberating upon any grievance in Church or State," it was necessary that public notice be given by seven householders of the vicinity in which it was to be held. These seven persons had to include in their notice their addresses and descriptions of themselves. These notices either had to be published in a local paper or given to a local clerk of the peace at least five days before the proposed assembly. Meetings of such a nature without notice were unlawful assemblies, and had to be dispersed. If more than twelve persons should remain of such a meeting after it was ordered to disband, they were to be adjudged felons and to be punished by death. If, in the notice or in the meeting, anything should be proposed which provided for altering any established matter otherwise than by the authority of the " King, Lords and Commons in Parliament assembled," or which tended "to incite or stir up the people to hatred or contempt of the person of his Majesty, his heirs or successors, or of the government and constitution of this realm as by law established," it was the duty of the officers of the peace to disperse the assembly in the same manner, although notice had been given. In addition to this, any place where lectures, discussions, or debates on public or political matters were held, and where admission fees were charged, was to be considered a disorderly house, unless those who had a part in its management had secured a license. The officer of the peace could demand entrance to any place at which he suspected that such meetings were being held, and if he was refused admission the house was to be deemed disorderly, regardless of whether the license had been secured. Naturally, exceptions were made in favor of the official meetings which were held in the course of the local administration, and also in favor of universities and schools. But it was made practically illegal to hold any other public meeting at which an officer of the law was not present, and, a matter of great importance, it was left largely to the discretion of these officers to determine the character of the opinions which it was permissible to express on such occasions.[29]

It is not strange that the reformers in Parliament endeavored to prevent, by every means at their command, the passage of these two acts. Meetings were held for that purpose in all parts of England. The Duke of Bedford presided and Fox spoke at the one which was called in Westminster. The London Corresponding Society held a large meeting at which addresses were voted to Parliament and the king, and a few days later published a broadside explaining the principles of the society. The result of all this agitation was a popular opposition to the policies of the administration more threatening than any which had occurred since the outbreak of the war. Thurlow and Leeds refused to sanction the Seditious Meetings Bill, but, for the most part, the opposition came from the people at large. In Parliament the ministers were as supreme as ever, and the measures which had been proposed were designed to enable them to suppress opposition in any other quarter.[30]

The adherents of the administration were equally determined in their efforts to secure popular approval for the acts. In some instances they arranged that the loyal addresses, called into being by the attack on the king, should contain requests for the passing of such laws, though in at least one instance the personal intervention of the minister was necessary before such request was embodied.[31] It was

---

[29] 36 Geo. III, c. 8.

[30] Hansard, Parliamentary History XXXII, 244–556. Morning Chronicle, November 17, 19, 20, 25, 26, 1795; December 5, 1795. The Sun, December 3, 1795. The Courier, November 19, 1795. The Oracle, November 13, 17, 23, 25, 1795. The Times, December 8, 1795. History of Two Acts.
See also titles of other pamphlets and broadsides in the appended bibliography.

[31] The Oracle, November 20, 1795; December 3, 1795. The Times, December 4, 1795. Dropmore Papers III, 144–147.

evident from the first, however, that the opposition was conducting a hopeless fight.[32]   With the strong support which Pitt had at his command in Parliament, revolution was the only means by which his measures could have been successfully opposed.   Such a step had been hinted at as possible by both Fox and the London Corresponding Society, but had been seriously advocated by neither,[33] so that

[32] Morning Chronicle, November 9, 1795.   This paper, which warmly supported Fox, said concerning the "Two Acts:"—

"By this bill Ministers declare that his present Majesty, for some unexplained reason, requires that restraints upon liberty, unknown to the constitution of England since the happy revolution, shall be laid upon the people during his life, but that the same restraint will not be necessary afterwards!   They call this supporting the King! If this law shall pass, no body of men can assemble either for the redress of grievance, or the repeal of a tax; for the nomination of a candidate or the discussion of a turnpike bill, without being subject on the slightest inaccuracy, or heat of expression, or rather on the base and malignant misconstruction of a couple of Treasury spies, to the penalties of misdemeanour; and this they call maintaining the constitution!   Yet this bill will pass into law."

[33] Hansard, Parliamentary History XXXII, 385.   On November 23 Fox repeated what he had already said:—

"If the majority of the people approve of these bills, I will not be the person to inflame their minds, and stir them up to rebellion; but if, in the general opinion of the country, it is conceived that these bills attack the fundamental principles of our constitution, I then maintain, that the propriety of resistance, instead of remaining any longer a question of morality, will become merely a question of prudence.   I may be told that these are strong words; but strong measures require strong words.   I will not submit to arbitrary power, while there remains any alternative to vindicate my freedom."

The London Corresponding Society, in a broadside which was dated November 23, and addressed to the Parliament and the people of Great Britain, said in part:—

"This society have always cherished, and will ever be desirous to inculcate, their most decided abhorrence of all tumult and violence.   Anxious to promote the happiness, and therefore jealous of the rights of man, they have never failed to propagate nor to practice the constitutional doctrine of opposing by every peaceable and rational means the encroachments of power and corruption.   But they have never countenanced, nor ever will, any motive, measure or sentiment tending to excite commotion—to inflame the mind with sanguinary enthusiasm—or to extinguish the emotions of tenderness and humanity which ought particularly to characterize a free and enlightened nation.   At the same time, they do not wish to be understood as giving by this declaration any sort of countenance to the detestable and delusive doctrines of passive obedience and non-resistance," etc.

the minister was now more securely intrenched in his position than ever. He had the support of an overwhelming majority of those who could participate in the government; and he had also the authority to suppress any opposition to his policies which others might arouse. Thus as far as home affairs were concerned his task was reduced to convincing those who had to furnish the means for carrying on the war that such war was not only necessary but also likely to bring a return for what was being expended. To that problem he now gave his attention.

The financial difficulties which presented themselves were sufficient to tax the ingenuity even of Pitt, who had been accustomed to glory in that aspect of his administration. Since the beginning of the war he had made large increases both in the debt and in the amount raised by taxation. On December 7, 1795, when he brought forward his budget for the year, he estimated that a supply of £27,662,000 would be needed. He had previously secured a loan of £18,000,-000, but when he brought this fact to the attention of the house, the charge was made that the rate of this loan was unfavorable to the government, and Pitt himself confessed that it had been negotiated in a somewhat irregular manner. To aid in securing the remainder of the necessary amount, increased levies were proposed, including an additional duty of ten per cent. on the assessed taxes, a tax on legacies which were not inherited by lineal heirs, and an increase in the duties on horses kept for pleasure, on tobacco, printed cottons and calicoes, and salt. Resolutions incorporating these items were introduced in the house by Pitt at the conclusion of his speech, and were severally agreed to.[34]

On the day after his financial suggestions had been ratified, Pitt brought forward a message from the king, which announced that the government of France was now such that it was capable of making peace, and that England was ready to begin negotiations for that purpose.[35] In vain

---

[34] Hansard, Parliamentary History XXXII, 556–569. Morning Chronicle, December 9, 1795.
[35] Hansard, Parliamentary History XXXII, 569.

Sheridan pointed out that four members of the Directory had had a part in sending Louis XVI to his death, and that the ministers had no certain evidence to prove that the government of the Directory would keep its treaties any better than had the government which preceded it. In reply to such criticisms Pitt and Dundas affirmed that France had exhausted her resources, and was therefore at a point where it was to her advantage to make peace, while England on the other hand had made even more important conquests than could have been expected at the beginning of the war, and had ruined the marine and destroyed the commerce of her rival.[36] It may have been true, as Sheridan asserted, that if this announcement of pacific intentions had been made before the negotiation of the loan, it would have resulted in an advantage to the government of nearly a million pounds. But it is very probable that the minister acted more consistently than the opposition orator realized. The policy which Pitt now inaugurated offered two possibilities, either of which would have been of material assistance in obtaining the ends which he had previously pursued. What those ends were, it is not necessary to repeat. Even when he was busiest in his efforts to induce a counter-revolution in France in favor of the dethroned house, he had been careful at all times to refrain from identifying his cause with the fate of the French monarchy. He had admitted that the restoration of the Bourbons would be a most satisfactory termination of the war, but he had never made it one of his chief contentions. He regarded aid to the royalists as merely a justifiable method of warfare. His purpose was to weaken his enemy, though he confessed that he would be glad if the result should be a return of the exiled family. He had not departed from the program which had been announced to Holland before the outbreak of the war, that if the republic in France should

---

[36] Hansard, Parliamentary History XXXII, 570–608.

For an account of the purpose of the ministers in the king's message, see Grenville's letter to Wickham, December 25, 1795. Wickham, Correspondence of William Wickham I, 228.

become permanent, England would follow the other powers in acknowledging it. His purpose at this time was similar to that which had led him to embark in the contest. He desired to reduce the power of France and to aggrandize England. He now believed that the French had been brought to such a state of exhaustion that they would, in a large measure, submit to any terms of peace which he might see fit to impose.[37] If this should prove to be true, England had only to make the announcement which was contained in the king's message to insure a speedy negotiation. Should such a negotiation terminate successfully, all criticism of his measures would be overwhelmed in the general satisfaction at the conclusion of a successful war. On the other hand, if France should refuse to take advantage of such an opportunity, it would yet serve an equally useful purpose, for the fact that the announcement had been made would enable the administration to command a heartier support for the financial measures which had been brought forward. That the alternatives were not dissociated in the mind of the minister may be inferred from the terms of the king's message. But should the French refuse to make peace then one and perhaps two more campaigns would be necessary, and for these the means had to be procured. This announcement opened the way for more direct proposals to the French, and it was highly probable that such advances would be useful in making it clear to Englishmen that further sacrifices were necessary before a satisfactory peace could be concluded.

Thus Pitt had begun a game in which it was impossible for him to lose, since either position which the French might take would necessarily further his purposes. Regarded from this point of view, the succeeding events are easy of explication. The question which has to be considered is

---

[37] Dropmore Papers III, 80–86. This memorandum on the state of France, made in the summer of 1795 and based on the reports of English agents, is an interesting addition to the evidence concerning the opinions of the English ministers with regard to the exhaustion of that country.

not whether the English minister desired peace, or was
sincere in his efforts to attain it, but rather the nature of
the terms which he insisted on demanding.

When it became evident that the French were not eager to
accept England's offer of a negotiation, the administration newspapers announced that, though the ministers
wished to obtain peace, the time had not arrived when
it was wise to make too great sacrifices to secure that end.
The True Briton stated explicitly that France must renounce her conquests and indemnify England before peace
would be desirable.[38] Even though the French should
be disposed to agree to such terms, the paper continued,
their newly adopted constitution interposed obstacles which
it would be difficult to overcome; for it gave constitutional support to the incorporation in the Republic, one
and indivisible, of acquisitions which, according to the
demands of England, had to be given up before a peace
could be established. In fact, however, the attitude of the
French government seems to have been the same as that of
the English ministers. The Directory, in announcing on
the 12th Nivôse (January 2) their readiness to negotiate
for peace, added that the obstinacy of the powers with
which they were at war had redoubled their means of conquest.[39] Again, the same body in its message to the
Council of Ancients, on the 5th Pluviose (January 25),
requesting a tax in kind, asserted that the enemies of
France had spoken of peace merely in order to cause the
French to relax their preparations, and that they would
never know peace until they had rendered it impossible for
their foes "to pursue their disastrous projects."[40] This
was regarded in England as a tacit refusal by France to
make peace except on her own terms, and the partizans of
the ministers so accepted it and urged it as a justification
for continuing the war.[41]

[38] True Briton, January 23, 26, 1796.
[39] Debrett, State Papers IV, 253.
[40] Debrett, State Papers IV, 184.
[41] True Briton, February 2, 1796.

The measure which was now proposed by the government was not inconsistent with the sentiments already expressed in the True Briton. England and her allies had nothing to lose in making the first advances to France, if that power had determined not to make peace on terms acceptable to them. The English ministers even conceived that they would gain popular support if such a proposal should be rejected by the French. On the other hand, if peace should result on the terms which they were prepared to demand, the project would certainly have proved worth while. Such, at any rate, were the arguments which Lord Grenville used to justify the proposal to the king, and they accord so closely with what would have been expected that there is no reason to doubt that they represented the real views of the ministers.[42] Although the other powers did not join England in this attempt, it was with their consent that Wickham, the English minister in Switzerland, on March 8, 1796, transmitted a note to Barthélemy, the French minister to the same country. In this note the French were requested to give written answers to three questions: whether there was a disposition in France to send ministers to a congress for reestablishing a general peace; whether there was a disposition to communicate to Wickham the grounds of pacification which would be acceptable to France; and whether France had any other method to propose for arriving at a general peace.[43] The reply of the Directory was delivered to Wickham on March 26. In substance, it said that the French ardently desired peace, but were in doubt as to whether the English ministers had the same wishes, since a congress such as had been proposed would necessarily render the negotiations endless

---

[42] Dropmore Papers III, 169, Grenville to George III, January 30, 1796, referring to a despatch to the British minister at Vienna in which this project was proposed.

Stanhope, Life of William Pitt V, Appendix, 30. In a letter to the king, on January 30, 1796, Pitt had used arguments of a similar nature to support a negotiation.

[43] Debrett, State Papers IV, 254. Wickham, Correspondence of William Wickham I, 269–293. Dropmore Papers III, 172–174.

and seem to indicate that England merely desired to get the benefit of the favorable impression which the first overtures would give. However, the reply went on to say, the Directory was ready to consider any proposals which did not involve a breach of the existing laws of the republic.[44]

The English ministers thus occupied a somewhat anomalous position. They had made the adoption of the new constitution the qualifying act which rendered France capable of carrying on a peace negotiation, yet they now demanded, as a sine qua non, terms of pacification which disregarded the express provisions of that constitution. For this reason it does not seem likely that the ministers seriously anticipated any immediate success in their proposal for a congress. Indeed, Lord Grenville confessed as much when he said in his note to Wickham that the Directory played the game of the English administration even better than had been hoped.[45] The next move was to publish these two notes with an announcement that the state of affairs which they disclosed made the continuation of the war absolutely necessary. This was done on April 10, when the answer of the Directory reached London.[46] The

[44] Debrett, State Papers IV, 255. After expressing doubt of the sincerity of England, the note of the Directory continued:—

"However that may be, the Executive Directory, whose policy has no other guides than openness and good faith, will follow in its explanations, a conduct which shall be wholly conformable to them. Yielding to the ardent desire by which it is animated, to procure peace for the French Republic, and for all nations, it will not fear to declare itself openly. Charged by the Constitution with the execution of the laws, it cannot make, or listen to any proposition that would be contrary to them. The Constitutional act does not permit it to consent to any alienation of that, which, according to the existing laws, constitutes the territory of the Republic.

"With respect to the countries occupied by the French armies, and which have not been united to France, they, as well as other interests, political and commercial, may become the subject of a negotiation, which will present to the Directory the means of proving how much it desires to attain speedily to a happy pacification."

[45] Wickham, Correspondence of William Wickham I, 343. Grenville to Wickham, April 15, 1796.

[46] True Briton, April 11, 1796. Debrett, State Papers IV, 256. Omitting any estimate of the propriety of the action either of the

True Briton made haste to deny that Pitt had departed from his demands of indemnity for the past and security for the future as necessary conditions of peace.[47]

The diplomatic movements which now follow must be studied in the light of various circumstances that were favorable to the policy which Pitt was evidently pursuing. First, it was believed in official circles that if the people of France could be convinced of the responsibility of their government for the continuation of the war, their influence would assist in securing the terms of peace which England was willing to accept;[48] and it was thought that formal communications would supplement the efforts which England still continued to make to foment internal discontent in France. Second, the later financial measures of Pitt were not meeting with his customary success; the circumstances which had attended the award of the loan had not increased the respect of the financial interests for him, with the exception, perhaps, of the lenders; the admitted irregularities which had been involved in its negotiation had been dignified by a parliamentary investigation, which, at Pitt's own suggestion, had been intrusted to a select committee, instead of to the whole house, as Sheridan requested; and it was not difficult for the report to be manipulated so that the chancellor of the exchequer should be acquitted of any more serious offence than carelessness, though the evidence which was brought forward did not place the affair in a very creditable light. The natural result was that it became more difficult for the government to secure a loan except through the same firm, from which £7,500,000 had been obtained on April 15, 1796,[49] and thus

English minister or of the French government, it would seem in any case that Pitt would have acted in a manner inconsistent with his previous policy if he had undertaken to negotiate a treaty on the conditions which the Directory offered.

[47] True Briton, April 20, 1796. Reply to an editorial in the Morning Chronicle.

[48] Wickham, Correspondence of William Wickham I, 343. It has already been shown that Grenville and Pitt expressed this idea in the letters to the king preliminary to Wickham's note.

[49] Hansard, Parliamentary History XXXII, 763-831. Journals of the House of Commons I, 310-360.

the voluntary subscription measure of the following December was made necessary.[50]   But it was not only with his loans that Pitt was encountering difficulties.   Parliament refused to agree to both his tax on legacies in land and that on prints and calicoes.   This opposition evidently came from the landed and commercial classes, and, as a consequence, it became exceedingly important for Pitt to convince them that an honorable peace could not be obtained.[51]

From these facts it is apparent that Pitt had many objects which he hoped to attain by manifesting a readiness to go more than half way in a negotiation, even though he should not succeed in effecting an immediate peace.   So long as the French persisted in adhering to the provisions of their constitution, the English minister was safe in offering them any terms provided he demanded at the same time that France give up territories that had already been incorporated in the Republic.   It may be urged that such a policy would only encourage the French to persevere in maintaining their equally impossible demands.   But our object is simply to ascertain the purpose of the English minister, not to determine its wisdom or propriety.   The fact seems to be that for the reasons which have been described he now made another attempt to treat with France.

Pitt was possibly influenced, in the measures which he now adopted, by the declaration of principles put forth by his supporters in the parliamentary election of 1796.   The platform of the administration party had been " Peace with honour," but, under the existing system of election, popular sentiment in only a few instances had any effective influence in determining the choice of the representatives.   It is not probable, therefore, that the minister was much concerned to give further proof of sincerity in thus assuming an attitude ostensibly favorable to peace.   It is more reasonable to conclude that the primary considerations which determined his course of action were the state of the English

---

[50] True Briton, April 16, 1796.
[51] Hansard, Parliamentary History XXXII, 1032–1041.

exchequer and the situation on the Continent. He thought that Austria would probably embrace a favorable opportunity for making peace with France, and in order to prevent such a step, proposed to offer additional financial aid to the emperor. Nevertheless, he did not think that a policy of subsidy could be successful with Austria for more than one campaign, after which he believed that England would be left to fight France and Holland, and probably Spain, single-handed. He felt confident, however, that his country could successfully oppose them all. In the meantime, he was willing to have Lord Grenville attempt a reconciliation of Prussia with Austria and thus bring about a new concert of action between the three powers, though he owned that he did not think such an effort would meet with success. From his point of view, therefore, the item of chief importance was to keep Parliament in a mood favorable to his financial projects.[52]

Lord Grenville's program was not well received by the king, and still less so by the Court of Berlin.[53] Therefore, the ministry determined, September 2, 1796, to send through the Danish ministers a request for a passport for a British agent to go to Paris. The purpose of this mission was, of course, to open a way to a pacification, if suitable terms could be obtained. In reality, however, this was not anticipated, and the result at which the minister aimed was to put on record the fact that his administration had made every reasonable offer, and that the French alone were responsible for the continuation of the war. If the Directory should consent to enter into a preliminary discussion of terms, the English agent was to insist that France could not retain the Austrian Netherlands. On the other hand, although England had agreed not to conclude the war until Austria had been secured in the possession of the territories which belonged to her at the commencement of hostilities, it was well known that the emperor did not desire to retain

---

[52] Dropmore Papers III, 214. Pitt to Grenville, June 23, 1796.
[53] Dropmore Papers III, 215–243.

12

the Austrian Netherlands, but was anxious to exchange them for some other principality, preferably Bavaria. It is evident, therefore, that Pitt did not yet feel that peace was imperative, unless terms which were agreeable to him could be obtained. Since France was not to be allowed to retain the Austrian Netherlands it may reasonably be inferred that the English ministry expected to make material concessions in other directions to France. In a measure, this was true. As an ultimatum, " not to be offered without fresh instructions," the English government was ready to restore all the conquests which had been made from France, and would permit the French to retain Savoy, Nice, " all the conquered countries on the Rhine not belonging to Austria, and the Spanish part of St. Domingo." In addition, the Dutch were to receive back the Spice Islands and other East India possessions. England would retain only " Ceylon, the Cape and Cochin," which her minister described as " the most valuable of her conquests." It will be noted, however, that the English agent was not empowered to agree to these proposals, or even to suggest them as an ultimatum, except by express instruction from his government. But even if this should be done, and the French should accept these terms, it would be necessary that Austria be consulted before the final agreements were reached.[54]

The Danish representatives readily agreed to act as intermediaries, but the Directory again played the game of the English minister better than he expected, or even desired. It sent no reply to the British communication, but De La Croix, the French minister of foreign affairs, verbally informed the Danish representative at Paris " that the Executive Directory of the French Republic would not, for the future, receive nor answer any overtures or confidential papers transmitted through any intermediate channel from the enemies of the Republic; but that if they would send persons furnished with full powers and official papers, these

---

[54] Dropmore Papers III, 239–242. The plan is detailed in a minute which was submitted to the king and several members of the cabinet before it was put into execution.

might, upon the frontiers, demand the passports necessary for proceeding to Paris."[55]   This decision was transmitted to the English ministers on September 23, 1796.   If it meant anything, it implied that the Directory believed itself to be in a position to dictate the terms of peace.   Under those circumstances the French government could not be expected to disregard that provision of the constitution upon which it had formerly insisted so vigorously.   At this juncture Pitt was about to launch his financial measure which depended for success in no small part upon his ability to convince the men of means in England that he had used every reasonable method to secure peace.   Therefore, in order, as far as possible, to secure unanimity at home, and at the same time to convince the people of France that their government alone was responsible for the continuance of the war, he decided to press the matter to an issue with the French Directory.

Grenville, in a letter to his brother, September 24, substantiates this view of the situation:—

The Directory has sent us the most insolent answer that can be conceived; but as the substance of it is in some degree ambiguous with respect to the main question of granting or refusing the passport, it has been thought better not to leave a loophole of pretence to them or their adherents here, to lay upon us the breaking the business off.   Another note is therefore to be sent today, by a flag of truce from Dover, in which the demand of the passport is renewed in such terms as seem most likely to bring that point to a distinct issue, aye or no.   In other times this last step would not only have been superfluous, but humiliating; in the present moment, the object of unanimity here in the great body of the country, with respect to the large sacrifices they will be called upon to make, is paramount to every other consideration.[56]

The French readily sent the desired passport, and, in order to give the attempt greater dignity, Lord Malmesbury was substituted for F. J. Jackson, minister of legation at Madrid, whom the British government at first intended to

---

[55] Debrett, State Papers V, 169–171.
[56] Buckingham, Court and Cabinets II, 350.   Auckland, Journal and Correspondence IV, 358.   Pitt gave expression to similar views in a letter to Auckland.

send to Paris. The details of the negotiations which ensued are not within the scope of this study. It is sufficient to say that each government endeavored to induce the other to make some demand that would definitely fix the blame for terminating the discussion. From its own point of view, each was successful. The terms which England proposed were substantially those which had been agreed upon by the cabinet before the communication was made through the Danish ministers. Again the French refused to consider the surrender of the Austrian Netherlands on the ground that the Republic was one and indivisible. Thus each party was able to appeal to its constituency with plausible arguments. In reality, matters remained about as before. When a point of importance arose, Malmesbury insisted on communicating with his court before giving a decision. This insistence, as appears from his correspondence, was due in part to the desire of the English ministers to secure all information possible concerning the internal condition of France, and to arrange that Malmesbury should provide for a continuance of such information through other channels after the termination of his mission. The French government seemed to suspect something of this sort, and, on December 19, notified the English envoy that since he was acting merely as a transmitter of despatches, he was performing a useless function. They, therefore, ordered him to leave Paris in forty-eight hours, intimating at the same time their willingness to carry on the negotiation by means of couriers.[57]

The details of this affair were given to the public as soon as the notes were passed, and after the dismissal of Malmesbury the entire correspondence was published in both countries as a justification of their respective shares in the negotiations. But, in the meantime, Pitt had successfully carried through one of the measures which formed a very vital part of his plan. On December 1, 1796, the govern-

---

[57] For information concerning this mission see Debrett, State Papers V, 171–214. Malmesbury, Diaries and Correspondence III, 260–366. Dropmore Papers III, 258–290.

ment authorized a voluntary subscription of £20,000,000. For each hundred pounds the subscribers were to receive five per cent. stock with a face value of one hundred and twelve pounds and ten shillings. The loan was to run for three years, but might be paid off two years after the conclusion of peace.[58] Within less than a week the entire amount had been subscribed.[59] It must not be assumed that every subscription was made from purely patriotic motives. Pitt, Grenville, and the other members of the cabinet were said to have put themselves to some inconvenience to take the ten thousand pounds which they each received. Still, Lord Sheffield wrote to Auckland while the subscription was in progress: "The terms appear, on a slight view, so favourable and so exempt from risk, that I cannot think there will be much difficulty in finding subscribers, although there may be great uncertainty in finding the money. If I had ever engaged in such speculations, if I had any money, or could get any, I should subscribe as a *good thing.*"[60] That there was some foundation for this allegation may be inferred from the fact that the Duke of Bedford, one of Fox's warmest supporters and a consistent opponent of the administration, subscribed for £100,000.[61] However, it was perhaps natural that, in a case of such evident necessity, the terms of the loan should be made sufficiently attractive to induce the subscriptions, which were of so great importance for carrying on the operations of government. At any rate, as a result of this measure the ministers could now regard more cheerfully the subsidy which Austria was demanding.

It is not within the province of this discussion to recount the further reverses, both military and financial, which caused the cabinet, on February 26, 1797, to order the Bank of England to suspend specie payment.[62] In spite of this suspension, the ministers went on with their efforts to

---

[58] True Briton, December 2, 1796.
[59] True Briton, December 5, 1796.
[60] Auckland, Journal and Correspondence III, 365.
[61] Buckingham, Court and Cabinets II, 351.
[62] Ross, Correspondence of Cornwallis II, 325.

secure the advances for which Austria was clamoring. On April 4 Lord Grenville wrote to the English minister at Vienna that the prospect for success in the matter was bright.[63] But, five days later, the cabinet decided to ask the emperor of Russia to intervene for the purpose of negotiating a peace, the chief reason assigned for this step being the embarrassment of public finances in England.[64] However, the reports that Austria was meditating a separate negotiation became more current, and it was finally learned that the preliminaries to a treaty between that power and France had been signed. As a result, on June 1 a note was sent to Paris by the English ministers expressing a desire to renew the negotiations which had been broken off.[65] This time Pitt earnestly desired peace on any reasonable terms, and, as the subsequent negotiations made manifest, was willing to make concessions which he had previously refused. Why he failed to secure a peace and was obliged to continue the war does not concern us here.

The minister had now practically confessed that his measures had been unsuccessful, and that his policy had been a failure. To those who asked for causes, if the True Briton may still be considered as the exponent of the views of the administration, the answer was summed up in the term, "the French Revolution." The plans of the minister had not been in fault. The execution of them was not susceptible to serious criticisms. It was the French Revo-

---

[63] Dropmore Papers III, 308.

[64] Dropmore Papers III, 310. In part, the minute of the meeting was as follows:—

"It was agreed humbly to submit to your Majesty as the opinion of this meeting, that, under the various circumstances of difficulty and danger in which his Majesty's dominions and those of his allies are placed by the result of the late unfavourable events, and most particularly by the increasing embarrassments of the public finances of this kingdom, it is become indispensably necessary that steps should be taken for making a joint application on the part of his Majesty and of the Emperor to the Emperor of Russia for his intervention with a view of opening and conducting negociations for peace; and also that measures should be adopted for concurring with the Court of Vienna in any immediate negociation which may be rendered necessary by the urgency of increased pressure from any further progress of the French in Corinthia."

[65] Dropmore Papers III, 327. Debrett, State Papers VI, 207.

lution against which his abilities had been measured, and because of which his efforts had been brought to naught. Such was the verdict of his editorial partizan. But, if the conclusions which have been reached in the course of this study are valid, for once the True Briton was mistaken. The French Revolution, as a political upheaval, dependent on radical doctrines, had been a factor of minor importance in causing the international situation in which England was implicated. France and England had merely been engaged in their old struggle for dominance, and, temporarily, Pitt was beaten at his own game.[66]

---

[66] The True Briton, March 21, 1797.

CONCLUSIONS.

The object of this inquiry has been to trace the influence of the French Revolution upon the people and politics of England from 1789 to 1797. As a result the following conclusions may be presented as established with some degree of certainty.

In its early stages the French Revolution was regarded favorably by the majority of Englishmen but was considered a subject rather for speculation than as vital to the interests of England. Gradually this favorable view of the revolution gave way to one that was distinctly hostile, due as is commonly supposed to the influence and writings of Edmund Burke. We believe, however, that this change of opinion may be attributed in slight measure if at all to the advocacy of the great orator but was effected by the deliberate efforts of the adherents of William Pitt in order to secure his political advantage. The end which Pitt had in view was the division of the Whig party and the supremacy of his own government. Pitt's first opportunity to weaken the Whig party came with the controversy between Fox and Burke on the subject of the French Revolution, in which Pitt adopted the view of Burke that the revolution was a great menace to England and the world. He upheld this view not as a matter of conviction but as a matter of policy, for owing to his defeat on the Russian program and to dissensions in his own cabinet he was in danger of losing his control. The propaganda which he inaugurated for the purpose of dividing the opposition and of gaining Whig adherents of his policy was continued with increased activity until the autumn of 1792, and to this propaganda, particularly after the spring of 1791, either consciously or unconsciously, Burke lent his aid.

The wasted condition of France and the apparently dis-

organized state of public institutions there, after the downfall of the monarchy, seemed to Pitt to offer a favorable
opportunity for the territorial enlargement of England and
the humiliation of her old-time rival. The attempt of the
French Republic to open the Scheldt in November, 1792,
afforded a plausible pretext for provoking war, and immediately Pitt took steps to establish himself more firmly in
power at home and to force from France a declaration of
war against England and Holland. In both respects he
was successful. The French declared war in February,
1793; and, as the result of his efforts during the year 1792,
prominent Whig aristocrats promised him open support,
and after a campaign designed to arouse fears of revolution
in England, they entered into a formal coalition with the
Tories in July, 1794.

Having accomplished his immediate purpose, Pitt was
next concerned with the important task of drawing the
English people to his support and of obtaining the means
for carrying out his continental projects. In this task he
was hampered by financial crises and bad harvests, which
served to increase the political unrest in the kingdom, particularly in 1795 and 1796, and caused the reform societies
already organized among the lower classes to increase in
numbers. In order to prevent any results from this source
injurious to the interests of the administration he caused
repressive statutes to be enacted that gave the government
control over public meetings. From the clergy of the established church, who aided the adherents of the administration in their propaganda of loyalty, he secured sincere
and even passionate support. To the purposes for which
he had begun the war he adhered even when negotiating for
peace, until the spring of 1797, when military reverses on the
Continent and financial difficulties at home forced him to
meet France more than half way in order to secure a peace.

The societies for promoting parliamentary reform, which
were active in England during this period, do not appear to
have found their inspiration, either for organization or con-

tinuance, in the French Revolution, nor do they appear to have advocated anything more than a radical reform in the system of representation in the House of Commons. There is no trace anywhere in England during these years of any considerable bodies of men who upheld or propagated either the republican principles of Thomas Paine or the extravagant doctrines of the French revolutionists.

It is, therefore, reasonable to conclude that the uprising in France played but a minor rôle in the domestic history of England in the years from 1789 to 1797, except as far as it was used by Pitt and his colleagues for their own political purposes as a pretext for reviving the old-time struggle with France for supremacy in the commercial and the colonial world.

BIBLIOGRAPHY OF SOURCES.

Only those works which have been consulted and found to pertain to the subjects discussed in this study are included in this list, since because of a lack of space it is not possible to mention the numerous secondary treatises on the period which have been used. The manuscripts cited are designated by the names of the men who collected the papers among which they are to be found. The newspapers quoted are for the most part contained in the British Museum and the Library of Congress. Unfortunately the files at both places are incomplete, and frequently only scattering copies have been preserved. The titles given here do not imply, therefore, that it has been possible to examine all the papers for the entire period which has been treated.

MANUSCRIPTS.

The Auckland Papers, Vols. XXIV–XLII. British Museum Additional MSS. 34,435–34,453.

The Duke of Leeds' Political Memoranda, 1774–1796. British Museum Additional MSS. 27,918.

Pamphlets and Journals of the Duke of Leeds, 1771–1796. British Museum Additional MSS. 28,570.

The Correspondence of Francis, Fifth Duke of Leeds, 1789–1798. Vols. V–VIII. British Museum Additional MSS. 28,064–28,067. Cited as "Leeds MSS."

Francis Place, Papers of the London Corresponding Society. 7 vols. British Museum Additional MSS. 27,811–27,817.

The Pelham Papers, Vol. IV. British Museum Additional MSS. 33,090.

The Correspondence of the Association for Preserving Liberty and Property against Republicans and Levellers, presented by John Reeves, Esq. 10 vols. British Museum Additional MSS. 16,919–16,929. Cited as "Reeves MSS."

NEWSPAPERS AND PERIODICALS.

The Annual Register.
The Argus (daily).
The Bath Chronicle (weekly).
The British Critic (monthly).
The British Gazetteer (Elizabeth Johnson's) (w).
The British Journal (Felix Farley's) (w).
The Courier (d).
The Critical Review (m).
The Diary; or, Woodfall's Register (d).
The Edinburgh Advertiser (tri-weekly).
The European Magazine (m).
The Evening Mail (t-w).
The Gazetteer; or, New Daily Advertiser (d).
The General Evening Post (t-w).
The Gentleman's Magazine (m).
Lloyd's Evening Post (t-w).
Lloyd's List.
The London Chronicle (t-w).
The London Gazette (semi-weekly).
The Monthly Mirror.
The Monthly Review.
The Morning Chronicle (d).
The Morning Herald (d).
The Morning Post and Daily Advertiser.
The Oracle and Public Advertiser (d).
The Public Advertiser (d).
The St. James Gazette (t-w).
The Star (d).
The Sun (d).
The Telegraph (d).
The Times (d).
The True Briton (d).
The Universal Magazine (m).
The Whitehall Evening Post (t-w).
The World (d).

BIOGRAPHY, CORRESPONDENCE, ETC.

ABBOT, CHARLES, *1 Baron Colchester.* Diary and Correspondence of. Ed. by his son Charles, *Lord Colchester.* 3 vols. 1861.

AMYOT, THOMAS. The Speeches in Parliament of Rt. Hon. William Windham. 3 vols. 1812.

BARING, MRS. HENRY. The Diary of the Rt. Hon. William Windham, 1784–1810. 1866.

BARRETT, CHARLOTTE. Diary and Letters of Madame D'Arblay. 6 vols. 1905.

BENTHAM-EDWARDS, M. The Autobiography of Arthur Young. 1898.

BRITISH HISTORICAL MANUSCRIPTS COMMISSION. Thirteenth Report, Appendix, Part VIII, Manuscripts and Correspondence of James, First Earl of Charlemont. Vol. II, 1784–1799.

—— Twelfth Report, Appendix, Part IV, Manuscripts of Philip Vernon Smith, Esq., pp. 343–374.

—— Thirteenth Report, Appendix, Part III; Fourteenth Report, Appendix, Part V; Fifteenth Report, J. B. Fortescue MSS. III, The Manuscripts of J. B. Fortescue, Esq., preserved at Dropmore. 3 vols. Cited as "Dropmore Papers."

—— Fifteenth Report, Appendix, Part VII, The Manuscripts of the Marquis of Ailesbury.

—— Fifteenth Report, Appendix, Part VI, The Manuscripts of the Earl of Carlisle, preserved at Castle Howard. Cited as "Carlisle Papers."

—— Fifteenth Report, Appendix, Part I, The Manuscripts of the Earl of Dartmouth, Vol. III.

BROUGHAM, HENRY, *Baron Brougham and Vaux*. Historical Sketches of Statesmen who flourished in the Time of George III. 3 vols. 1855–56.

BROWNING, OSCAR (Ed.) The Despatches of Earl Gower, the English Ambassador at Paris. 1885.

—— (Ed.) The Political Memoranda of Francis Godolphin, Fifth Duke of Leeds. Camden Society, N. S., V. 35. 1884.

BURKE, EDMUND. Works. (Bohn Edition.) 9 vols. 1854–1857.

CARTWRIGHT, F. D. (Ed.) The Life and Correspondence of Major John Cartwright. 2 vols. 1826.

COLQUHOUN, J. C. William Wilberforce; his Friends and his Times. 2d ed. 1867.

CONWAY, MONCURE D. The Life of Thomas Paine. 2 vols. 1892.

—— The Writings of Thomas Paine. 4 vols. 1895.

CUNNINGHAM, PETER. The Letters of Horace Walpole, Earl of Orford. 9 vols. 1861.

DEBRETT, JOHN. A Collection of State Papers, Relative to the War against France. 11 vols. 1794–1802.

—— and Almon, John. The Parliamentary Register, 1774–1803. 92 vols. in 84. 1775–1804.

EDEN, WILLIAM, *1 Baron Auckland*. Journal and Correspondence. 4 vols. 1861–62.

ELLIOT, SIR GILBERT, *1 Earl of Minto*. Life and Letters of, from 1751 to 1806. 3 vols. 1874.

FITZWILLIAM, CHARLES WILLIAM, *5 Earl of Fitzwilliam,* and Bourke, *Lt.-Gen. Sir Richard* (Eds.)   The Correspondence of Rt. Hon. Edmund Burke between the years 1744–1797.   4 vols.   1844.

FOX, HENRY RICHARD VASSALL, *Lord Holland.*   Memoirs of the Whig Party during my Time.   Ed. by his son, Henry Edward, *Lord Holland.*   2 vols.   1852–54.

GALT, J.   George III, his Court, and Family.   2 vols.   2d ed.   1821.

GIBSON, EDWARD, *1 Baron Ashbourne.*   Pitt; some Chapters of his Life and Times.   2d ed.   1898.

GRENVILLE, RICHARD PLANTAGENET T.N.B.C., *2 Duke of Buckingham and Chandos.*   Memoirs of the Court and Cabinets of George III.   4 vols.   1853–55.

HAMMOND, J. L. LEBRUN.   Charles James Fox, a Political Study.   1908.

HANSARD, T. C.   The Parliamentary History of England.

HARCOURT, LEVESON VERNON.   The Diaries and Correspondence of the Rt. Hon. George Rose.   2 vols.   1860.

HARDY, THOMAS.   Memoir.   1832.

HARRIS, JAMES, *1 Earl of Malmesbury.*   Diaries and Correspondence.   Ed. by his grandson, the 3 Earl.   4 vols.   1844.

——   Series of Letters of, [and of] His Family and Friends.   Ed. by his grandson the Earl of Malmesbury.   2 vols.   1870.

HOLCROFT, THOMAS.   Memoirs.   3 vols.   1815.

HOWELL, T. B., Howell, T. J., and Cobbett, W.   A Complete Collection of State Trials and Proceedings for High Treason.   33 vols.   1809–26.

HUTTON, CATHARINE.   The Life of William Hutton, F.A.S.S., including a particular Account of the Riots at Birmingham in 1791.   2d ed.   1817.

HUTTON, JAMES (Ed.)   Selections from the Letters and Correspondence of Sir James Bland Burges.   1885.

JACOB, T. EVAN.   The Life of William Pitt.   1890.

JENNINGS, LOUIS J. (Ed.)   The Correspondence and Diaries of the late Rt. Hon. John Wilson Croker.   3 vols.   1884.

LANDOR, WALTER SAVAGE.   Charles James Fox, A Commentary on his Life and Times.   Edited by Stephen Wheeler.   1907.

The Lives and Trials of the Reformers.   1836.

MARTENS, GEORG FRIEDRICH VON.   Recueil de traités d'alliance, de paix, de trève, de neutralité, de commerce, de limites, d'échange, etc.   8 vols.   1761–1808.

MAXWELL, RT. HON. SIR HERBERT.   The Creevey Papers.   1904.

MILES, CHARLES POPHAM (Ed.)   The Correspondence of William Augustus Miles on the French Revolution.   2 vols.   1890.

MOORE, THOMAS.   Memoirs of the Life of the Rt. Hon. Richard Brinsley Sheridan.   1825.

MORLEY, JOHN. Edmund Burke. A Historical Study. 1867.
——— Burke. 1888.
MORRIS, ANNE CARY (Ed.)   The Diary and Letters of Gouverneur Morris. 2 vols. 1888.
PELLEW, HON. GEORGE, D.D. The Life and Correspondence of Henry Addington, *1 Viscount Sidmouth.* 3 vols. 1847.
PRIESTLEY, JOSEPH. Memoirs of Dr. Joseph Priestley. 1806.
PRIMROSE, ARCHIBALD PHILIP, *5 Earl of Rosebery.* Life of William Pitt. 1891.
PRIOR, JAMES. A Memoir of the Life and Character of Rt. Hon. Edmund Burke. 1824.
PROTHERO, ROWLAND E. (Ed.)   The Private Letters of Edward Gibbon, 1753–1794. 2 vols. 1896.
The Riots at Birmingham July 1791. 1863.
ROSS, CHARLES. The Correspondence of Charles, First Marquis of Cornwallis. 2d ed. 3 vols. 1859.
RUSSELL, JOHN, *1 Earl Russell* (Ed.)   Memorials and Correspondence of Charles James Fox. 2 vols. 1853.
RUTT, JOHN TOWILL (Ed.)   The Theological and Miscellaneous Works of Joseph Priestley. 25 vols. 1817–1832.
SALOMON, FELIX. William Pitt der Jüngere. Erste Band. 1906.
Sheridan and his Times. By an Octogenarian. 2 vols. 1859.
SMYTH, MRS. GILLESPIE. Memoirs and Correspondence of Sir Robert Murray Keith. 2 vols. 1849.
SMYTH, WILLIAM. Memoir of Mr. Sheridan. 1840.
SPARKS, JARED. The Life of Gouverneur Morris. 3 vols. 1832.
STANHOPE, PHILIP HENRY, *Viscount Mahon, 5 Earl Stanhope.* The Life of the Rt. Hon. William Pitt. 4 vols. 1861–62.
TOMLINE, GEORGE, D.D. Memoirs of the Life of the Rt. Hon. William Pitt. 3 vols. 1822.
TROTTER, JOB BERNARD. Memoirs of the latter years of the Rt. Hon. Charles James Fox. 1811.
TWISS, HORACE. The Public and Private Life of Lord Chancellor Eldon. 2 vols. 1844.
VALE, G. The Life of Thomas Paine. 1871.
WATKINS, JOHN. Memoirs of the Public and Private Life of R. B. Sheridan. 2 vols. 1817.
WICKHAM, WILLIAM (Ed.)   The Correspondence of William Wickham. 2 vols. 1870.
WILBERFORCE, R. I., and Wilberforce, S. (Eds.)   The Correspondence of William Wilberforce. 2 vols. 1840.
——— The Life of William Wilberforce. 5 vols. 1838.
WOLCOTT, JOHN. Works. 5 vols. 1812.
WRAXALL, SIR N. W. Posthumous Memoirs of his own Times. 3 vols. 1836.

WRIGHT, J.   The Speeches of the Rt. Hon. Charles James Fox in the House of Commons. 6 vols. 1815.

PAMPHLETS, TRACTS, ETC.

An Abstract of the History and Proceedings of the Revolution Society in London. 1789.

An Account of the Proceedings of a Meeting of the Inhabitants of Westminster in Palace Yard, November 26, 1795. 1795.

An Account of the Proceedings of a Meeting of the People in a Field near Copenhagen House, November 12, 1795. 1795.

An Account of the Proceedings of the London Corresponding Society . . . in St. George's Fields, June 29, 1795. 1795.

An Account of the Seizure of Citizen Thomas Hardy . . . with some Remarks on the Suspension of the Habeas Corpus Act. 1794.

An Account of the Trial of Thomas Fysche Palmer, etc. 1793.

An Account of the Trial of Thomas Muir, etc. 1793.

Adam Smith, Author of an Inquiry into the Wealth of Nations, and Thomas Paine, Author of the Decline and Fall of the English System of Finance, etc. 1796.

ADAMS, JOHN. Observations on Paine's Rights of Man, etc. (English Edition.) 1791.

ADAMS, WILLIAM. Thoughts on the Anti-monarchical Tendency of the Measures of the British Minister, etc. 1796.

The Address and Declaration of the Society of Constitutional Whigs, Independents, and Friends of the People . . . November 5, 1792.

The Address and Report on the Enquiry into the General State of the Poor . . . for the County of Hampshire. 1795.

An Address in Verse to the Author of the Poetical and Philosophical Essay on the French Revolution. 1793.

An Address of a Buckinghamshire Farmer to his fellow Subjects . . . December 5, 1792.

The Address of the British Constitutional Society for a Parliamentary Reform, etc. April 14, 1794.

An Address to Rt. Hon. William Pitt on Some Parts of his Administration, etc. 1797.

An Address to the Association of the Parish of St. Martin's in the Fields, etc.

An Address to the Bishops upon the Subject of a late Letter from one of their Lordships to certain of the Clergy in his Diocese. 1790.

An Address to the Common Sense and Understanding of the People, etc. 1790.

An Address to the English Nation; with a slight sketch of the existing Grievances, etc. 1796.

An Address to the Hon. Edmund Burke from the Swinish Multitude. 1793.

An Address to the Inhabitants of Great Britain and Ireland, etc. 1793.

An Address to the Inhabitants of Great Britain and Ireland in Reply to a Printed Report of the London Corresponding Society. February, 1794.

An Address to the People of England. 1796.

An Address to the Public from the Friends of Freedom Assembled . . . February 1, 1793. 1793.

An Address to the Public from the Society for Constitutional Information. 1780.

The Advantage of a National Observance of Divine and Human Laws. By a Country Postmaster. 1796.

Advice to Sundry Sorts of People by John Nott, Frameworkknitter, first cousin to John Nott, the Sinker-Maker.· 1791(?).

Advice to the People on the Prospect of a Peace. By a Freeholder of the County of Surrey. 1796.

AGUTTER, WILLIAM. Christian Politics . . . a Sermon preached September 2, 1792. 1792.

——— Observations on the General Fast of the Year 1796. 1796.

——— The Sin of Wastefulness, etc. 1796.

AIKIN, DR. JOHN. An Address to the Dissenters of England, etc. 1790.

The Alarm, Being Britanica's Address to her People.

ANDERSON, RALPH. A Letter to Sir John Sinclair, etc. 1797.

Annual Parliaments, the Ancient and most Salutary Rights of the Commons of Great Britain. 1780.

An Answer from John Bull to Thomas Bull, December 22, 1792.

Answer to a Letter from a Welsh Freeholder . . . by a Clergyman of the Diocese of St. David's. 1790.

An Answer to Dr. Priestley's Letters to the Rt. Hon. Edmund Burke . . . By a Layman of the Established Church. 1791.

An Answer to the Second Part of the Rights of Man in two Letters to the Author. 1792.

An Answer to Thoughts on Parliamentary Reform. 1784.

The Anti-Gallican. 1793.

The Anti-Gallican Songster. 1793.

The Anti-Levelling Songster. 1793.

An Appeal to Britons. By a Friend. 1794.

An Appeal to the Common Sense of the British People on the Subjects of Sedition and Revolution. Philodemos. 1793.

Ask and You Shall Have, etc. 1795.

Assassination of the King! or the Conspirators exposed. 1795.

13

Association Papers, containing the Publications, etc., of the Loyal Associations. June 21, 1793.

At a General Meeting of the London Corresponding Society, held at Globe Tavern in the Strand, January 20, 1794, the following Address to the People, etc.

At a Meeting of the Society for Constitutional Information held February 15, 1782, it was resolved, etc. 1782.

At a Time when the recent Exertions of the Government, etc. December 4, 1792. (An Address published by the Crown and Anchor Association.)

An Authentic Account of the Riots in Birmingham, etc. September 26, 1791.

Authentic Copies of Mr. Pitt's Letter to his Royal Highness, the Prince of Wales, and his Royal Highness' Reply. 1789.

An Authentic Copy of a Petition praying for a Reform in Parliament, presented by Charles Grey, Esq., May 6, 1793.

An Authentic Copy of the Duke of Richmond's Bill for a Parliamentary Reform. 1783.

BALL, GEORGE, D.D. A Sermon preached in the Cathedral of Worcester March 7, 1795. 1795.

BANCROFT, THOMAS, M.A. Sermon preached at the Cathedral Church, Chester, December 9, 1793. 1793.

BARBAULD, A. L. An Address to the Opposers of the Repeal of the Corporation and Test Acts. 1790.

BARLOW, JOEL. Advice to the privileged Orders in the several States of Europe, etc. 2d ed. 1792.

BARNARD, THOMAS. Observations on the Proceedings of the Friends of the Liberty of the Press, December 22, 1792 . . . 1793.

BARRY, REV. EDWARD. A Dispassionate Address to the Subjects of Great Britain. 1793(?).

BATHURST, REV. HENRY. A Sermon preached before the House of Commons . . . February 28, 1794. 1794.

BAXTER, J. Resistance to Oppression the Constitutional Right of Britons, etc. 1795.

BEADON, RICHARD. A Sermon preached before the Lords Spiritual and Temporal . . . April 19, 1793. 1793.

BELSHAM, WILLIAM. Remarks on the Nature and Necessity of a Parliamentary Reform. 1793.

——— Memoirs of the Reign of George III. to the Session of Parliament ending A.D. 1793. 6 vols. 1796. Seventh vol., 1801.

——— Remarks on the Bill for the better Support and Maintenance of the Poor. 1797.

BENNET, REV. G. A Display of the Spirit and Design of those who under Pretext of a Reform Aim at the Subversion of the Constitution and Government of this Kingdom, etc. 1796.

BENTHAM, JEREMY. A Protest Against Law, Taxes, etc. 1795.

BENTLEY, ——, ESQ. A Letter to the Rt. Hon. Charles James Fox upon the Dangerous and Inflammatory Tendency of his late Conduct in Parliament. 1793.

BIGGE, THOMAS. Considerations on the State of Parties, etc. 1794(?).

BINNS, ABRAHAM. Remarks on the Publication entitled a Serious Admonition to the Disciples of Thomas Paine. 1796.

Birmingham Society for Constitutional Information. Address, etc., November 4, 1793.

Birmingham Society for Constitutional Information, first instituted . . . November 20, 1792.

Bishop Sherlock's Argument against a Repeal of the Corporation and Test Acts, etc. 1787.

BLACK, WILLIAM. Reasons for preventing the French under the Cover of Liberty from Trampling upon Europe. 1793.

BLAKE, MARK, ESQ. A Letter to the Clergy of the Church of Scotland. 1794.

BLEWVIS, MR. Observations and Reflections on the Origin of Jacobin Principles, etc. 1794.

The Book of Babs, etc. 1795(?).

BOOTHBY, BROOKE. A Letter to the Rt. Hon. Edmund Burke. December 27, 1790.

BOUSELL, JOHN. The Standard of the Lord of Hosts exalted, etc. 1790.

BOWLES, JOHN. A short Answer to the Declaration of the Persons calling themselves the Friends of the Liberty of the Press. 1793.

—— Objections to the Continuance of the War examined and refuted. 1794.

—— Reflections submitted to the Consideration of the combined Powers. 1794.

—— Farther Reflections submitted to the Consideration of the combined Powers. 1794.

—— The Dangers of a Premature Peace, etc. 1795.

—— Two Letters addressed to a British Merchant. 1796.

—— French Aggressions proved, etc. 1797.

—— A third Letter to a British Merchant. 1797.

—— The Retrospect; etc. 1798.

BRAND, JAMES. A Sermon preached February 28, 1794. 1794.

BRAND, REV. JOHN. A Defence of the Pamphlet ascribed to John Reeves, Esq., etc. 1796.

—— An Historical Essay on the Principles of Political Associations in a State, etc. 1796.

A Brief History of Birmingham. 1797.

A Calm Inquiry into the Office and Duties of Jurymen in Cases of
High Treason, etc. 1794.

A Candid Inquiry into the Nature of Government and the Right
of Representation. 1792.

CARTWRIGHT, JOHN. The Legislative Rights of the Commonalty
Vindicated, etc. 1777.

—— Give us our Rights, etc. 1778.

—— A Letter to the Earl of Abingdon, etc. 1778.

—— The People's Barrier against undue Influence and Corruption, etc. 1780.

—— A Letter to the Duke of New Castle, etc. 1792.

—— The Commonwealth in Danger, etc. 1795.

—— A Letter to the High Sheriff of the County of Lincoln,
etc. 1795.

—— The Constitutional Defence of England, etc. 1796.

—— An Appeal on the Subject of the English Constitution.
1797(?).

The Catechism of Man, etc. 1796(?).

The Causes of the present Complaints fairly stated and fully refuted. 1793.

CAWTHORNE, JOSEPH. A Letter to the King in Justification of a
Pamphlet entitled Thoughts on the English Government, etc.
1796.

CHALMERS, LIEUT. COL. Strictures on a Pamphlet written by Thomas
Paine on the English System of Finances, etc. 1796.

CHALMERS, GEORGE. (FRANCIS OLDYS.) The Life of Thomas Pain
with a Review of his Writings, etc. 1792.

—— The Abridged Life of Thomas Pain, etc. 1793.

A Charge delivered by the Chairman of the Constitutional Association held at Norwich, December 26, 1792.

The Charge delivered by the Rt. Hon. Sir James Eyre, Lord Chief
Justice of his Majesty's Court of Common Pleas, . . . in the
High Treason Trials, October, 1794.

CHELSUM, REV. JAMES. The Duty of Relieving the French Refugee
Clergy stated, etc. 1793.

CHRISTIE, THOMAS. Letters on the Revolution in France, etc. 1791.

CHRISTOPHILUS. A Serious Address to Rev. Dr. Priestley occasioned by reading his familiar Letters, etc. 1790.

Church and King. . . . By Pasquin Shaveblock, Esq., Shaver Extraordinary. 1795.

A Circumstantial History of the Transactions at Paris on the Tenth
of August, etc. 1792.

Citizen Thelwall, Fraternity and Unanimity to the Friends of Freedom, etc. 1795(?).

The Civil and Ecclesiastical System of England defended and fortified. 1791.

CLARKE, REV. THOMAS B. The Benefits of Christianity contrasted with the pernicious Influence of Modern Philosophy on Civil Society, etc. 1796.

CLAYTON, REV. JOHN. The Duty of Christians to Magistrates, etc. 1791.

COBBETT, EDWARD. Observations on the Emigration of Dr. Joseph Priestley. 1794.

COELLOGON, REV. C. E. DE. God and the King, etc. 1790.

—— The peculiar Advantages of the English Nation, etc. 1792.

A Collection of the Letters which have been addressed to the Volunteers of Ireland on the Subject of a Parliamentary Reform. 1783.

COLLINS, THOMAS, D.D. An Assize Sermon, etc. 1794.

Comments on the proposed War with France, on the State of Parties, etc. 1793.

A Comparative Display of the Different Opinions of the most distinguished British Writers on the Subject of the French Revolution. 2 vols. 1793.

A Concise Sketch of the intended Revolution in England, etc 1794.

Confiscation Considered, etc. 1795.

Confusion's Masterpiece, etc. 1794.

Considerations on Lord Grenville's and Mr. Pitt's Bills concerning Treasonable and Seditious Practices and Unlawful Assemblies. By a Lover of Order. 1796(?).

Considerations on Mr. Paine's Pamphlet on the Rights of Man. 1791.

Considerations on Public Economy, etc. 1796.

Considerations on the Preliminaries to the Commencement of the War. . . . By the Author of the Crisis Stated. 1794(?).

Considerations on the Universality and Uniformity of the Theocracy, by a Layman of the Church of England. 1796.

A Constitutional Guide to the People of England at Present unrepresented, etc.

Constitutional Letters in Answer to Mr. Paine's Rights of Man. 1792.

The Contrast, or two Portraits of the Rt. Hon. Charles James Fox, etc. 1793.

A Controversial Letter of a new kind to the Rev. Dr. Price from a Clergyman of the Church of England. 1790.

Convention Bill. A Notice of a Meeting, etc. December 18, 1795.

COOPER, SAMUEL, D.D. The first Principles of Civil and Ecclesiastical Government, etc. 1791.

—— Hand-bill, dated December 4, 1796.

COOPER, THOMAS. A Reply to Mr. Burke's Invective against Mr. Cooper and Mr. Watt, etc. 1792.

Copy of a Letter from Rt. Hon. Lord Carys-fort to the Huntingfordshire Committee, etc. 1780.

A Copy of the Declaration and Articles subscribed by the Members of Administration, etc. 1789.

A Copy of the Duke of Richmond's Letter on Parliamentary Reform, etc., printed for the Sheffield Society for Constitutional Information. 1792.

A Cordial Drop, etc. 1793(?).

The Correspondence of Rev. C. Wyvill with the Rt. Hon. William Pitt. 1796.

The Correspondence of the Revolution Society in London with the National Assembly, etc. 1792.

Corruption Exposed: Being Remarks on the Trial of George Rose, Esq., etc. 1792.

A Country Curate's Advice to Manufacturers, etc.

COURTENAY, REV. HENRY R. A Sermon preached before the Lords Spiritual and Temporal, etc. 1795.

COXE, REV. WILLIAM. A Letter to Rev. Dr. Richard Price, etc. 1790.

The Crisis Stated, etc. 1793.

A Critical Review of the Ipswich Journal, etc. 1790.

CROFT, GEORGE, D.D. The Test Laws Defended, etc. 1790.

CRUDEN, JOHN, ESQ. An Address to the Loyal Part of the British Empire, etc. 1796(?).

The Curses and Causes of War pointed out, etc. 1795.

Cursory Remarks on Mr. Pitt's new Tax of imposing a Guinea per Head on every Person who wears Hair Powder. By Brutus. 1795.

Cursory Remarks on Paine's Rights of Man. 1792.

Curtis Rescued from the Gulph, etc. 1792.

DALLES, WILLIAM. Thoughts upon the present Situation, etc. 1793.

DALYRIMPLE, A. Mr. Fox's Letter to his worthy and independent Electors of Westminster, etc. 1793.

DAMPIER, THOMAS, D.D. A Sermon preached . . . July 23, 1793. 1793.

The Danger of repealing the Test Act, etc. 1790.

DAY, THOMAS. Reflections upon the Present State of England and the Independence of America. 1783.

Declaration of the Merchants, Bankers, Traders, and other Inhabitants of London made . . . December 5, 1792.

The Decline and Fall, Death, Dissection and Funeral Procession of his most Contemptible Lowness, the London Corresponding Society, etc. 1796.

Extermination, or an Appeal to the People of England on the Present War with France. 1793 or 1795(?).

Extract from the Sussex Weekly Advertiser of December 24, 1792. 1793.

Extracts from Books and other Small Pieces in Favour of Religious Liberty and the Rights of Dissenters. 2 pts. 1789. 1790.

Extracts from Dr. Priestley's Works, etc. 1792.

Facts, Reflections and Queries, submitted to the Consideration of the associated Friends of the People. 1792.

Facts Submitted to the Consideration of the Friends of Civil and Religious Liberty, etc. 1790(?).

A faithful Narrative of the last Illness, Death, and Interment of the Rt. Hon. William Pitt, etc. 1795.

FANCOURT, WILLIAM L. Britons and Fellow Countrymen, etc. December 3, 1792.

Fast Day as observed at Sheffield, etc. 1794.

Faustus; a Fragment of a Parody, etc. 1793.

A Few Minutes Advice to the People of Great Britain on Republics. 1792.

A Few Words, but no Lies; from Roger Bull to his Brother Thomas. 1792(?).

FIELD, WILLIAM. A Second Letter addressed to the Inhabitants of Warwick, etc. 1791.

FINCH, REV. THOMAS. Address to the Poor of Northupps in the County of Norfolk, etc. 1795.

Five Minutes Advice to the People of Great Britain on the present alarming State of public Affairs, etc. 1792.

FLEMING, S. An impartial Statement of the Merits and Services of Opposition, etc. 1796(?).

Followers of Reason Vindicated, etc. 1795.

FOOTE, S., JR. Reform, a Farce modernized from Aristophanes. 1792.

FOWNES, JOSEPH. An Enquiry into the Principles of Toleration, etc. 1790.

FOX, CHARLES JAMES. A Speech . . . Spoken at the Whig Club December 4, 1792.

——— A Letter to the Worthy and Independent Electors of the City and Liberty of Westminster. January 26, 1793.

FOX, WILLIAM. A Discourse on National Fasts, particularly in Reference to April 19, 1793. 1793.

——— The Interest of Great Britain respecting the French War. 3d ed. 1793.

——— Thoughts on the Death of the King of France. 1793.

——— A Defence of the Decree of the National Convention of France for Emancipating Slaves in the West Indies. 1794.

—— A Defence of the War against France. 1794.

—— A Discourse occasioned by the National Fast of February 28, 1794.

—— On Jacobinism. 1794.

—— The Friend, a weekly Essay. Nos. 1–23. 1796.

FRANCIS, PHILIP. Draught of a Resolution and Plan intended to be proposed to the Society of Friends of the People. 1795.

Fraternity, Humanity, Peace. May 17, 1795.

Friendly Remarks upon some Particulars of his Administration in a Letter to Mr. Pitt by a near Observer. 1796.

A full, accurate, and impartial History of the Campaign, etc. 1794.

A full and particular Account of the Birth, Parentage and Education, Life, Character and Behaviour of that most notoriously notified Malefactor, Willy Pitto, etc. 1796(?).

A full, true, and particular Account of the Conquest of France by the King of Prussia and the Duke of Brunswick, etc. 1792.

GARDINER, REV. JOHN. A Sermon preached . . . April 19, 1793. 1793.

—— A Sermon preached . . . February 25, 1795. 1795.

Garrick's Jests; or Gems in high glee, containing all the Jokes of the Wits of the present Age, viz: Mr. Garrick, Mr. Fox, Mr. Burke, etc.

A general Reply to the several Answers . . . of a Letter written to a Noble Lord by the Rt. Hon. Edmund Burke. 1796.

GERRALD, a Fragment, etc. 1795(?).

GERRALD, JOSEPH. A Convention the only Means of Saving us from Ruin, etc. 1793.

GIFFORD, JOHN. A Narrative of the Transactions personally relating to the unfortunate Louis XVI, King of France . . . from June 20, 1791, to January 21, 1793. 1793.

—— A plain Address to the Common Sense of the People of England, etc. 1793.

—— A Letter to the Earl of Lauderdale . . . Containing Strictures on his Lordships Letters to the Peers of Scotland. 1794.

—— The Reign of Louis XVI, etc. 1794.

—— A Letter to Hon. Thomas Erskine, etc. 1797.

—— A second Letter to Hon. Thomas Erskine, etc. 1797.

—— A short Address to the Members of the loyal Associations, etc. 1798.

—— A Letter to the Earl of Lauderdale . . . with a Preface . . . from Rt. Hon. Edmund Burke, etc. 1800.

GILBANK, REV. W. The Duties of Man, etc. 1793.

Glorious News for Old England. . . . A New Song. 1795(?).

GOLDSMITH, OLIVER. The English Constitution, etc. 1792.

GOODENOUGH, REV. SAMUEL. A Sermon preached . . . February 28, 1794. 1794.

GORDON, REV. GEORGE. A Sermon preached February 28, 1794. 1794.

GROSE, REV. JOHN. A Sermon preached February 28, 1794. 1794.

GURNEY, JOSEPH (Stenographer) The whole Proceedings of the Trial and Information against Thomas Paine, etc. 1793.

—— The Trial of Thomas Hardy for High Treason, etc. 4 vols. 1794.

—— The Whole Proceedings on the Trial of Thomas Walker of Manchester, etc. 1794.

—— The Trial of Robert Thomas Crossfield for High Treason, etc. 1796.

—— The Trial of William Stone for High Treason, etc. 1796.

H. R. H. Dr. Price and the Rights of Man, etc. 1791.

HALES, CHARLES. The Bank Mirror; etc. October, 1796.

HALLORAN, REV. L. H. A Sermon for December 19, 1797. 1797.

HAMILTON, JAMES E. A Letter to the People of England upon the Present Crisis. 1793(?).

HARLEY, ROBERT, ESQ. An Essay upon the public Credit, etc. 1797.

HART, JOHN. An Address to the Public on the Subject of the Starch and Hair Powder Manufactories, etc. 1795.

HARVEY, CHARLES, ESQ. A Charge delivered to the Grand Jury of the City and County of Norwich, January 18, 1793. 1793.

HAWES, R. Peas for the Swine and Grapes for the Citizens, etc. 1793.

HAWKER, ROBERT, D.D. The invaluable Blessings of our religious and Civil Government, etc. 1793.

—— An Appeal to the People of England on the Subject of the French Revolution, etc. 1794.

HAWKINS, REV. W. Regal Rights Consistent with National Liberties, etc. 1795.

HAWTRY, REV. CHARLES. Various Opinions of the philosophical Reformers Considered, etc. 1792.

HAYES, REV. SAMUEL. A Sermon preached . . . July 20, 1792. 1792.

—— A Sermon preached . . . January 27, 1793. 1793.

HEDDESFORD, REV. GEORGE. Topsy Turvey, etc. 1793.

HERVEY, FRED. A new Friend on an old Subject, etc. 1791.

HEWAT, ALEXANDER, D.D. The firm Patriot, etc. 1795.

—— Religion essential to the Being and Happiness of Society, etc. 1796.

HEY, RICHARD. Happiness and Rights, etc. 1792.

HEYWOOD, SAMUEL. The Right of Protestant Dissenters to a Complete Toleration Asserted, etc. 1789.

High Treason!! Narrative of the Arrest, Examination by the Privy
   Council and Imprisonment of P. T. Le Maitre, etc. 1795.
HILL, REV. GEORGE. The present Happiness of Great Britain, etc.
   1792.
Hints to Opposition in a Letter Addressed to Rt. Hon. C. J. Fox.
   1795.
Hints to the People of England for the year 1793, etc. 1792.
Historical Memoirs of Religious Dissensions, etc. 1790.
The History of a Good Bramin, etc. 1795.
A History of the late important Period from the Beginning of his
   Majesty's Illness to the Settlement of the Executive Gov-
   ernment, etc. 1789.
The History of Two Acts, etc. 1796.
HOBSON, REV. JOHN. A Series of Remarks upon a Sermon preached
   at St. Philip's Church, Birmingham, etc. 1790.
HODGSON, E. (Stenographer)   The Genuine Trial of Thomas Paine,
   etc. 1793.
HODSON, REV. FRODSHAM. A Sermon preached . . . March 8, 1797.
   1797.
HODSON, REV. SEPTIMUS. Sermons on the present State of Re-
   ligion in this Country, etc. 1793.
——— An Address to the different Classes of Persons in Great
   Britain on the present Scarcity and high Price of Provisions,
   to which is an Appendix Containing a Table of the average
   Price of Wheat from 1595–1795. 1795.
——— The great Sin of witholding Corn, etc. 1795.
HOLCOMBE, REV. WILLIAM. Self Correction a Duty we owe to our
   Country in Times of public Calamity, etc. 1796.
HOLCROFT, THOMAS. A Letter to the Rt. Hon. William Windham,
   etc. 1795.
——— A Narrative of Facts relating to a Prosecution for High
   Treason, etc. 1795.
HOLLOWAY, JOHN. A Letter to the Rev. Dr. Price, etc. 1789.
HOLMES, ROBERT, D.D. A Sermon preached . . . March 9, 1796.
   1796.
HORSLEY, SAMUEL. A Review of the Case of the Protestant Dis-
   senters, etc. 1790. (First ed. 1787.)
——— A Sermon preached . . . January 30, 1793. 1793.
HUGHES, REV. RICE. A Letter on the Meeting at Crown and Anchor
   on July 14, 1791, etc. 1791.
HUGHES, WILLIAM. Justice to a Judge, etc. 1793.
HUMPHREYS, REV. JOHN. Regard due to Divine Judgments Con-
   sidered, etc. 1794.
HUNT, ISAAC. Rights of Englishmen, etc. 1791.

HUNTER, REV. THOMAS. The Inseparable Union of Religion and Patriotism, etc. 1794.

HUNTER, WILLIAM. A Letter to Dr. Priestley F.R.S. in Answer to his Letter to the Rt. Hon. William Pitt, etc. 1787.

HUNTINGFORD, REV. GEORGE ISAAC. A Sermon preached . . . April 19, 1793. 1793.

Impartial Memoirs of the Life of Thomas Paine, etc. 1793.

Important Thoughts on the Test Acts, in a Letter to a Friend, etc.

An Inquiry into the Causes of the present Derangement of the public Credit in Great Britain, etc. 1793.

JACKSON, REV. ROGER. A Charge delivered to the Grand Jury . . . January 15, 1793.

JACKSON, WILLIAM, D.D. A Sermon preached . . . February 25, 1795. 1795.

JACOMB, ROBERT. A Letter vindicating Dissenters from the Charge of Disloyalty, etc. 1793.

JARDINE, DAVID. Seasonable Reflexions on Religious Fasts, etc. 1794.

JEBB, A. Two Pennyworth of Truth for a Penny, etc. 1793.

JENYNS, SOAME, ESQ. Thoughts on a parliamentary Reform. 1793.

JEPSON, REV. WILLIAM. Letters to Thomas Payn, etc. 1791.

John Bull in Answer to his Brother Thomas, etc. 1792(?).

John Bull to his Brother. 1792(?).

John Bull's Answer to his Brother Thomas's Second Letter, December 28, 1792.

John Frost this Day at twelve O'clock, etc. 1793.

JONES, ABRAHAM. The State of the Country in the Month of November, 1794. 1794.

JONES, JOHN. The Reason of Man, etc. 1793.

JONES, JOHN GALE. Sketch of a Speech delivered at the Westminster Forum, December 9–30, 1794. 1795.

—— Sketch of a Political Tour through Rochester, Chatham, Maidstone, Gravesend, etc. 1796.

JONES, WILLIAM. The Principles of Government in a Dialogue between a Scholar and a Peasant. 1782.

Jordan's Complete Collection of all the Addresses and Speeches of Hon. C. J. Fox, Sir A. Gardiner and J. H. Tooke, Esq., etc. 1796.

KEATE, REV. WILLIAM. A free Examination of Dr. Price's and Priestley's Sermons, etc. 1790.

—— Quotation against Quotation, etc. 1790.

KEITH, REV. G. S. An impartial and comprehensive View of the present State of Great Britain, etc. 1797.

KING, EDWARD. Considerations on the Utility of the National Debt. 1793.

KING, WALKER, D.D. Two Sermons preached . . . August 19, 1793. 1793.

KIPPIS, ANDREW. A Sermon preached at the Old Jewry, November 4, 1788, etc. 1788.

—————— An Address delivered at the Interment of the late Dr. Price. 1791.

—————— A Sermon preached . . . February 28, 1794. 1794.

Knaves-Ace Association. Resolution adopted at a Meeting of Placemen Pensioners, etc. 1793.

KNOX, WILLIAM. Considerations on the present State of the Nation, etc. 1789.

—————— A friendly Address to the Members of the several Clubs in the Parish of St. Ann's, Westminster, etc. 1793.

LANGFORD, REV. W. Obedience to the established Laws and Respect to the Person of the Administrator, etc. 1793.

LARCHER, ANDREW. A Remedy for establishing universal Peace and Happiness, etc. 1794 (?).

The last dying Words of Tom Paine, etc. 1794.

LEE, R. (Citizen) The Excellence of the British Constitution, etc. October 2, 1795.

—————— The Voice of the People, etc. 1795.

—————— Warning to Tyrants, etc. 1795.

—————— The Wrongs of Man, etc. 1795.

—————— The Rights of Nobles, etc. 1795.

—————— The Rights of Princes, etc. 1795.

—————— The Rights of Prints, etc. 1795.

—————— The Rights of Man, etc. 1795.

—————— The Blessings of War, etc. 1795.

—————— The Rights of the Swine, etc. 1795.

—————— Rare News for Old England, etc. 1795.

LEIGH, REV. W. A Sermon preached . . . February 25, 1795. 1795.

A Letter addressed to the Inhabitants of Great Britain, etc. December 11, 1792.

A Letter addressed to the Inhabitants of Great Britain, etc. January 9, 1793.

A Letter from his Grace the Duke of Richmond . . . with Notes by a Member of the Society for Constitutional Information. 30th ed. 1795.

A Letter from Irenopolis to the Inhabitants of Eleutheropolis, etc. 2d ed. 1792.

A Letter from the Rt. Hon. Lord Petre to the Rt. Rev. Dr. Horsley, etc. 1790.

A Letter of Thanks . . . to the Rt. Hon. Edmund Burke, etc. 1792.

A Letter on the present Associations, interspersed with various Remarks, etc. 1793.

A Letter to a Friend in the Country . . . by a Member of one of the Inns of the Court. 1792.

A Letter to a Noble Earl from a Member of Parliament, etc. 1797.

A Letter to a Nobleman containing Considerations on the Laws relating to Dissenters, etc. 1790.

A Letter to his Grace, the Duke of Richmond in Answer to his Queries, etc. 1783.

A Letter to John Clayton, Containing a Defence of Protestant Dissenters, etc. 1791.

A Letter to John Horne Tooke, Esq., etc. 1789.

A Letter to Lord Ashburton from Mr. Horne, etc. 1782.

A Letter to Mr. Miles, occasioned by his late scurrilous Attack on Mr. Burke, etc. 1796.

A Letter to the Most insolent Man alive, William Pitt. 1789.

A Letter to the public Meeting of the Friends of the Repeal of the Test and Corporation Acts, etc. 1790.

A Letter to the Rt. Hon. Charles James Fox from a Westminster Elector. 1794.

A Letter to the Rt. Hon. Charles James Fox on the late Conduct of his Party. 1789.

A Letter to the Rt. Hon. Edmund Burke from a Dissenting Country Attorney, etc. 1791.

A Letter to the Rt. Hon. Edmund Burke in Reply to his Reflections, etc. 1790.

A Letter to the Rt. Hon. Henry Dundas . . . by the London Corresponding Society, etc. 1794.

A Letter to the Rt. Hon. Henry Dundas, Esq., or an Appeal to the People of Great Britain, etc. 1794.

A Letter to the Rt. Hon. William Pitt, Chancellor of the Exchequer, on the Conduct of the Bank Directors, etc. 1796.

A Letter to the Rt. Hon. William Pitt on his Apostacy from the Cause of Parliamentary Reform, etc. 1793.

A Letter to the Rt. Hon. William Pitt on the present alarming Crisis, etc. 1796.

A Letter to the Rt. Rev. Lord Bishop of Landaff . . . by a Country Curate. 1792.

A Letter to the Rt. Rev. Samuel, Lord Bishop of St. David's . . . by a Welsh Freeholder. 1790.

Letters from a Country Gentleman to a Member of Parliament, etc. 1789.

Letters from a Gentleman in Scotland to his Friend in England, etc. 1794.

Letters to a Friend on the Test Laws . . . by a Chaplain in the Navy. 1791.

Letters to the People of England against the Repeal of the Test and Corporation Acts, by a Graduate of Oxford. 1790.

Letters to the People of Great Britain respecting the present State of Public Affairs. 1795.

Letters to Thomas Paine; in Answer to his late Publication on the Rights of Man, etc. 1791.

LEWELYN, WILLIAM. An Appeal to Man against Paine's Rights of Man. 1793.

LEWIS, REV. T. The Happiness of Living under the British Government, etc. 1793.

Liberty and Equality; treated in a short History Addressed from a poor Man to his Equals. 1792.

The Life and Character of Robert Watt, etc. 1795.

The Life, Death and Wonderful Achievements of Edmund Burke. 1792.

LOFFT, CAPEL. An History of the Corporation and Test Acts, etc. 1790.

—— Remarks on the Letter of the Rt. Hon. Edmund Burke concerning the Revolution in France, etc. 1790.

—— A Vindication of the short History of the Corporation and Test Acts. 1790.

—— Remarks on the Letter of Mr. Burke to a Member of the National Assembly. 1791.

The London Corresponding Society at a general Meeting, etc. November 12, 1795.

Look before you Leap; or a healin' sa' for the Crackit Crowns . . . by Tam Thrum, an auld Weaver. 1792.

LOWTH, REV. ROBERT. A Sermon preached . . . March 17, 1793. 1793.

MACKENZIE, HENRY. The Life of Thomas Paine. 1793.

MACKINTOSH, JAMES. Vindiciae Gallicae, etc. 1791.

McLEOD, A. A warm Reply to Mr. Burke's Letter. March 19, 1796.

McLEOD, NORMAN. Letters to the People of North Briton on Parliamentary Reformation, etc. 1793.

MACOMAS, DR. Letters addressed to the Rt. Hon. William Pitt, etc. 1793.

MADAN, REV. SPENCER. A Letter to Dr. Priestley in Consequence of his familiar Letters, etc. 1790.

—— The principal Claims of the Dissenters, etc. 1790.

—— The Duty and Necessity of Humiliation, etc. 1795.

MAINWARING, WILLIAM. A Charge to the Grand Jury of Middlesex, etc. 1792.

The Malcontent. A Letter from an Associator to Francis Plowden, Esq., etc. 1794.

MANNERS, REV. M.   The Citizen's Obligation, etc.   1792.

MARGAROT, MAURICE.   A Letter to the Rt. Hon. Henry Dundas, etc. 1792.

MARSH, HERBERT.   The History of the Politics of Great Britain and France Vindicated from a late Attack of Mr. William Belsham.   1801.

MARTIN, JOHN.   An Essay on the Liberty of Man.   1794.

MAULE, REV. J.   A Sermon preached . . . February 28, 1794.   1794.

MAXWELL, JAMES.   A Touch on the Times, etc.   1793.

The Measures of the Ministry to prevent a Revolution, etc.   1794.

The Member's and Elector's useful Companion for the present General Election, etc.   1790.

The Memorials of M. Le Brun, Secretary for Foreign Affairs to the French Republic, on the Situation of Affairs between Great Britain and France December 17, 1792, etc.   1793.

The Merits of Mr. Pitt and Mr. Hastings as Ministers in War and Peace impartially stated.   1794.

MILES, W. A.   The Conduct of France towards Great Britain Examined.   1793.

—— A Letter to Earl Stanhope.   1794.

—— A Letter to the Duke of Grafton, etc.   1794.

—— Authentic Correspondence with Le Brun, etc.   1796.

—— A Letter to Henry Duncombe, etc.   1796.

MILN, REV. ROBERT.   The Rise and fatal Effects of War, etc.   1794.

A Miniature of Thomas Paine, etc.   1792(?).

Mr. Adam's Speech in Defence of R. T. Crossfield, etc.   1796.

Mr. Justice Ashursts' Charge to the Grand Jury, etc.   November 19, 1792.

Mr. King's Speech at Egham with Thomas Paine's Reply, etc. 1793.

Mr. St. George, a true Story . . . by John Bull.   1795(?).

Modern Madness; or the Constitutionalists Dissected.   By Solomon Searchem, Esq.   1792.

More Reasons for a Reform in Parliament.   1793.

MORGAN, WILLIAM.   A Review of Dr. Price's Writings on the Subject of the Finances of this Kingdom.   1792.

—— Facts addressed to the Serious Attention of the People of Great Britain, etc.   1796.

—— An Appeal to the People of Great Britain on the present Alarming State of the public Finances and Public Credit.   1797.

MORRES, HERVEY.   Impartial Reflexions upon the present Crisis, etc. 1796.

MOSER, JOSEPH.   An Examination of the Pamphlet entitled Thoughts on the English Government, etc.   1796.

My Brethren and fellow Protestants, etc.   1793(?).

14

NARES, REV. R. Principles of Government deduced from Reason, etc. 1792.
——— Principles of Government adapted to General Instruction and Use. 1793.
NARES, REV. WILLIAM. Man's best Right, etc. 1793.
——— A short Account of the Character and Reign of Louis XVI, etc. 1793.
The National Advocates, a Poem affectionately inscribed to Hon. Thomas Erskine and Vicary Gibbs, Esq. 1795.
National Sins the Cause of national Sufferings, etc. 1797.
NEALE, REV. GEORGE. A Letter to Rt. Hon. Edmund Burke, etc. 1796.
The Necessity of a Speedy and Effectual Reform in Parliament, etc. 1792.
NEWTON, REV. JOHN. The imminent Danger and the only Sure Resource of this Nation, etc. 1794.
NOCH, LAELIUS. A Short Sketch of the Revolution in 1688. 1793.
O'BRYEN, DENNIS. Utrum Horum? The Government or the Country. 1796.
Observations on Dr. Price's Revolution Sermon and on the Conduct of the Dissenters, etc. 1790.
Observations on the Reflections of the Rt. Hon. Edmund Burke . . . in a Letter to the Rt. Hon. Earl Stanhope. 1790.
Official Copies of the Correspondence of Lord Malmesbury, Minister Plenipotentiary to the French Republic, and the Executive Directory of France. 1796.
Oh, Dear! What Can the Matter be? 1793.
O'LEARY, REV. ARTHUR. A Sermon preached . . . March 8, 1797. 1797.
One Pennyworth of Advice to the loyal Associations of Great Britain. 1793.
One Pennyworth of Truth from Thomas Bull to his Brother John. 1792.
One Pennyworth More, or a Second Letter from Thomas Bull to his Brother John. December 12, 1792.
Opinions delivered at a numerous and respectable Meeting in the Country, etc. 1793.
Oppression!!! The Appeal of Captain Sperry, late Editor of the Argus, to the People of England, etc. 1795.
The Origin and Plan of a general Association of Householders, etc. 1796.
The Original Address of the Constitutional Society. 1780(?).
OWEN, REV. JOHN. Righteous Judgment, etc. 1794.
Paine and Burke Contrasted. . . . Published by Anonymous Persons who sign themselves True Friends of the People. 1792.

Paine, Sin and the Devil, tres juncti in uno. Intercepted Correspondence from Satan to Citizen Paine.

PAINE, THOMAS. The Address and Declaration of the Friends of Universal Peace and Liberty, etc. 1791.

——— The Rights of Man, etc. 1st part. 1791.

——— An Address to the Republic of France, etc. 1792.

——— A Letter addressed to the Addressers, etc. 1792.

——— A Letter to Mr. Secretary Dundas, June 6, 1792.

——— Miscellaneous Articles. 1792.

——— The Rights of Man, etc. 2d part. 1792.

——— Two Letters to Lord Onslow and one to Mr. Henry Dundas, etc. 1792.

——— Prospects on the War and Paper Currency, etc. 1793. (Written in 1787.)

——— Reasons for wishing to preserve the Life of Louis Capet, etc. 1793(?).

——— The Age of Reason, etc. 1794.

——— A Dissertation on the first Principles of Government, etc. 1795.

——— The Rights of Man for the Use and Benefit of all Mankind. 1795.

——— The Decline and Fall of the English System of Finance. 1796.

PALEY, WILLIAM, D.D. Reasons for Contentment, etc. 1793.

——— A Sermon preached . . . July 22, 1795. 1795.

PALMER, SAMUEL. A Vindication of modern Dissenters, etc. 1790.

PARR, SAMUEL. A Sequel to the printed Paper lately circulated in Warwickshire, etc. 1792.

PARRY, WILLIAM. Remarks on the Resolutions passed at a Meeting of the Noblemen and Clergy of the County of Warwick, etc. 1790.

——— Thoughts on such penal religious Statutes as affect Protestant Dissenters, etc. 1791.

Part of a Letter from Robert Adair to the Rt. Hon. C. J. Fox, etc. 1796.

PASQUIN, ANTHONY, ESQ. Legislative Biography, etc. 1795.

PATJE, C. L. A. (Herbert March, tr.) An Essay on the English National Credit. 1797.

PATTON, CHARLES. An Attempt to establish the Basis of Freedom, etc. 1793.

Pax in Bello; or, a few Reflexions on the Prospects of Peace, etc. 1796.

PEACOCK, REV. D. M. Considerations on the Structure of the House of Commons, etc. 1794.

Pearls Cast before Swine by Edmund Burke, scraped together by Old Hubert. 1794(?).

PEARSON, EDWARD, B.D. A Sermon preached . . . November 5, 1793. 1793.

——— A Sermon preached . . . January 30, 1794.

PEDDIE, REV. JAMES. The Revolution the Work of God and a Cause of Joy, etc. 1789.

PENN, WILLIAM. Vindiciae Britannicae, etc. 1794.

The People's Friend; or, the Mysteries of St. Stephen's Chapel unfolded. 1795(?).

PERCEVAL, WILLIAM. The Duties and Powers of public Officers and private Persons with Respect to Violations of the public Peace. 1793(?).

The pernicious Effects of the Art of Printing upon Society, etc. 1796(?).

The pernicious Principles of Thomas Paine exposed in an Address to Labourers and Mechanics, by a gentleman.

Personal the best Pledges of public Reform. . . . By a Clergyman in the Diocese of Canterbury. 1795.

PETRE, ALEXANDER. Strictures on the Character and Principles of Thomas Paine. 1792.

PHAIL, JAMES M. Remarks on the present Times, exhibiting the Causes of the high Price of Provisions, etc. 1795.

A Picture of the Times. Published weekly. 1796.

PIGGOTT, CHARLES. A political Dictionary, etc. 1795.

Pitti-Clout and Dun-Cuddy, a political Eclogue wherein is expressed in courtly Lays the inviolable Attachment of the Treasury Shepherds, etc. 1795.

Pitt's Ghost. Being an Account of the Death, Dissection, Funeral Procession, Epitaph . . . of the much lamented Minister of State. 1795(?).

A plain and earnest Address to Britons, especially Farmers . . . by a Farmer. 1792.

Plain Thoughts of a plain Man, etc. 1797.

A Plan for the periodical Abolition of all Taxes raised by Means of Collectors, etc. 1795.

PLAYFAIR, WILLIAM. Inevitable Consequences of a Reform in Parliament. 1792.

——— Better Prospects to the Merchants and Manufacturers of Great Britain. 1793.

——— A general View of the actual Force and Resources of France, January, 1793. 1793.

——— Thoughts on the present State of French Politics, etc. 1793.

—— For the Use of the Enemies of England. A real statement of the Finances, etc. 1796.

—— A History of Jacobinism, its Crimes, Cruelties and Per-
fidies, etc. 2 vols. 1798.

PLOWDEN, FRANCIS, ESQ. The Case stated. 1791.

—— Jura Anglorum. The Rights of Englishmen. 1792.

—— A short History of the British Empire during the last
twenty Months, etc. 1794.

—— Church and State, etc. 1795.

A Poetical Effusion on the religious and political Principles of Dr.
Priestley. 1791.

A political Debate on Christian Principles; or, the Correspondence
between Rev. John Newton and Rev. David Williamson. 1793.

A political Dictionary for the Guinealess Pigs, etc. 1795(?).

Political Observations on the Test Act. 1790.

The Political Salvation of Great Britain by Means entirely new
. . . by a Gentleman independent of Parties. 1797.

The Poll Tax. An Ode by Grizzle Bald Pate, Esq. 1795.

The poor Man's Answer to the rich Associations. 1793(?).

POPE, SIMEON. A Letter to Rt. Hon. William Curtis . . . on the
national Debt, etc. 1796.

POTTER, JOHN. A Treatise on the Law of Elections, etc. 1790.

POULTER, REV. EDMUND. A Sermon on the present Crisis, preached
. . . December 9, 1792. 1793.

A practical philosophical Essay on the French Revolution, etc.
1796.

Precious Morsels. Features of Sundry great Personages, etc.
1795(?).

The present State of the British Constitution deduced from Facts
by an Old Whig. 1793.

PRICE, DR. RICHARD. Observations on the Nature of Civil Liberty,
etc. 1776.

—— Additional Observations on the Nature and Value of Civil
Liberty, etc. 1777.

—— Two Tracts on Civil Liberty, etc. 1778.

—— Observations on the Importance of the American Revolution, etc. 1784.

—— A Discourse on the Love of Country, etc. 1789.

—— The Preface and Additions to the Discourse on the Love
of Country. 1790.

—— Britain's Happiness, and its full Possession of Civil and
religious Liberty, etc. 1791.

PRIESTLEY, DR. JOSEPH. A Letter to the Rt. Hon. William Pitt on
the Subject of Toleration, etc. 1787.

—— The Conduct to be observed by Dissenters in order to procure the Repeal of the Corporation and Test Acts, etc. 1789.

—— Familiar Letters addressed to the Inhabitants of Birmingham, etc. 1790.

—— Familiar Letters addressed to the Inhabitants of Birmingham in Refutation of several Charges, etc. 1790.

—— An Address to the Students of New College, Hackney,
etc. 1791.

—— An Appeal to the Public on the Subject of the Riots in
Birmingham, etc. 1791.

—— A Discourse occasioned by the Death of Dr. Price, etc.
1791.

—— Dr. Priestley's Letter to the Inhabitants of Birmingham,
etc. 1791.

—— The Duty of Forgiveness of Injuries, etc. 1791.

—— Letters to Rt. Hon. Edmund Burke occasioned by his Reflections on the Revolution in France. 1791.

—— A Sermon preached . . . April 19, 1793. 1793.

—— Letters addressed to the Philosophers and Politicians of
France, etc. 1794.

—— The present State of England compared with Antient
Prophecies, etc. 1794.

—— The Use of Christianity, especially in dangerous Times,
etc. 1794.

Principle and Practice combined; or, the Wrongs of Man . . . by
one who signs himself a Patriot. 1792.

Proceedings and Speeches at the Meeting, November 17, 1795, at
St. Andrew's Hall, Norwich, etc. 1795.

Proceedings in an Action for Debt between Rt. Hon. C. J. Fox,
Plaintiff, and J. Horne Tooke, Esq., etc. 1792.

Proceedings in the National Assembly of France on the Admission
of Mr. William Priestley, etc. 1792.

Proceedings of the Association for preserving Liberty and Property
against Republicans and Levellers, etc. 1792.

Proceedings of the Friends of the Abuse of the Liberty of the Press
on December 21, 1792. 1793.

Proceedings of the Friends of the Abuse of the Liberty of the
Press December 22, 1792; January 19, and March 9, 1793. 1793.

Proceedings of the Society of Friends of the People . . . in the
year 1792. 1793.

The Proceedings on the Trial of Daniel Isaac Eaton upon Indictment for publishing a supposed Libel, etc. 1793.

The Proclamation . . . A poetical Epistle from Harry Gay to his
Friend, Richard Quiet. 1792.

A Protest against Paine's Rights of Man, etc. 1792.

Public Documents declaratory of the Principles of the Protestant Dissenters, etc. 1790.

RAMSEY, WILLIAM (Stenographer)   The Trial of Rev. Thomas Fysche Palmer, etc. 1793.

―――― The Proceedings in Cases of High Treason under a special Commission of Oyer and Terminer, etc. 1794.

―――― The Trial of Joseph Gerrald, etc. 1794.

―――― The Trial of Maurice Margarot, etc. 1794.

―――― The Trial of William Skirving, Secretary to the British Convention, etc. 1794.

―――― The Tribune, Consisting Chiefly of the political Lectures of John Thelwall, etc. 1796.

RAY, REV. JAMES.   To the Christian World. A plain Sermon, etc. 1795(?).

Reasons against National Despondency; in Refutation of Mr. Erskine's View, etc. 1797.

Reasons for national Penitence, recommended for the Fast, etc. 1794.

Reasons for Seeking a Repeal of the Corporation and Test Acts submitted . . . By a Dissenter. 1790.

REEVES, JOHN, ESQ.   The Grounds of Alderman Wilkes and Boydell's Petition for Peace examined and Refuted. 1795.

―――― Thoughts on the English Government, etc. 1795.

Reflexions on the Consequences of his Majesty's Recovery, etc. 1789.

Reflexions on the present State of the Resources of the Country. 1796.

Reform or Ruin; Take your choice, etc. 1797.

The Reformers. A Satirical Poem, etc. 1793.

A Refutation of Mr. Pitt's alarming Assertion, made on the last Day of the Last session of Parliament, etc. 1794.

Reign of the English Robespierre, addressed to the Nation. 1795.

Remarks addressed to Rev. Charles Weston, Chairman of the Committee of the Durham County and City Association, etc. 1793.

Remarks on a Pamphlet published as Mr. Fox's Speech at the Opening of Parliament, etc. 1793.

Remarks on the Proceedings of the Society who style themselves the Friends of the People, etc. 1792.

RENNEL, MAJOR.   War with France the only Security of Britain, etc. 1794.

RENNELL, REV. THOMAS.   The Connexion of the Duty of Loving the Brotherhood, Fearing God, and Honouring the King, etc. 1793.

―――― The Principles of French Republicans essentially founded on Violence and Blood-guiltiness, etc. 1793.

Report of the Committee of the Friends of the People . . . appointed to examine the State of Representation in Scotland. 1793(?).

Report of the Constitutional Society on the Treason and Sedition Bills. 1795.

The Retort Politic on Master Burke . . . from a Tyro of his own School, but another Class. 1796.

The Resolutions of the first meeting of the Friends of the Liberty of the Press, etc. 1793.

Resolutions . . . of the Society associated for the Purpose of Obtaining a Parliamentary Reform, etc. 1792.

A Review of the Case of the Protestant Dissenters, etc. 1790.

Revolutions without Bloodshed; or Reformation preferable to Revolt. 1794.

RICH, DAVID D. The Case of the Labourers in Husbandry stated, etc. 1795.

The Rights and Duties of Man united in a Series of Letters from a Gentleman in London to a Friend in the Country, etc. 1792.

Rights of Citizens, etc. 1791.

The Rights of Government not incompatible with the Rights of Man, etc. 1791.

The Rights of Monarchy. A Poem, etc. 1792.

Rights of Nature against the Usurpation of Establishments, etc. 1796.

The Rights of the Devil; or, the Jacobin's Consolation, etc. 1793.

RILAND, REV. JOHN. The Rights of God, etc. 1792.

ROBINSON, REV. THOMAS. An Address to the Loyal Leicester Volunteers, etc. 1795.

—— A serious Exhortation to the Inhabitants of Great Britain with Reference to the Approaching Fast. 1795.

A Rod in Brine; or, a Tickler for Tom Paine . . . by an Oxford Graduate. 1792.

ROSE, JOHN. An impartial History of the late Disturbances at Bristol, etc. 1793.

ROUS, GEORGE. Thoughts on Government, etc. 1791.

—— A Letter to the Rt. Hon. Edmund Burke, etc. 1792(?).

RUSSEL, W. Reform and Revolution, etc. 1796.

ST. JOHN, JOHN. A Letter from a Magistrate to Mr. William Rose of Whitehall, etc. 1791.

SAUNDERS, CHRISTOPHER, LL.D. Who were the Aggressors? etc. 1797.

SCOTT, JAMES, D.D. A Sermon preached . . . April 19, 1793. 1793.

SCOTT, JOHN. A Letter to the Rt. Hon. Edmund Burke, etc. 1791.

—— Observations on Mr. Belsham's Memoirs of the Reign of George III. 1796.

SCOTT, THOMAS. An impartial Statement of the Scriptural Doctrines in Respect of Civil Government, etc. 1792.
——— An Estimate of the religious Character of the State of Great Britain, etc. 1793.
SCURLOCK, REV. DAVID. Thoughts on the Influence of Religion in Civil Government, etc. 1792.
Seeds of Sedition. Important Discovery to the honourable Committee of Sedition Hunters in Nottingham. 1793.
SEMPHILL, HUGH, *Lord.* A Short Address to the Public, etc. 1793.
A Sequel to Sir William Jones's Pamphlet on the Principles of Government, etc. 1784.
A Serious Exhortation to the Electors of Great Britain, etc. 1796(?).
A Sermon preached at the Cathedral Church of St. Paul, London, May 28, 1795, by Henry, Lord Bishop of Bristol. 1795.
SHARP, GRANVILLE. A circular Letter to the several petitioning Counties, Cities and Towns, etc. 1780.
The Shaver's new Sermon for the Fast Day . . . by Pasquin Shaveblock, Shaver Extraordinary. 1795.
A Short Account of the Character and Reign of Louis XVI, etc. 1793.
SIBLEY, MANOAH (Stenographer) The Genuine Trial of Thomas Hardy, etc. 2 vols. 1795.
Simpkin Redivus to Simon, etc. 1796.
SINCLAIR, SIR JOHN. Thoughts on the Naval strength of the British Empire. 1795.
SINCLAIR, JOHN. Lucubrations during a short Recess, etc. 1783.
Sins of Government, Sins of the Nation . . . by Volunteer. 1793.
A Sketch of the Campaign of 1793, etc. 1795.
A Sketch of the Reign of George III. from 1780 to the close of 1790. 1791.
A Small whole Length of Dr. Priestley from his printed Works, etc. 1792.
SMITH, JAMES. The Golden Calves of Dan and Bethel, etc. 1795.
The Soldier's Friend. . . . Written by a Substitute. 1793.
Some Remarks on the British Constitution, etc. 1793.
SOMERVILLE, THOMAS, D.D. The Effects of the French Revolution, etc. 1793.
——— Observations on the Constitution and present State of Britain. 1793.
Sound Reasons and solid Argument for Reform in Parliament, etc. 1795(?).
Specimens of the Manner in which public Worship is conducted in dissenting Congregations. 1793.

Speculations on the Establishing of a unique Tenure of Land, etc. 1795.

A Speech in which the Question of a War with France is stated and examined by a Lover of his Country. 1793.

A Speech intended to have been spoken at the general Meeting of the Friends of Parliamentary Reform, etc. 1790.

The Speech of Alexander the Coppersmith, LL.D. Spoken . . . January 19, 1793.

The Speech of Hon. Thomas Erskine at a Meeting of the Friends of the Liberty of the Press, etc. 1792.

The Speech of John Thelwall at the second Meeting of the London Corresponding Society at Copenhagen House, etc. 1795.

The Speech of Thomas Day on the Necessity of a Reform in Parliament, etc. 1794.

The Speeches at length of Rt. Hon. C. J. Fox, T. Erskine, etc. 1797.

SPENCE, THOMAS.   The End of Oppression, etc.   1795(?).

——— Spence's Recantation, etc.   1795(?).

STANHOPE, CHARLES, *Earl*.   A Letter to the Rt. Hon. Edmund Burke, etc.   1790.

——— Speech in the House of Peers. . . . Printed by the London Corresponding Society.   1794.

The State of the Representation in England and Wales delivered to the Society of Friends of the People, etc.   1793.

STEWART, JOHN.   Good Sense; Addressed to the British Nation, etc. 1794.

——— The Tocsin of Britannica, etc.   1794.

——— Second Peal of the Tocsin, etc.   1794.

STONE, REV. FRANCIS.   Political Reformation on a large scale, etc. 1789.

——— An Examination of the Rt. Hon. Edmund Burke's Reflections, etc.   1792.

The Story of Sheridan, etc.   1790.

Strictures on Mr. Burke's two Letters addressed to a Member of Parliament.   1796.

Strictures on the Letter of the Rt. Hon. Mr. Burke on the Revolution in France.   1791.

Substance of the Speech of Rev. Mr. Walker at the general Meeting of the County of Nottingham, etc.   1780.

A Summary View of the principal Cities and Towns of France, etc. 1797.

A Supplement to the Trial of Thomas Paine . . . by a Gentleman present at the Time.   1793.

SUTTON, REV. CHARLES M.   A Sermon preached . . . February 28, 1794.   1794.

SUTTON, REV. THOMAS. A Sermon preached . . . January 30, 1793. 1793.

Symond's Abstracts of the Two Bills, etc. 1796(?).

SYMONS, REV. J. The Ends and Advantages of an established Ministry, etc. 1792.

—————— A Sermon preached . . . February 28, 1794. 1794.

—————— Unanimity the Security of the Nation, etc. 1795.

TATHAM, EDWARD, D.D. Letters to the Rt. Hon. Edmund Burke on Politics. 1791.

—————— A Sermon preached . . . November 5, 1791. 1791.

—————— A Sermon Suitable to the Times, etc. 1792.

Temperate Comments on Intemperate Reflections, etc. 1791.

A Ten Minutes Address to Englishmen by a loyal Subject. 1793.

Ten Minutes Advice to the People of England on the two Slavery Bills, etc. 1795.

Ten Minutes Caution from a plain Man to his fellow Citizens. 1792.

Ten Minutes Reflection on the late Events in France recommended by a plain Man to his fellow Citizens. 1792.

THELWALL, JOHN. John Gilpin's Ghost, etc. 1795.

—————— The natural and constitutional Right of Britons to annual Parliaments, universal Suffrage, etc. 1795.

—————— Peaceful Discussion, not tumultuary Violence the Means of redressing national grievance, etc. 1795.

—————— Political Lectures. 1795.

—————— An Appeal to popular Opinion against Kidnapping and Murder. 1796.

—————— Democracy Vindicated. An Essay on the Constitution and Government of the Roman State from the posthumous Works of Walter Moyle with Preface and Notes by John Thelwall. 1796.

—————— Prospectus of a Course of Lectures, etc. 1796.

—————— Sober Reflections on the Seditious and Inflammatory Letter of Rt. Hon Edmund Burke to a Noble Lord. 1796.

THOMAS, REV. ROBERT. The Cause of Truth, etc. 1797.

THORP, ROBERT, D.D. An Establishment in Religion and religious Liberty, etc. 1792.

Thoughts on a Letter addressed to the Rt. Hon. Thomas Conolly, etc. 1790.

Thoughts on a Parliamentary Reform. 1784.

Thoughts on a Peace with France, etc. 1796.

Thoughts on the Cause of the present Failures. 1793.

Thoughts on the late Riot at Birmingham. 1791.

Thoughts on the Letter of Edmund Burke to the Sheriff of Bristol on the Affairs of America, etc. 1778.

Thoughts on the Resolutions of the Protestant Dissenters, etc. 1790.

Thoughts upon the present Situation, etc. 1793.

Three Letters to Dr. Price, Containing Remarks on his Observations on the Nature of Civil Liberty, etc. 1776.

Three Words on the War. 1793.

To Britons! A Tract in the Form of a Discourse by a Lay-Brother. 1793(?).

To the Great and Learned among Christians, etc. 1793.

Tom Paine's Jests, etc. 1794.

A Tour through the Theater of War in the Months of December, 1792, and January, 1793, etc. 1793.

Towers, Joseph. An Oration delivered at the London Tavern on the 4th of November, 1788, etc. 1788.

———— Thoughts on the Commencement of a new Parliament, etc. 1790.

———— Tracts on political and other Subjects published at various Times, etc. 1796.

Townshend, Thomas. A Summary Defence of the Rt. Hon. Edmund Burke, etc. 1796.

Tracts published and distributed gratis by the Society for Constitutional Information. 1783.

Treason Triumphant over Law and the Constitution, etc. 1795.

Tremlitt, Thomas. Strictures on the proposed Plan for adopting a Loan, etc. 1796.

The Trial of Daniel Isaac Eaton for publishing a supposed Libel, etc. 1794.

Trial of George Rose at the Suit of Mr. Smith. 1791.

The Trial of Henry Yorke for a Conspiracy, etc. 1795.

The Trial of John Horne Tooke on a Charge of High Treason, etc. 1794.

The Trial of Robert Watt, late Wine Merchant of Edinburgh, for High Treason, etc. 1794.

The Trial of Thomas Paine for writing a Libel, etc. 1792.

The Trial of William Winterbotham . . . for Seditious Words, etc. 1794.

The Trials of Robert Watt and David Downie for High Treason, etc. 1794.

The Trials of the Birmingham Rioters at Warwick, etc. 1791.

A Trip to the Island of Equality, etc.

The True Briton's Catechism, etc. 1793.

Trueheart, J. The Soldier's Answer to the Pamphlet entitled the Soldier's Friend, etc. 1793(?).

Truth and Reason against Place and Pension, etc. 1793.

Truth and Treason; or, a Narrative of the Royal Procession to the House of Peers, October 29, 1795. 1795.

TURNER, REV. DANIEL. An Exhortation to Peace and Loyalty, and the Support of Government, etc. 1792.

Two Letters addressed to a British Merchant a short Time before the expected Meeting of Parliament. 1796.

Two Letters addressed to his Grace the Duke of Bedford and the People of England. 1796.

Two Letters from Norman McLeod, Esq., M. P., to the Chairman of the Friends of the People, etc. 1792.

Two Speeches of Thomas Day at the general Meeting of the Counties of Cambridge and Essex, etc. 1780.

VANSITTART, NICHOLAS. An Inquiry into the State of the Finances of Great Britain, etc. 1796.

Verses written on Seeing the Execution of Robert Watt. 1794.

Very familiar Letters addressed to Dr. Priestley . . . by John Nott, Button Burnisher. 1790.

Very familiar Letters addressed to Mr. John Nott, Button Burnisher, by Alexander Armsling, Whip Maker and Abel Sharp, Spur Maker. 1790.

VIETTE, M. DE. Dumourier unmasked, etc. 1793.

A View of the Relative State of Great Britain and France at the Commencement of the Year 1796.

Views of the Ruins of the principal Houses destroyed during the Riots at Birmingham. 1791.

The Village Association, or the Politics of Edley, etc. 1793(?).

VINCENT, WILLIAM, D.D. A Discourse addressed to the People of Great Britain, etc. 1792.

A Vindication of the Duke of Bedford's Attack on Mr. Burke's Pension, etc. 1796.

A Vindication of the London Corresponding Society, etc. 1794(?).

A Vindication of the Rt. Hon. Edmund Burke's Reflections on the Revolution in France, etc. 1791.

Vindiciae Landavensis; or, Strictures on the Bishop of Landaff's late Charge, etc. 1792.

The Virtues of Hazel; or, Blessings of Government. 1794.

The Voices of Truth to the People of England, etc. 1797.

WADDINGTON, S. F., ESQ. Remarks on Mr. Burke's two Letters, etc. 1796(?).

WAKEFIELD, DANIEL, ESQ. Observations on the Credit and Finances of Great Britain, etc. 1797.

WAKEFIELD, GILBERT. An Address to the Rt. Rev. Dr. Samuel Horsley, etc. 1790.

—— The Spirit of Christianity Compared to the Spirit of the Times in Great Britain. 1794.

—— A Reply to the Letter of Edmund Burke to a Noble Lord. 1796.

WALKER, CHARLES, ESQ. Reflections on Government in General, etc. 1796.

WALKER, GEORGE. The Dissenter's Plea, etc. 1789(?).

WALKER, REV. ROBERT. The Sentiments and Conduct becoming Britons in the present Conjuncture, etc. 1794.

WALLACE, LADY EGLANTINE. The Conduct of the King of Prussia and General Dumourier investigated. 1793.

War. (A broadside.)   December 31, 1792.

War with France the only Security of Britain at the present momentous Crisis . . . by an Old Englishman. 1794.

A Warning Voice to the People of England on the true Nature . . . of the two Bills now before Parliament. 1795.

WATSON, RICHARD. A Charge delivered to the Clergy of the Diocese of Landaff, etc. 1792.

—— Two Sermons preached in the Cathedral Church of Landaff, etc. 1795.

The Welsh Freeholder's Vindication of his Letter, etc. 1791.

WESTON, CHARLES, D.D. Authority of Government and Duty of Obedience, etc. 1793.

—— A Sermon preached . . . January 30, 1793.   1793.

Whig and No Whig. A Political Paradox. 1789.

The Whig Club; a Sketch of Modern Patriots. 1795.

A Whig's Apology for his Consistency in a Letter from a Member of Parliament to his Friend. 1795.

WHITAKER, REV. E. W. National Calamities the Consequence of National Guilt, etc. 1795.

The Whole Proceedings on the Trials of Mr. William Stone for High Treason, etc. 1796.

WILLIAMS, REV. J. H. Two Sermons preached . . . April, 1793, and February, 1794.   1794.

—— War the Stumbling Block of a Christian, etc. 1795.

WILLIAMS, WILLIAM. A Reply to Mr. Burke's two Letters on the Proposals for Peace, etc. 1796.

—— Rights of the People, etc. 1796.

WILLS, REV. THOMAS. The Scriptural Fast, etc. 1794.

WILSON, JOSEPH. A Letter Commercial and Political addressed to Rt. Hon. William Pitt. 1793.

WINTERBOTHAM, WILLIAM. The Commemoration of National Deliverances and the Dawning Day, etc. 1794.

WOLCOTT, JOHN (Peter Pindar). Odes to Mr. Paine, etc. 1791.

WOLSTONCROFT, WILLIAM. A Vindication of the Rights of Men, etc. 1790.

Wonderful Exhibition!!! Gulielimo Pittachio, the sublime Wonder of the World, etc. 1794.

WOOLSEY, ROBERT. Reflections upon Reflections, etc. 1790.

WOOLY, REV. W. A Cure for Canting, etc. 1794.

Words in Season to the Traders and Manufacturers of Great Britain. 1792.

WORKMAN, JAMES. An Argument against Continuing the War. 1795.

———— A Letter to his Grace the Duke of Portland, etc. 1797.

WRIGHT, THOMAS. The Death of a Great Man, etc. 1791.

WYVILL, CHRISTOPHER. A State of the Representation of the People of England, etc. 1793.

———— Political Papers, etc. 1794 +.

YORKE, HENRY. These are the Times that try Men's Souls, etc. 1793.

YOUNG, ARTHUR. (A broadside.) December 18, 1792.

———— The Example of France a Warning to Great Britain, etc. 1793.

———— The Use and Abuse of Money, etc. 1794.

———— The Constitution Safe without Reform, etc. 1795.

———— An Idea of the Present State of France. 1795.

———— An Enquiry into the State of the Public Mind among the lower Classes, etc. 1798.

———— Travels in France, etc.

INDEX.

15